Pro JMX:
Java Management Extensions

J. JEFFREY HANSON

Pro JMX: Java Management Extensions
Copyright ©2004 by J. Jeffrey Hanson

ISBN (pbk): 1-59059-101-1

Printed and bound in the United States of America 12345678910

Trademarked names may appear in this book. Rather than use a trademark symbol with every occurrence of a trademarked name, we use the names only in an editorial fashion and to the benefit of the trademark owner, with no intention of infringement of the trademark.

Technical Reviewers: Robert Castaneda and Nathan Lee

Editorial Board: Steve Anglin, Dan Appleman, Gary Cornell, James Cox, Tony Davis, John Franklin, Chris Mills, Steven Rycroft, Dominic Shakeshaft, Julian Skinner, Martin Streicher, Jim Sumser, Karen Watterson, Gavin Wray, John Zukowski

Assistant Publisher: Grace Wong

Project Manager: Beth Christmas

Copy Editor: Ami Knox

Production Manager: Kari Brooks

Production Editor: Lori Bring

Proofreader: Thistle Hill Publishing Services, LLC

Compositor: Kinetic Publishing Services, LLC

Indexer: Nancy Guenther

Artist: Kinetic Publishing Services, LLC

Cover Designer: Kurt Krames

Manufacturing Manager: Tom Debolski

Distributed to the book trade in the United States by Springer-Verlag New York, Inc., 175 Fifth Avenue, New York, NY, 10010 and outside the United States by Springer-Verlag GmbH & Co. KG, Tiergartenstr. 17, 69112 Heidelberg, Germany.

In the United States: phone 1-800-SPRINGER, email orders@springer-ny.com, or visit http://www.springer-ny.com. Outside the United States: fax +49 6221 345229, email orders@springer.de, or visit http://www.springer.de.

For information on translations, please contact Apress directly at 2560 Ninth Street, Suite 219, Berkeley, CA 94710. Phone 510-549-5930, fax 510-549-5939, email info@apress.com, or visit http://www.apress.com.

The source code for this book is available to readers at http://www.apress.com in the Downloads section.

*This book is dedicated to Russell's orchard
and heaven on the hood of my '68 Mustang.*

Contents at a Glance

Contents

About the Author

 **J. Jeffrey Hanson** is the chief architect at eReinsure.com, Inc., where he directs architecture and design for J2EE-based frameworks, applications, and systems for the reinsurance industry. Jeff Hanson has more than 18 years of experience in the software industry, including filling the role of lead architect for the Route 66 platform at Novell and chief architect at Zareus, Inc.

Jeff's experience includes analysis, design, and implementation for systems, applications, and platforms in the newspaper publishing industry, mortgage lending industry, retail banking, word processing, and developer services. Jeff has also authored numerous articles and books for the software industry.

About the Technical Reviewers

Rob Castaneda is principal architect at CustomWare Asia Pacific, where he provides architecture consulting and training in EJB/J2EE/XML-based applications and integration servers to clients throughout Asia and America. Rob's multinational background, combined with his strong real-world business experience, enables him to see through the specifications to create realistic solutions to major business problems. He has also contributed to and technically edited various leading EJB and J2EE books.

Nathan Lee is a senior architect at CustomWare Asia Pacific, where he leads the assurance product development group delivering testing, management, and monitoring tools based on Java and JMX. Nathan has traveled extensively throughout the Asia Pacific region training and mentoring clients in J2EE/XML, workflow, and integration technologies. Nathan holds a bachelor of engineering (software) degree with first class honors.

Introduction

Pro JMX: Java Management Extensions is written from the perspective of a J2EE application architect. This book can help developers and IT-management staffs to build systems and applications that can be monitored, managed, and upgraded in real-time using standard Java-based tools.

Who This Book Is For

This book was written for application and system developers, architects, designers, and support staffs. The code examples contained herein will help developers with each concept. I provide architecture diagrams to ease the learning curve for architects and designers. Real-world examples will allow business people to understand the many uses for JMX.

This book was written with the assumption that people reading it have a background in Java software development sufficient to understand an intermediate level of Java-based programming concepts. This book should appeal to system managers and management system designers as well as software developers, designers, and architects who are interested in learning JMX.

How This Book Is Organized

The chapters of the book attempt to take you through each JMX section in a logical step-by-step manner in order to build on previous concepts while introducing new concepts. The content for each chapter is briefly summarized as follows:

Chapter 1 will introduce you to some of the challenges that management systems face today and how JMX is positioned to meet these challenges effectively. I will present the main concepts and components that work together to form the architecture and frameworks of JMX. Some of the problems solved by JMX are already solved in the enterprise using other technologies; JMX also integrates these technologies into the Java platform in a flexible, dynamic fashion.

Chapter 2 discusses the instrumentation level of JMX and how it enables devices, services, applications, and other resources to be easily exposed as manageable resources to any Java-enabled system or application.

Chapter 3 looks at the manner in which JMX defines management agents and how JMX agents interact with MBeans and management applications. We will also investigate how JMX defines services with respect to agents.

Chapter 4 introduces the concept of MBean servers and how they function as abstraction layers between managed resources and management applications. Instances of MBeans are never directly accessed by management applications; instead, the MBean server acts as a proxy object between MBeans and external components.

Chapter 5 presents a brief overview of how management systems must meet different challenges including controlling, monitoring, updating, and reporting the state of devices, applications, and services; converting management data into readable form; providing Quality of Service (QoS) and repairing errors to minimize system downtime; and providing accounting and auditing services for resources and users.

Chapter 6 introduces you to the JMX distributed services level and shows how it is used along with other JMX technologies. Chapter 6 particularly looks at how JMX defines the concept of connectors in order to join client and server components.

Chapter 7 further explores connectors and how a connector is attached to a JMX MBean server to make it accessible to remote Java clients. The chapter discusses how the client end of a connector exports essentially the same interface as the MBean server, and how all connectors have the same Java technology–based interface, allowing management applications to use the connector most suited to their networking environment and even change connectors transparently as needs evolve.

Chapter 8 will teach you how a JMX agent may register its connector servers with its infrastructures, and how a JMX client may query these infrastructures in order to find and connect to the advertised servers.

Chapter 9 discusses the client duties and features of the JMX distributed services level. The client/server interaction of JMX exposes a transparent communication model. The reason for this transparency is that JMX exposes an API to a remote client that is as close as possible to the API defined by JMX for access to instrumentation within a local agent.

Chapter 10 discusses the JMX Remote security features, including connector security based on password authentication and file access control, connector security that uses a subject delegation model, and fine-grained connector security.

Chapter 11 discusses how widespread JMX has become in the software industry by looking at some of the companies that have adopted JMX and some of their products in which JMX is used.

Chapter 12 summarizes the book, showing the different components, frameworks, and APIs that JMX offers to provide a comprehensive management implementation and design platform.

CHAPTER 1

Introducing JMX

TODAY'S SERVICE-DRIVEN APPLICATION environments present formidable challenges to businesses in all industries. Resources, such as applications, devices, services, and processing power, are dynamically appearing, changing, and disappearing at a rate that is seemingly impossible to manage. Companies are forced to hire additional IT staff and outsource work to try to solve this formidable dilemma.

Current technologies fall disappointingly short of providing engineers with the flexibility and power they need to solve the problems that resource management trends are creating, such as dynamic service locating, multiprotocol support, processor sharing, and peer-to-peer management. Although resources are actively evolving, current technologies remain stagnant. Proactive capabilities are mandatory requirements for management systems today, because statically designed systems fail to address the needs of new resources as they become available.

The goal of the Java Management Extensions (JMX) architecture is to present a standardized modular architecture that is flexible and powerful enough to meet these challenges. JMX is an architectural specification and programming interface that defines a comprehensive array of dynamic management technologies and frameworks for standardizing resource management using the Java programming language. This book discusses JMX concepts in general as well as JMX concepts specifically pertaining to client and server communications.

In this chapter, I will introduce you to some of the challenges that management systems face today and how JMX is positioned to meet these challenges effectively. I will present the main concepts and components that work together to form the architecture and frameworks of JMX. Some of the problems solved by JMX are already solved in the enterprise using other technologies; JMX also integrates these technologies into the Java platform in a flexible, dynamic fashion.

System and Resource Management Challenges

Service-driven development is rapidly replacing the client-server model that, until now, was safely entrenched in the fabric of enterprise systems. As an enterprise developer, you have likely faced the challenge from internal or external customers to solve resource management problems involving open systems where services and resources are deployed at will.

1

In the past, you could confidently assume that experts specializing in system analysis would design, install, and configure a static solution for system and resource management, after the development of a system or product was completed. This is no longer the case. In order to keep up with the ever-changing climate of distributed services, system and resource management must be addressed from the design stage to deployment, taking into account such important issues as Service Level Agreements (SLAs).

Leaving system and resource management to be addressed as an afterthought makes it difficult to find and keep competent system managers and analysts. This causes enterprise applications and systems to be very costly and difficult to install, maintain, and upgrade.

You have most likely found that system and resource management must be addressed at the very onset of a project in order to ensure that it becomes a core part of applications and services as they are deployed or upgraded. More than just an important step, this is a fundamental requirement if services are to be dynamically upgraded, modified, and maintained. JMX has emerged as a management standard and is poised to help you meet this requirement.

Distributed environments such as those found in Web-enabled storefronts, online banking, and corporate intranets encounter resources such as applications, devices, and services in a random and explosive fashion. For example, financial data might be coming in and going out as accounting processes are performed; printers and mobile devices are added and removed from the network as engineering and sales processes take place; and employee data is added, removed, and updated as staff changes are made in human resources. Figure 1-1 shows a typical arrangement of resources in a distributed system.

As you can see, resource management encompasses software resources, personnel resources, and hardware resources. Management of this mixed bag of devices, services, applications, and so on can become a nightmare without the proper tools. See the sidebar "Management Technologies Today" for a sampling of such tools.

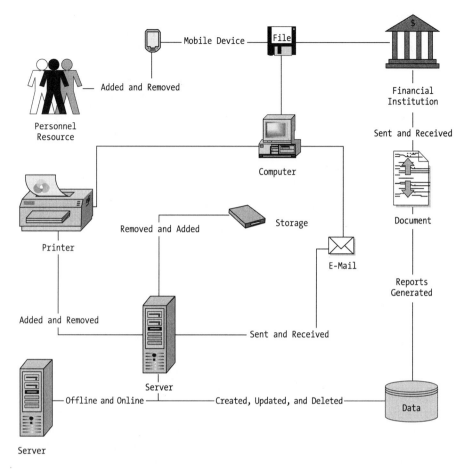

Figure 1-1. A typical arrangement of enterprise resources

Management Technologies Today

Today's management systems employ a wide array of protocols, technologies, and toolsets, as illustrated by a survey of management technologies currently in use:

- The Simple Network Management Protocol (SNMP) has emerged as the standard for networks based on the Internet Protocol (IP). SNMP is essentially a request-reply, network monitoring, and control protocol running over UDP, TCP, or IPX. SNMP operates between a management station and an agent.

- The Common Management Information Protocol (CMIP) is an Open Systems Interconnection–based network management protocol that supports information exchange between network management applications and management agents. CMIP was developed and funded by government and corporations to replace SNMP.

- The Distributed Management Task Force (DMTF) Common Information Model/Web-Based Enterprise Management (CIM/WBEM) standard defines a management information model and an XML-based interface to describe the language, naming, meta schema, and mapping techniques to other management models such as the SNMP management information base (MIB) and the DMTF management information format (MIF).

- The Application Instrumentation and Control (AIC) standard is a C language application programming interface (API) for exposing application metrics and thresholds. AIC allows information to be extracted from application programs at runtime.

- Other proprietary enterprise management technologies are provided by Tivoli, Computer Associates, BMC Software, HP, and the OMI Web Services initiative.

Now let's take a closer look at JMX.

JMX Overview

Java development is revolutionizing enterprise application development, which is resulting in a vast number of exciting new ways to present data, resources, and services to clients. With this comes the increasing need for a standard way to manage all of these new systems, resources, and services. This is where JMX comes in. JMX defines a term known as *instrumentation*, which specifies a mechanism for adorning Java components in such a way as to expose the most appropriate set of management interfaces. Augmenting or instrumenting these resources with management capabilities in a universal and flexible manner is of utmost importance for Java to move forward as a primary enterprise development environment.

Java is a dynamic, flexible, and portable development environment for developers of applications, systems, devices, and services. However, applying static management solutions against such dynamic resources would not afford you the gains necessary to solve the management requirements of most enterprises. What makes more sense is a standard management architecture that is as flexible, dynamic, and portable as the development environment itself. JMX offers just such a solution. As the name implies, JMX is a set of extensions to the Java programming language that allows any Java component to become innately manageable.

How JMX Works

JMX provides an easy, flexible, standard mechanism to instrument Java objects with management interfaces. JMX instrumentation is completely independent from the rest of its management infrastructure, which enables a resource to be augmented with manageable characteristics regardless of how its hosting application might be implemented. This allows developers to focus on their area of expertise and eliminate the usually sizable investment in retraining needed to become proficient in some proprietary management technology.

Because JMX is becoming a ubiquitous management standard, developers can instrument their components according to the JMX specification and be confident that all JMX-enabled management tools can manage them. Even non-JMX management tools can manage JMX components with the addition of an adaptor to serve as a bridge between JMX and the non-JMX tools.

JMX exploits the inherent runtime-discovery features of the Java programming language to expose a management solution that is dynamic and flexible enough to be easily made interoperable with existing management systems. Since JMX shields a management application from the information models and communication protocols, new services can be deployed and updated at runtime without stopping and restarting any of the core system components.

Statically designed management systems prove extremely difficult to integrate with other management systems. Even statically designed systems based on the same standard can be very hard to integrate, because the slightest degree of deviation from the standard quickly exposes the fact that changes must be recompiled and systems must be stopped and restarted.

Dynamic management systems, however, are capable of being modified and extended regardless of system downtime or recompiling issues. JMX provides a powerful architecture for building systems that embrace the dynamic approach. JMX offers an unprecedented means to create dynamic systems by allowing each component to describe itself with a degree of granularity that is needed for each situation. The ability of each component to describe itself in as detailed a manner as needed enables management systems and platforms to take advantage of useful features such as hot deployment and runtime discovery.

Implementing JMX

JMX enables configuration settings to be viewed, edited, and removed at runtime. You can use JMX to dynamically load, initialize, modify, and monitor applications, their components, and their configuration information.

Implementations of the JMX specification are rapidly emerging as JMX becomes pervasive throughout the Java 2 Enterprise Edition (J2EE) development community. The reference implementation provided by Sun is a usable product that is freely available for downloading. J2EE application server vendors such as JBoss, IBM, BEA, and others are making JMX a core part of their server architecture.

> **NOTE** *Although many J2EE application server vendors are integrating JMX into the core architecture of their server products to facilitate management functionality, they are also finding that JMX provides powerful features for applications and services. We will explore this part of JMX throughout this book as well.*

Next we will take a look at the JMX architecture.

JMX Architecture

JMX defines a three-level architecture. This design promotes a clean separation of processing that allows resources to be instrumented for almost any situation that faces enterprise systems and applications. The flexible and generic nature of JMX helps to protect systems from changes that inevitably occur with management technologies. This model provides a high degree of flexibility by enabling different segments of the developer population to focus on the level that best fits their respective companies' business.

The three levels of JMX are as follows:

* *Instrumentation level:* This level, aimed at the Java developer community, defines a specification for instrumenting manageable resources. A managed resource can be an application, a service, a device, etc. A managed resource is exposed as a Java object called a managed bean (MBean) and is instrumented so that it can be managed by JMX-compliant applications.

  MBeans could be regarded as JavaBeans that expose application-specific management interfaces. MBeans are registered with an MBean server, and all access to the MBean must go through the MBean server. MBeans allow resources to expose their particular management functionality to management applications and systems. For example, an MBean can be instrumented to start and stop an application or service.

- *Agent level:* This level, aimed at the management application community, defines a specification for implementing management agents. Management agents are composed of specific business logic, an MBean server, a set of MBeans, a group of agent services, and optionally one connector or protocol adaptor. Agents act as proxies to managed resources, making them available to management applications. Agents that provide a connector or protocol adaptor not only can be located on the same machine as the resources they control, but can also be distributed across a network.

- *Distributed services level:* This level, aimed at the management application community, defines a specification for implementing remote MBean clients. This level defines management interfaces and components that can operate on remote agents or groups of remote agents.

  The distributed services level consists of one or more components called *connectors* and *protocol adaptors.* Connectors and protocol adaptors enable access to agents from remote management applications or systems. Remote management applications supporting protocols such as SNMP, Hypertext Transfer Protocol (HTTP), JMS (Java Messaging Service), and others can access the managed resources and control them in a universally similar manner. Multiple management systems using heterogeneous protocols can access the managed resources simultaneously. This enables managed resources to be made available to existing enterprise management systems.

In addition to the three levels, which I will discuss in more detail in the following sections, JMX provides a number of APIs that define a specification for interacting with existing management environments. These APIs, referred to as the *Additional Management Protocol APIs,* help developers build platform-independent management applications for most common industry standards.

Figure 1-2 shows a high-level view of the JMX architecture.

JMX allows centralized management of MBeans. An *MBean* is a Java object that exposes a specific interface and conforms to certain naming patterns. If a resource's management interface conforms to these requirements, that resource is considered an MBean. The management interface of a resource is the information and set of controls that a management application needs in order to operate on a resource.

MBeans are controlled by an object known as an *MBean server.* The MBean server functions as a registry for MBeans and exposes their management interfaces to other objects seeking to manipulate them. An MBean server is contained within an agent, which acts to expose the MBean server, and therefore exposes the registered MBeans as well. Any MBean registered with an MBean server is visible to management applications that interact with the MBean server's agent.

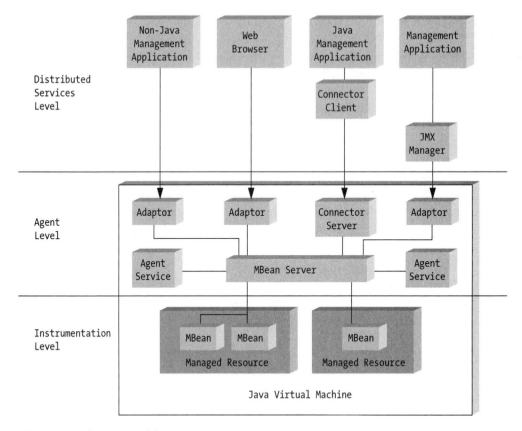

Figure 1-2. The JMX architecture

Instrumentation Level

The JMX instrumentation level defines APIs and technologies that allow developers to augment any Java-accessible resource with manageable features. The instrumentation API defines how applications expose data, operations, and events to interested management systems and applications. The instrumentation layer exposes a manageable resource as one or more MBeans, which I define in more detail in the following sections.

JMX Manageable Resources

A *manageable resource* is any entity that can be exposed using the Java programming language. A manageable resource can be an application, a service, a component, a device, or any other software entity that can be exposed in Java. The instrumentation of these managed resources in fact relies on the Java programming language. This implies that a resource must be a Java object or at least be packaged as a Java object, as in the case of a native component that is exposed using the Java Native Interface (JNI).

As mentioned previously, an MBean is a Java object in JMX that defines a resource to be managed. The specification for MBeans closely follows the JavaBeans component model in a number of ways. This close relationship between MBeans and JavaBeans enables an easy transition for JavaBeans into the realm of JMX manageability. This allows any JMX agent to act as a management container for JavaBeans that have been instrumented as MBeans. MBeans are never exposed directly by an MBean server; instead they are exposed indirectly using an alias that is stored in a Java Object known as an *ObjectName*.

JMX defines four types of MBeans: standard, dynamic, open, and model MBeans. Each type of MBean fits a different level of instrumentation capability:

- *Standard MBeans* are the least complex of the four types of MBeans. Standard MBeans expose their management interface using an actual Java language interface that defines the attributes and operations that should be manageable.

- *Dynamic MBeans* must also implement a specific Java interface; however, this interface defines methods that expose manageable attributes and operations in a generic way. The details of the manageable attributes and operations are left up to the MBean itself to be determined at runtime, thus allowing for greater flexibility.

- *Model MBeans* are extended dynamic MBeans that allow the specific managed resource to be determined at runtime. This is made possible by requiring a JMX implementation to provide a generic ModelMBean object that can be used as a proxy for other objects that wish to be managed. The actual managed resource object is passed to the ModelMBean object at runtime and referred to, in-proxy, by the ModelMBean's generic interface. The generic ModelMBean then delegates all calls made to methods defined in the DynamicMBean interface to the managed resource to handle.

- *Open MBeans* are also dynamic MBeans that rely on a small, predefined set of universal Java types and advertise their functionality using a descriptively rich set of metadata information.

Notification Model

JMX defines an event model that allows MBeans to broadcast notification events. The JMX event model is similar to the JavaBeans event model, because objects register as listeners with an MBean in order to receive events that are transmitted by the MBean. The MBean notification model expands on the

JavaBeans event model, in that the MBean notification model enables a listener object to register once with a broadcasting MBean and receive all events that the broadcasting MBean transmits. Notification events can be transmitted by MBeans and by an MBean server.

The JMX notification model defines the following components:

- The `javax.management.Notification` class: Extends the `java.util.EventObject` class, which indicates any type of notification event.

- The `javax.management.NotificationListener` interface: Extends the `java.util.EventListener` interface, which is implemented by objects desiring to receive notification events transmitted by MBeans.

- The `javax.management.NotificationFilter` interface: Extends the `java.io.Serializable` interface, which is implemented by objects that serve as filters for notification events. This interface allows notification listeners to filter notification events that are transmitted by an MBean.

- The `javax.management.NotificationBroadcaster` interface: Implemented by an MBean that transmits notification events. This interface defines methods that allow objects to register as listeners with an MBean. Methods are also provided that return information about the notification events that can be transmitted by the broadcasting MBean.

- The `javax.management.NotificationEmitter` interface: Extends `javax.management.NotificationBroadcaster` and is implemented by broadcasters that transmit notification events. Like the `javax.management.NotificationBroadcaster` interface, this interface defines methods to allow objects to add or remove themselves as listeners to notifications transmitted from broadcasters; however, this interface provides slightly more control for removing listeners.

MBean Metadata Classes

The instrumentation specification defines metadata classes that describe the management interface of an MBean. These classes are used by an MBean server to manually perform introspection on standard MBeans and to allow dynamic MBeans to describe themselves. These classes describe the attributes, operations, constructors, and notifications of MBeans.

An agent exposes information about its MBeans using the MBean metadata classes. All MBean clients interested in the management interface of an MBean interact with the MBean's metadata objects and extract information from them as needed.

Some types of MBeans extend the basic metadata classes in order to provide additional information. For example, open MBeans and model MBeans both provide extended instances of the basic MBean metadata classes. Because all metadata classes extend the basic metadata classes, the information from the basic metadata classes is always available.

Agent Level

The JMX *agent level* defines management agents that register, contain, and expose an MBean server, MBeans, and agent services, such as monitoring, event notification, timers, and dynamic loading of Java classes.

Agents

An *agent* is a software component composed of an MBean server, a set of MBeans, agent services, and at least one protocol adaptor or connector. An agent acts as a liaison between MBeans and MBean clients.

An agent exposes a number of functions to MBean clients either locally or remotely. MBean clients interact with an agent to manage MBeans by getting their attribute values, changing their attribute values, or invoking operations on them. MBean clients can interact with an agent to get notifications transmitted by any MBean. MBean clients can instantiate and register new MBeans from Java classes already loaded into the agent's Java Virtual Machine (JVM) or new classes loaded from the local machine or downloaded from the network.

MBean Servers

An *MBean server* acts as a registry for MBeans registered with an agent. The MBean server is a component that provides services to interested objects, allowing them to manipulate and manage MBeans. All operations or interactions on an MBean must be performed through interfaces on the MBean server.

An MBean server is found or created by an agent that uses static methods of a factory class. This flexible creation mechanism allows an agent to contain more than one MBean server.

The javax.management.MBeanServer interface and javax.management. MBeanServerConnection interface define the operations available by an agent. An implementation of the agent specification must provide a class that implements the `javax.management.MBeanServer` interface and/or `javax.management.MBeanServerConnection` interface.

An MBean server transmits notifications when MBeans are registered or deregistered. A specific subclass of the `javax.management.Notification` class is used for this purpose. This class contains a list of object names involved in the notification. The MBean server does not broadcast notifications itself; instead it uses a delegate MBean, which implements the `javax.management.NotificationBroadcaster` interface to broadcast the notifications in its place.

Agent Services

An agent must expose certain mandatory services, and can contain other optional services. These agent services can perform management operations on MBeans registered in an MBean server and are often implemented as MBeans themselves. If they are implemented as MBeans, they can also be controlled by an MBean server. The JMX specification defines the following agent services:

- Dynamic class loading using a component known as a *management applet,* or *M-Let.* This service retrieves and instantiates classes from an arbitrary location specified by a URL.

- Monitors that observe an MBean attribute's value at specified intervals and notify other objects if target conditions, called *gauges,* have been met.

- Timers that provide a scheduling mechanism to trigger notifications at certain dates and times or at certain predefined intervals.

- A relation service that enables multiple user-defined associations between MBeans using roles. The relation service maintains the consistency of a relation by monitoring MBean operations and deregistrations to ensure that if a relation becomes invalid, the MBean is removed from the relation.

Distributed Services Level

An agent can make itself available to remote management tools using any number of communication protocols. Once an agent has made itself available remotely, a client running in a different process or on a different machine can manipulate the agent and the MBeans registered in the agent. Some common protocols used by remote agents include the SNMP, HTTP, the Simple Object

Access Protocol (SOAP), and others. For example, agents that expose an HTTP interface allow management applications to control them using a Web browser. This can be very useful when an agent resides behind a firewall.

Agents that provide support for a common protocol, such as SNMP, allow many existing network management tools to control them and the MBeans that they contain. This allows companies to leverage the investment they have made training existing employees.

The distributed services level specifies concepts defining entities that operate on agent-level components. Some of the components provided by the distributed level include the following:

- *Connector components* that provide transparent interaction between an agent and management applications. This interaction is defined as transparent because it behaves in the same fashion regardless of whether the agent is local or remote.

- *Protocol adaptors* that define interfaces to agents so that the agents may provide the means for clients of the protocols to interact with the agents using semantics of each given protocol. Examples are HTTP and SNMP.

- *Message exchanges* between a connected client and server and the sequence these message exchanges must follow.

- *Lookup services* that define how JMX agents register their connector servers and how clients can query the agents to find and connect to their servers.

An agent depends on protocol adaptors and connectors to make it accessible from management applications outside of the JVM in which it resides. Each protocol adaptor provides unique management views of an agent over a specific protocol. Connectors expose the same interface to a client regardless of the underlying protocol, allowing transparent access to an agent. Both protocol adaptors and the server components of connectors act as liaisons between agents and remote management applications.

> **NOTE** *To be accessed remotely, an agent must provide at least one protocol adaptor or connector. However, an agent can provide multiple protocol adaptors or connectors in order to be accessible from any number of heterogeneous management applications simultaneously.*

Protocol adaptors and connectors, which I discuss in the next sections, are usually implemented as MBeans themselves, conferring upon them the same benefits that manageable resources enjoy, such as hot deployment, runtime modifications, and others.

Protocol Adaptors

Protocol adaptors allow management applications to access an agent and manipulate it using any given protocol that the adaptor supports, such as HTML, SOAP, or SNMP. Protocol adaptors provide a management view of the JMX agent through a given protocol. These views include the agent's services and the agent's MBeans that are suitable for the given protocol, such as a Web browser view for an HTML adaptor. Protocol adaptors are used when management applications rely on a specific protocol, as is often the case with legacy applications.

Connectors

Connectors are used to connect an agent with remote management applications over an assortment of protocols. Connectors are comprised of a server component in the agent and a connector client in the management application. All connectors for a given agent expose the same Java interface. This allows management applications to choose the interface that fits the needs of the application most precisely. As the management application changes over time, the connector used by the application can change without modifying the associative code between the application and the agent.

Figure 1-3 shows a typical use of protocol adaptors and connectors.

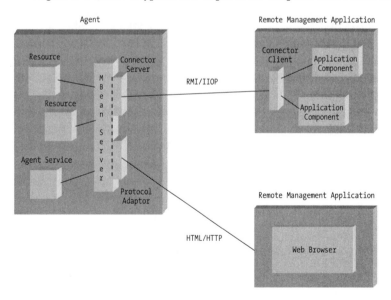

Figure 1-3. Protocol adaptors and connectors

As you can see, JMX is a very modular framework of objects, components, and services that work together to form a cohesive platform for management systems and services.

Modular Server Architecture

Increasingly, development platforms that are based on J2EE are exposing business logic as services. In fact, many of the J2EE APIs are strikingly similar to CORBA services. JMX provides an ideal management framework for service-based systems. With the loose coupling JMX defines between managed resources and end products, services exposed as MBeans can be created, modified, or replaced without starting and stopping the environment in which they are deployed. This kind of hot deployment can even be applied to the services themselves. For example, if a system is designed to access services indirectly instead of keeping references to them, the services can be interchanged without any interaction by the client and without bouncing the server.

J2EE is a collection of APIs, specifications, and frameworks that make up an extraordinary architecture for distributed enterprise development. However, even with the direction and framework pieces that J2EE provides, a system over time can become burdened with monolithic code that is handicapped with tightly coupled components and services. JMX enforces a loose coupling and encourages a component-oriented development model. Thus, a J2EE system that is designed with JMX as an inherent facet of its architectural foundation shields itself from the troubles that can quickly emerge in a monolithic environment.

Any object that can be exposed as a Java object can be instrumented as an MBean and registered with an MBean server. This enables all components in the Java and J2EE space to be exposed as MBeans and to be managed by JMX-aware applications and services. This ability that JMX has to permeate a system with its management semantics facilitates building truly modular, service-oriented enterprise systems.

JMX certainly fits the bill as a management architecture, but platform vendors and application server vendors are finding that the modular characteristic of JMX provides a perfect climate for automated component and service integration. The combination of modularity and inherent manageability is making JMX the primary focus for future service-based system and application designs.

For a system to mature successfully with fewer maintenance headaches, it must be modular in nature. Indeed, throwing more people at a project in order to expedite milestone completion dates only works if the project is based on a modular foundation. JMX is modular at its very core. Any project that uses JMX as its foundation can arguably increase headcount to a satisfactory advantage.

Each level, instrumentation, agent, and distributed service is composed of a number of different components, which can be depicted as a three-level model. Figure 1-4 is a graphical look at the three levels and their relationships.

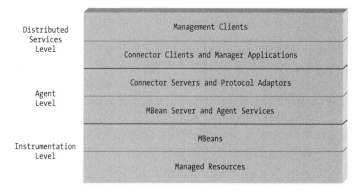

Figure 1-4. The three levels of JMX and their relationships

JMX establishes its management ground rules on the principle of instrumented resources. To instrument a resource, a developer augments the resource with semantics that are defined by the MBean model outlined in the JMX specification. A resource is instrumented in a standard or dynamic fashion. Resources instrumented as standard MBeans are Java objects that implement a given interface conforming to certain naming and design patterns similar to the JavaBeans component model. Resources instrumented as dynamic MBeans are Java objects that implement a specific interface, but resolve the actual management values dynamically at runtime.

Properly instrumented resources are automatically recognized and manageable by any JMX agent. Instrumented resources can also be managed by any non-JMX management tool that can interact with an agent and operate on MBeans using the Java programming language.

To get acquainted with the instrumentation level and the MBean architecture, I will show you how to write a simple date-time service class and instrument it as a standard MBean.

Writing Your First MBean

To acquaint you with the instrumentation level and the MBean architecture, I have provided the code for a simple MBean. This example will encapsulate a simple date-time service class instrumented as a standard MBean.

```
package com.apress.jhanson.services;

import java.util.Calendar;
import java.text.DateFormat;

public class DateTimeService
{
    public String getDate()
```

```
   {
      Calendar rightNow = Calendar.getInstance();
      return DateFormat.getDateInstance().format(rightNow.getTime());
   }

   public String getTime()
   {
      Calendar rightNow = Calendar.getInstance();
      return DateFormat.getTimeInstance().format(rightNow.getTime());
   }
}
```

Now instrument your DateTimeService class as a standard MBean. You will expose both the Date and Time properties as manageable attributes. This involves two steps: First, you must define your MBean interface and then you must modify the DateTimeService class to declare it as implementing the MBean interface. The MBean interface is named the same as your DateTimeService class with the word *MBean* appended on the end:

```
package com.apress.jhanson.services;

public interface DateTimeServiceMBean
{
   public String getDate();
   public String getTime();
}
```

The DateTimeService class is now modified to implement the MBean as follows:

```
public class DateTimeService implements DateTimeServiceMBean
```

Writing Your First Agent

In order to test your instrumented class, write a simple agent. You will use your agent to manage any service MBeans that you write, so you deftly name the agent *ServiceAgent,* as shown here:

```
package com.apress.jhanson.agents;

import com.apress.jhanson.services.*;
import javax.management.*;
```

```
public class ServiceAgent
{
    public static void main(String[] args)
    {
        try
        {
            MBeanServer mbServer =
                MBeanServerFactory.createMBeanServer();

            ObjectName oName =
                new ObjectName("services:name=DateTime,type=information");

            mbServer.registerMBean(new DateTimeService(), oName);
        }
        catch(MBeanRegistrationException e)
        {
            e.printStackTrace();
        }
        catch(NotCompliantMBeanException e)
        {
            e.printStackTrace();
        }
        catch(MalformedObjectNameException e)
        {
            e.printStackTrace();
        }
        catch(InstanceAlreadyExistsException e)
        {
            e.printStackTrace();
        }
    }
}
```

Now, you will modify your agent to allow you to view your results. Note
that in the following code, the com.sun.jdmk.comm package is imported from the
jmxtools.jar file, which ships with the reference implementation:

```
package com.apress.jhanson.agents;

import com.apress.jhanson.services.*;
import javax.management.*;
import com.sun.jdmk.comm.*;
```

```
public class ServiceAgent
{
    public static void main(String[] args)
    {
        try
        {
            MBeanServer mbServer =
                MBeanServerFactory.createMBeanServer();

            ObjectName oName =
                new ObjectName("services:name=DateTime,type=information");

            mbServer.registerMBean(new DateTimeService(), oName);

            ObjectName adaptorOName =
                new ObjectName("adaptors:protocol=HTTP");

            HtmlAdaptorServer htmlAdaptor = new HtmlAdaptorServer();
            mbServer.registerMBean(htmlAdaptor, adaptorOName);
            htmlAdaptor.start();
        }
        catch(MBeanRegistrationException e)
        {
            e.printStackTrace();
        }
        catch(NotCompliantMBeanException e)
        {
            e.printStackTrace();
        }
        catch(MalformedObjectNameException e)
        {
            e.printStackTrace();
        }
        catch(InstanceAlreadyExistsException e)
        {
            e.printStackTrace();
        }
    }
}
```

After running your agent, you can view the MBeans that are registered with it by opening a Web browser and going to the URL http://localhost:8082. This will display the page shown in Figure 1-5.

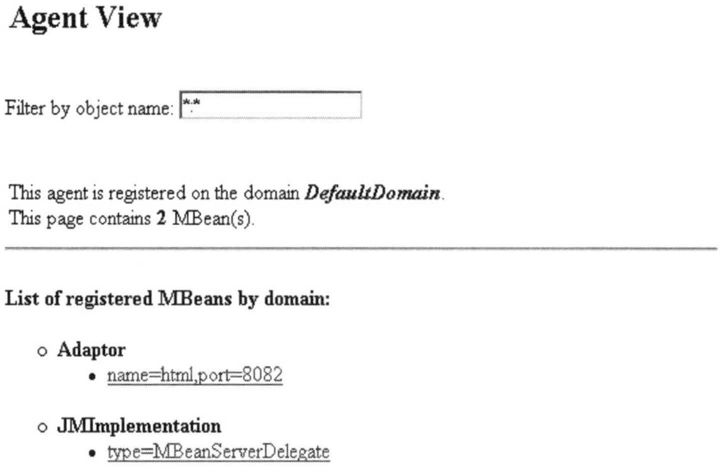

Agent View

Filter by object name: [*.*   ]

This agent is registered on the domain **DefaultDomain**.
This page contains **2** MBean(s).

List of registered MBeans by domain:

- **Adaptor**
  - name=html,port=8082

- **JMImplementation**
  - type=MBeanServerDelegate

Figure 1-5. The adaptor-generated HTML page

The Web page generated by your adaptor shows two MBeans: Adaptor and JMImplementation. If the links for either of these are selected, operations can be performed on either of the MBeans, and properties can be set as well.

Summary

Service-driven enterprise systems and applications present unique challenges when it comes to managing resources. Resources such as applications, devices, services, and processing power appear, change, and disappear at runtime, making static management technologies impotent in their attempts to maintain control. Businesses find themselves helpless, attempting to retrofit legacy management tools as a solution to these problems.

JMX presents a standardized modular architecture that can solve dynamic management requirements for systems of all sizes. JMX provides a framework and programming interface that defines a powerful array of management technologies that can be used to instrument resources and build dynamic management tools through the Java programming language.

The JMX specifications and the reference implementations can be found at http://java.sun.com/jmx. Also found at this site are useful articles, links to books, and code examples.

Now that you have been briefly introduced to the main concepts of JMX in this chapter, we will explore each of these concepts in depth.

CHAPTER 2

The Three-Level Model: Instrumentation and MBeans

TYPICAL ATTEMPTS AT ENABLING systems with management features entail some kind of clumsy post-development retrofitting that must settle for gathering inconsistent information that happens to be available from these systems by chance. JMX-based systems are engineered from their inception with management capabilities. JMX defines a mechanism, called *instrumentation*, for factoring components of any Java-accessible system in such a way as to expose the most appropriate interfaces and services to each particular community of developers.

Instrumentation in JMX is embodied within a structured framework for augmenting Java objects with attributes and operations that work together to form a management interface for the objects. These instrumented Java objects are contained and organized within a simple registry called an MBean server, which is maintained by a JMX agent. Management applications can access the instrumented objects by interacting with an agent using currently defined protocols and processes.

The JMX instrumentation-level APIs and technologies allow developers to augment any Java-accessible resource with manageable features. The instrumentation API defines how applications expose data, operations, and events to interested management systems and applications. The instrumentation layer exposes a manageable resource as one or more managed beans, or MBeans. The instrumentation level directs itself towards the Java developer community as a whole.

In this chapter, I will discuss the instrumentation level of JMX and how it enables devices, services, applications, and other resources to be easily exposed as manageable resources to any Java-enabled system or application.

An MBean Primer

In Chapter 1, I discussed how an MBean is a Java object that represents any entity that can be exposed using the Java programming language. There are four types of MBeans: standard, dynamic, open, and model.

An MBean exposes access to its behavior using Java methods, known in JMX as *operations*. An MBean exposes access to its state using standard JavaBean properties. JavaBean properties are fields that are modified using setter methods and accessed using getter methods (further information about JavaBeans can be found at `http://java.sun.com/beans`). Properties of an MBean are referred to as *attributes*. An MBean exposes changes to its state to interested listeners using *notifications*.

An agent discovers the management interface for an MBean using one of two mechanisms, *static* or *dynamic*. Static discovery relies on runtime introspection. Dynamic discovery relies on the MBean itself to return standard metadata objects containing the management information. Standard MBeans define their management interface statically; dynamic, open, and model MBeans expose their management interfaces dynamically using metadata objects.

All four of the MBean types serve unique purposes. However, dynamic MBeans, open MBeans, and model MBeans all share two common features: They all implement the `javax.management.DynamicMBean` interface or an extension of the `javax.management.DynamicMBean` interface, and they all expose their management information using `MBeanInfo` objects. `javax.management.MBeanInfo` objects are instances of the `javax.management.MBeanInfo` class. The `javax.management.MBeanInfo` class is used to present metadata about each MBean to interested management tools. The relationships between the four types of MBeans along with their metadata are demonstrated in Figure 2-1.

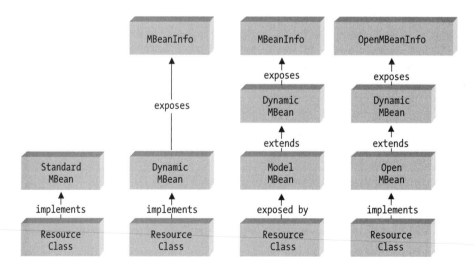

Figure 2-1. MBean relationships

MBeans are never directly exposed by an MBean server. Instead they are named and retrieved by an alias known as an `ObjectName`. We examine the structure of an `ObjectName` in the next section, as well as the details and uses of standard MBeans and dynamic MBeans.

Naming MBeans Using Object Names

An MBean is registered with an MBean server that is exposed by an agent. The MBean server uses an object known as an *object name* to uniquely identify the MBean. An object name is represented by `javax.management.ObjectName` and consists of two parts that are separated by a colon:

- *A domain name:* A domain name is any arbitrary, case-sensitive string of characters that represents a namespace meaningful to an application, business, user, etc.

- *A property list:* The property list of an object name is an arbitrary, unordered, comma-delimited list of one or more name/value pairs that are used to uniquely identify an MBean or provide information about an MBean.

The following examples are allowable object names:

`"mydomain:name=mymbean"`

`"DefaultDomain:type=service"`

`"com.jeffhanson:type=book,subject=jmx"`

In Chapter 1, I showed you how to register the `DateTimeService` MBean with the MBean server under an object name of `services:name=DateTime,type=information`. If you dissect this name, you find that the domain is *services* and the property list consists of two name/value pairs, *name=DateTime* and *type=information*.

The property list for an object name can be significant as it is used in query operations when locating MBeans. For example, you can apply the following string to a query operation on an MBean server to find all MBeans that belong to the domain *mydomain*:

`"mydomain:* "`

The following example finds all MBeans in the domain *mydomain* that have the key/value pair *type=service* anywhere in the property list of their domain name:

`"mydomain:type=service,*"`

Standard MBeans are the simplest MBeans to implement and use. Let's take a brief look at some of the more common features of a standard MBean.

Standard MBeans

A standard MBean exposes its management information statically in one of the following three ways:

1. By implementing an actual Java interface that defines the operations and attributes that express the MBean's desired management data. The name of the interface must be the same as the MBean's class name with the suffix MBean appended. For example, the MBean interface for an object whose fully qualified class name is com.apress.jhanson.User would be named com.apress.jhanson.UserMBean.

2. By extending the javax.management.StandardMBean class and passing the class of the management interface as the parameter to the javax.management.StandardMBean constructor.

3. By instantiating an instance of javax.management.StandardMBean and passing an instance of the MBean class and the class of the management interface as parameters to the javax.management.StandardMBean constructor.

I demonstrated the implementation of a standard MBean in Chapter 1 when I applied a management interface to the DateTimeService class. This involved defining an actual Java interface that the DateTimeService class implemented. The Java interface was named the same as the DateTimeService class with the addition of MBean appended to the end (i.e., DateTimeServiceMBean). Recall that the DateTimeServiceMBean interface defined two methods, getDate() and getTime(). This effectively exposed two read-only attributes, Date and Time, to the JMX architecture.

I will now show you how to make the attributes Date and Time read-write by adding a setter method for each attribute. You will also see how to introduce two operations on your MBean called stop() and start(). To do so, modify the MBean interface for your DateTimeService class to look like the following:

```
package com.apress.jhanson.services;

public interface DateTimeServiceMBean
{
    public void setDate(String newValue);
    public String getDate();
    public void setTime(String newValue);
```

```
    public String getTime();
    public void stop();
    public void start();
}
```

Dynamic MBeans

A dynamic MBean exposes its management information by returning standard
metadata objects from methods defined in the javax.management.DynamicMBean
interface. Since dynamic MBeans provide their actual management information
at runtime, they are much more flexible than standard MBeans. They also typically provide better performance than standard MBeans because they do not
require an agent to perform introspection on them to obtain their management
data. However, these benefits come at the cost of type safety, which can be dan-
gerous if extra caution is not taken. The DynamicMBean interface is a fairly simple
interface as can be seen by its definition:

```
package javax.management;

public interface DynamicMBean
{
    Object getAttribute(String s)
        throws AttributeNotFoundException,
                MBeanException,
                ReflectionException;

    void setAttribute(Attribute attribute)
        throws AttributeNotFoundException,
                InvalidAttributeValueException,
                MBeanException,
                ReflectionException;

    AttributeList getAttributes(String[] strings);

    AttributeList setAttributes(AttributeList list);

    Object invoke(String s, Object[] objects, String[] strings)
        throws MBeanException, ReflectionException;

    MBeanInfo getMBeanInfo();
}
```

As you can see, the DynamicMBean interface is quite straightforward. It provides four methods for dealing with attribute information (getAttribute,

setAttribute, getAttributes, and setAttributes), one method, invoke, that can be used to call one of its operations, and one method, getMBeanInfo, that returns its detailed metadata.

Although the DynamicMBean interface is straightforward and simple looking, it enables an implementation that provides a vast amount of information about an MBean. The MBeanInfo object, which is returned by the getMBeanInfo method, is a frontline access point for extensive information about an MBean's attributes, operations, notifications, and constructors.

Now, I will introduce how to implement the DynamicMBean interface and how you can apply it to the DateTimeServiceMBean in order to support a more dynamic implementation.

Implementing the DynamicMBean Interface

Let's modify the DateTimeService class to implement the DynamicMBean interface. Remember, when you implemented the DateTimeService MBean as a standard MBean in Chapter 1, you relied on an agent to introspect your MBeans in order to gather the management information about the MBean. So, once you have modified your MBean to implement the DynamicMBean interface, an agent will detect this and delegate the information-gathering duties to your MBean itself. Let's take a look at how this unfolds.

Eliminating the DateTimeServiceMBean Interface

The first thing you can do is eliminate the DateTimeServiceMBean interface. The DateTimeServiceMBean interface is no longer needed because you are not relying on the agent to detect this interface and use it as a reference for introspection. Once you have removed your reference to the DateTimeServiceMBean interface, you must modify the DateTimeService class to implement the DynamicMBean interface as shown:

```
package com.apress.jhanson.services;

import javax.management.*;
import java.util.Calendar;
import java.util.Iterator;
import java.text.DateFormat;
import java.lang.reflect.Constructor;
```

```java
public class DateTimeService
    implements DynamicMBean
{

    public static final boolean READABLE = true;
    public static final boolean WRITEABLE = true;
    public static final boolean ISIS = true;

    private String userConfiguredDate = null;
    private String userConfiguredTime = null;
    private MBeanAttributeInfo[] attributeInfo = new MBeanAttributeInfo[2];
    private MBeanConstructorInfo[] constructorInfo = new MBeanConstructorInfo[1];
    private MBeanOperationInfo[] operationInfo = new MBeanOperationInfo[2];
    private MBeanInfo mBeanInfo = null;

    public void setDate(String newValue)
    {
        userConfiguredDate = newValue;
    }

    public String getDate()
    {
        if (userConfiguredDate != null)
            return userConfiguredDate;
        Calendar rightNow = Calendar.getInstance();
        return DateFormat.getDateInstance().format(rightNow.getTime());
    }

    public void setTime(String newValue)
    {
        userConfiguredTime = newValue;
    }

    public String getTime()
    {
        if (userConfiguredTime != null)
            return userConfiguredTime;
        Calendar rightNow = Calendar.getInstance();
        return DateFormat.getTimeInstance().format(rightNow.getTime());
    }

    public void stop()
    {
    }
```

```
public void start()
{
}
```

Implementing the DynamicMBean Methods

In order to fulfill the requirements of the DynamicMBean interface, you need to provide an implementation for six methods: getAttribute, setAttribute, getAttributes, setAttributes, invoke, and getMBeanInfo.

The four methods dealing with attributes (getAttribute, setAttribute, getAttributes, and setAttributes) primarily involve testing a String or String array for an attribute name or names and either returning values or setting values accordingly. Notice that these examples include a lot of checking for null values and invalid names inside of the attribute and operation methods. You do this because there is no compile-time type checking performed on the parameters of these methods, so you must try to do as much checking as possible at runtime, in order to make up for the lack of compile-time checking and avoid invalid values.

```
public Object getAttribute(String attributeName)
    throws AttributeNotFoundException,
    MBeanException,
    ReflectionException
{
    if (attributeName == null)
    {
        IllegalArgumentException ex =
            new IllegalArgumentException("Attribute name cannot be null");
        throw new RuntimeOperationsException(ex, "null attribute name");
    }

    if (attributeName.equals("Date"))
    {
        return getDate();
    }

    if (attributeName.equals("Time"))
    {
        return getTime();
    }

    throw(new AttributeNotFoundException("Invalid attribute: "
                                    + attributeName));
}
```

The setAttribute Method

The setAttribute method sets the value of a specific attribute of your dynamic MBean. The only parameter required is an Attribute object containing the identification of the attribute to be set and a specified value. Multiple exceptions are potentially thrown by this method as follows:

- AttributeNotFoundException: Thrown if an invalid attribute is passed in

- InvalidAttributeValueException: Thrown if an invalid attribute value is passed in

- MBeanException: Thrown by the MBean's setter method for the attribute

- ReflectionException: Thrown while trying to invoke the MBean's setter method for the attribute

The following code illustrates how to apply the setAttribute method for two attributes, Date and Time:

```
public void setAttribute(Attribute attribute)
    throws AttributeNotFoundException,
    InvalidAttributeValueException,
    MBeanException,
    ReflectionException
{
    if (attribute == null)
    {
        IllegalArgumentException ex =
            new IllegalArgumentException("Attribute cannot be null");
        throw new RuntimeOperationsException(ex, "null attribute");
    }

    String name = attribute.getName();
    Object value = attribute.getValue();

    if (name == null)
    {
        IllegalArgumentException ex =
            new IllegalArgumentException("Attribute name cannot be null");
        throw new RuntimeOperationsException(ex, "null attribute name");
    }
```

```
if (value == null)
{
    IllegalArgumentException ex =
        new IllegalArgumentException("Attribute value cannot be null");
    throw new RuntimeOperationsException(ex, "null attribute value");
}
```

The isAssignableFrom method in the following code block is used to check whether one class reference can be assigned to another:

```
try
{
    Class stringCls = Class.forName("java.lang.String");
    if (stringCls.isAssignableFrom(value.getClass()) == false)
    {
        IllegalArgumentException ex =
            new IllegalArgumentException("Invalid attribute value class");
        throw new RuntimeOperationsException(ex, "Invalid attribute value");
    }
}
catch (ClassNotFoundException e)
{
    e.printStackTrace();
}
```

You now check to see which attribute is to be modified. In this example, you simply do String compares to test for equality.

```
if (name.equals("Date"))
{
    setDate(value.toString());
}
else if (name.equals("Time"))
{
    setTime(value.toString());
}
else
{
    throw(new AttributeNotFoundException("Invalid Attribute name; "
                                        + name));
}
}
```

The getAttributes Method

The getAttributes method retrieves the values of several attributes of your dynamic MBean. The only parameter for this method is an array of String objects that represents the list of names of the attributes to be retrieved. The return value is an AttributeList object containing the list of attributes retrieved.

```java
public AttributeList getAttributes(String[] attributeNames)
{
    if (attributeNames == null)
    {
        IllegalArgumentException ex =
            new IllegalArgumentException("attributeNames cannot be null");
        throw new RuntimeOperationsException(ex, "null attribute names");
    }

    AttributeList resultList = new AttributeList();

    if (attributeNames.length == 0)
        return resultList;

    for (int i = 0; i < attributeNames.length; i++)
    {
        try
        {
            Object value = getAttribute((String) attributeNames[i]);
            resultList.add(new Attribute(attributeNames[i], value));
        }
        catch (Exception e)
        {
            e.printStackTrace();
        }
    }

    return (resultList);
}
```

The setAttributes Method

The setAttributes method sets the values of several attributes of your dynamic MBean. The only parameter passed in is an AttributeList object containing the identification of the attributes to be set and a specified value. The return value is an AttributeList object containing the list of attributes that were set with their new values.

```
public AttributeList setAttributes(AttributeList attributes)
{
   if (attributes == null)
   {
      IllegalArgumentException ex =
         new IllegalArgumentException("attributes cannot be null");
      throw new RuntimeOperationsException(ex, "null attribute list");
   }

   AttributeList resultList = new AttributeList();

   if (attributes.isEmpty())
      return resultList;

   for (Iterator i = attributes.iterator(); i.hasNext();)
   {
      Attribute attr = (Attribute) i.next();
      try
      {
         setAttribute(attr);
         String name = attr.getName();
         Object value = getAttribute(name);
         resultList.add(new Attribute(name, value));
      }
      catch (Exception e)
      {
         e.printStackTrace();
      }
   }

   return (resultList);
}
```

The invoke Method

The invoke method tests a String for an operation name and, if the name is valid, makes the call to the appropriate operation.

The invoke method enables an operation to be invoked on your dynamic MBean. The parameters required are

- An operation name that represents the name of the operation to be invoked.

- An array of objects containing the parameter values to be passed to the operation that is invoked.

- An array of Strings containing the class names representing the parameter types of the operation that is invoked.

The return value, if applicable, is a generic Object.

```
public Object invoke(String operationName,
                     Object[] params,
                     String[] signature)
    throws MBeanException,
    ReflectionException
{
    if (operationName == null)
    {
        IllegalArgumentException ex =
            new IllegalArgumentException("Operation name cannot be null");
        throw new RuntimeOperationsException(ex, "null operation name");
    }

    if (operationName.equals("stop"))
    {
        stop();
        return null;
    }
    else if (operationName.equals("start"))
    {
        start();
        return null;
    }
    else
    {
        throw new ReflectionException(new NoSuchMethodException(operationName),
                                      "Invalid operation name: "
                                      + operationName);
    }
}
```

The getMBeanInfo Method

The getMBeanInfo method is the workhorse for providing metadata information about your MBean. This method must return information about attributes, operations, constructors, and notifications for your MBean. Each group of information is encapsulated within an instance of a JMX metadata class such as MBeanAttributeInfo, MBeanConstructorInfo, and MBeanOperationInfo. These metadata objects are then encapsulated within another metadata object, MBeanInfo, and returned.

```
public MBeanInfo getMBeanInfo()
{
    if (mBeanInfo != null)
        return mBeanInfo;

    attributeInfo[0] = new MBeanAttributeInfo("Date",
                                              String.class.getName(),
                                              "The current date.",
                                              READABLE,
                                              WRITEABLE,
                                              !ISIS);
    attributeInfo[1] = new MBeanAttributeInfo("Time",
                                              String.class.getName(),
                                              "The current time",
                                              READABLE,
                                              WRITEABLE,
                                              !ISIS);

    Constructor[] constructors = this.getClass().getConstructors();
    constructorInfo[0] =
        new MBeanConstructorInfo("Constructs a DateTimeService object",
                                 constructors[0]);

    MBeanParameterInfo[] params = null;
    operationInfo[0] = new MBeanOperationInfo("start",
                                              "Starts the DateTime service",
                                              params,
                                              "void",
                                              MBeanOperationInfo.ACTION);

    operationInfo[1] = new MBeanOperationInfo("stop",
                                              "Stops the DateTime service",
                                              params,
                                              "void",
                                              MBeanOperationInfo.ACTION);
```

```
        mBeanInfo = new MBeanInfo(this.getClass().getName(),
                                  "DateTime Service MBean",
                                  attributeInfo,
                                  constructorInfo,
                                  operationInfo,
                                  new MBeanNotificationInfo[0]);


        return (mBeanInfo);
    }
}
```

Now that you have completed the conversion from a standard MBean to a dynamic MBean, an agent can delegate management queries about your MBean to the MBean itself.

Model MBeans

Model MBeans are extensions of dynamic MBeans and, as such, return their management information using metadata objects as well. Model MBeans expose the same metadata objects that dynamic MBeans expose, as well as additional information. For example, the object returned from the getMBeanInfo method must be an instance of the ModelMBeanInfo interface, which exposes Descriptor objects in addition to the standard information.

Model MBeans can be instantiated and used as a template or proxy instead of defining your own MBean classes. This is especially useful as a mechanism for exposing a management interface for existing Java resources without modifying the existing classes. This also buffers an MBean implementation away from the differences that can sometimes crop up between JVM versions and vendors.

Open MBeans

Open MBeans are extensions of dynamic MBeans as well and also return their management information using metadata objects. Like model MBeans, open MBeans expose the same metadata objects that dynamic MBeans expose, as well as additional information. Open MBeans are restricted to using a finite set of universal Java data types to expose their information, in order to facilitate supporting a more complete set of objects at runtime.

MBean Notifications

JMX defines an event notification framework that is similar to the general event framework already in use in the Java programming language. The JMX event framework defines notifications that can be transmitted by broadcasters and received by listeners. Notification broadcasters can be MBeans or MBean servers.

The JMX event notification framework defines the following components:

- A Notification class: An event class that extends the java.util.EventObject class, which contains information about the notification event.

- A NotificationListener interface: This must be implemented by objects that wish to receive notifications sent by broadcasters.

- A NotificationFilter interface: Objects implementing this can be used by listener objects to filter events transmitted by broadcasters.

- A NotificationBroadcaster interface: This is implemented by broadcasters that transmit notification events. A broadcaster that implements this interface must allow objects to add and remove themselves as listeners to notifications transmitted by the broadcaster.

- A NotificationEmitter interface: This extends NotificationBroadcaster and is implemented by broadcasters that transmit notification events. Like the NotificationBroadcaster interface, this interface defines methods to allow objects to add or remove themselves as listeners to notifications transmitted from broadcasters; however, this interface provides slightly more control for removing listeners.

Within the JMX event framework, a listener only registers one time with a broadcaster in order to receive all events that the broadcaster will transmit. The listener then, optionally, applies appropriate filter objects to the events as they are received in order to pick and choose which events the listener wants. Figure 2-2 portrays the JMX event notification framework.

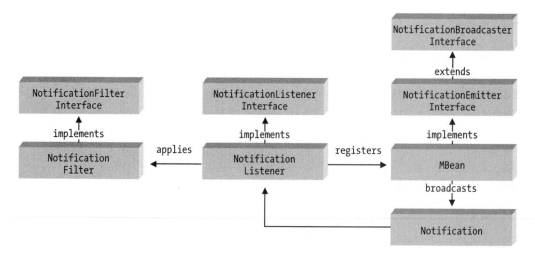

Figure 2-2. Notification framework

MBean Information and Metadata Classes

MBeans are exposed by an agent through instances of metadata classes. These metadata classes are the vehicles of information that client applications must understand in order to view and use information concerning attributes, operations, constructors, and notifications of an MBean.

The JMX MBean metadata classes are as follows:

- MBeanInfo: Instances of this class provide an MBean's class name and description. Instances of this class also encapsulate instances of other metadata classes containing information about the attributes, operations, constructors, and notifications of an MBean.

- MBeanFeatureInfo: This class is the superclass for all of the other metadata classes with the exception of the MBeanInfo class.

- MBeanAttributeInfo: Instances of this class encapsulate the information for a given attribute. This information includes the attribute's name, class name, description, whether the attribute is readable and/or writable, etc.

- MBeanConstructorInfo: Instances of this class encapsulate the information for a given constructor of an MBean. This information contains the signature of the constructor including the parameter types.

- MBeanOperationInfo: Instances of this class encapsulate the information for a given operation of an MBean. This information includes the operation's name, description, signature, and impact type. The impact type gives a loose approximation of the type of impact the operation will have on the system. For example, the impact type can be one of four values defined in the MBeanOperationInfo class: INFO, ACTION, ACTION_INFO, and UNKNOWN. An impact type of INFO means that the operation just returns information without causing any other type of impact. An impact type of ACTION means the operation will perform some action on the MBean and possibly other objects. ACTION_INFO means the operation will perform some action and return information.

- MBeanParameterInfo: Instances of this class encapsulate the information for a single parameter of an operation or constructor. This information includes the parameter's name, description, and type.

- MBeanNotificationInfo: Instances of this class describe the characteristics of the notifications that are transmitted by an MBean. This information includes the notification name, description, and notification types. The notification types are strings defining the types of notifications that the MBean may transmit. Each notification type is a string in dot notation, which is assigned by a broadcaster, describing the semantic meaning for each notification.

Let's look at how you modify the DateTimeService MBean to support notifications. For this example, you want to transmit a notification whenever the Date or Time attributes change and whenever the stop or start operations are called.

Adding Fields to Your MBean

The first thing you must do is add a couple of fields. You add a notificationInfo field that will contain the information about your notifications. You also add an instance of the NotificationBroadcasterSupport class to handle adding and removing of listeners and to do the actual notification transmission to the listeners. Finally, you add a notificationSequence field that will keep track of the number of notifications and act as the identifier of each notification.

```
private MBeanNotificationInfo[] notificationInfo = null;
private NotificationBroadcasterSupport broadcasterSupport =
                            new NotificationBroadcasterSupport();
private long notificationSequence = 0;
```

Modifying the setDate and setTime Methods

Next you need to modify the setDate and setTime methods to transmit an AttributeChangeNotification object whenever the Date or Time attributes are changed.

```
public void setDate(String newValue)
{
    String oldValue = getDate();
    String attrType = String.class.getName();
    String attrName = "Date";

    userConfiguredDate = newValue;
```

```
    AttributeChangeNotification notif =
        new AttributeChangeNotification(this,
                                        ++notificationSequence,
                                        System.currentTimeMillis(),
                                        "Date has been changed.",
                                        attrName, attrType,
                                        oldValue, newValue);


    broadcasterSupport.sendNotification(notif);
}

public void setTime(String newValue)
{
    String oldValue = getDate();
    String attrType = String.class.getName();
    String attrName = "Time";

    userConfiguredTime = newValue;

    AttributeChangeNotification notif =
        new AttributeChangeNotification(this,
                                        ++notificationSequence,
                                        System.currentTimeMillis(),
                                        "Time has been changed.",
                                        attrName, attrType,
                                        oldValue, newValue);


    broadcasterSupport.sendNotification(notif);
}
```

Modifying the stop and start Methods

Now, modify the stop and start methods to transmit generic Notification objects whenever they are called.

```
public void stop()
{
    Notification notif = new Notification("services.datetime.stop",
                                          this,
                                          ++notificationSequence,
                                          "DateTime service stopped.");
    broadcasterSupport.sendNotification(notif);
}
```

```
public void start()
{
    Notification notif = new Notification("services.datetime.start",
                                          this,
                                          ++notificationSequence,
                                          "DateTime service started.");
    broadcasterSupport.sendNotification(notif);
}
```

Enabling the MBean to Add and Remove Notification Listeners

Next, you add methods to enable your MBean to add and remove notification listeners. These methods are required in order to fulfill your implementation requirements for the NotificationEmitter interface. You delegate the actual *adding* and *removing* processes to the broadcasterSupport object.

```
public void addNotificationListener(NotificationListener listener,
                                    NotificationFilter filter,
                                    Object handback)
{
    broadcasterSupport.addNotificationListener(listener, filter, handback);
}


public void removeNotificationListener(NotificationListener listener)
    throws ListenerNotFoundException
{
    broadcasterSupport.removeNotificationListener(listener);
}


public void removeNotificationListener(NotificationListener listener,
                                       NotificationFilter filter,
                                       Object handback)
    throws ListenerNotFoundException
{
    broadcasterSupport.removeNotificationListener(listener, filter, handback);
}
```

Modifying the mBeanInfo Object

Now, modify the mBeanInfo object that you return from your getMBeanInfo method to include the new notification info.

```
mBeanInfo = new MBeanInfo(this.getClass().getName(),
                          "DateTime Service MBean",
                          attributeInfo,
                          constructorInfo,
                          operationInfo,
                          getNotificationInfo());
```

Creating the Notification Metadata Objects

And finally, you add a method to handle the creation of the notification information object. This method is necessary to complete the implementation requirements of the NotificationEmitter interface.

```
public MBeanNotificationInfo[] getNotificationInfo()
{
    if (notificationInfo != null)
        return notificationInfo;

    notificationInfo = new MBeanNotificationInfo[]
    {
        new MBeanNotificationInfo(new String[] { "service.user.start" },
                              Notification.class.getName(),
                              "DateTime service start."),
        new MBeanNotificationInfo(new String[] { "service.user.stop" },
                              Notification.class.getName(),
                              "DateTime service stop."),
        new MBeanNotificationInfo(new String[] {
                              AttributeChangeNotification.ATTRIBUTE_CHANGE },
                              AttributeChangeNotification.class.getName(),
                              "DateTime service attribute changes.")
    };

    return notificationInfo;
}
```

Summary

The three-level model that JMX defines presents different levels of technologies to different developer communities. This allows teams of developers to target the area of management that best suits their experience level and business needs.

The JMX instrumentation level allows developers to augment Java resources with management semantics from the very beginning of the development cycle. These augmented or instrumented resources, referred to as MBeans, provide the foundation for a comprehensive and powerful management platform. This design, along with the component-oriented nature of JMX, ensures that system and application services are not only manageable, but also very modular in nature.

CHAPTER 3

The Three-Level Model: Agents

WHENEVER THE TERM *agent* is brought up in software development circles, we tend to think of independent, nomadic components that roam about the Web searching, gathering, prying, and engaging in other potentially scary activities. However, in nonspecific terms, a generic software agent can be thought of as an autonomous component that communicates and interacts with other entities on behalf of one or more controlling entities. Extensions of generic agents include intelligent agents, proxy agents, master agents, subagents, and others.

A software agent has historically been thought of as including such properties as autonomy, reactivity, social ability, collaborative behavior, adaptability, and mobility. Although JMX agents are certainly not precluded from possessing these properties, they are generally defined in far simpler terms. JMX agents are software modules that link management applications with managed resources.

A software management agent can be generically defined as a software module representing a managed entity that stores and delivers management information to other interested devices or software applications over a given protocol. For example, within the realm of the Simple Network Management Protocol (SNMP), agents are loosely defined as network devices, such as hosts, bridges, hubs, routers, etc., that can be communicated with and monitored by a management application. Typically, a management agent responds to a management application's requests, performs actions requested by the management application, and may send notification messages to the application.

In this chapter, we will look at the manner in which JMX defines management agents and how JMX agents interact with MBeans and management applications. We will also investigate how JMX defines services in respect to agents.

The Agent Level of JMX

The JMX agent level defines management agents, which contain and expose an MBean server, agent services, and MBeans. The agent level of the JMX specification is aimed at the management solutions development community. The specifications for JMX agent design and implementation allow developers to build applications that manage resources without prior knowledge of the attributes or operations of the resources.

An agent facilitates access to managed resources by acting as the connecting link between management applications and registered MBeans. An agent is responsible for dispatching requests to the MBeans that it contains as well as broadcasting notifications to interested notification receivers that have previously registered with the agent. A JMX agent consists of several mandatory services, known as *agent services,* an MBean server, and at least one protocol adaptor or connector.

Services that a JMX agent must provide include a monitoring service, a timer service, a relation service, and a dynamic class-loading service. Additional services can be provided as well. These services are also registered as MBeans.

An agent can reside in a local JVM or in a JVM that is remote to interested management applications or remote to MBeans that the agent contains. Later, I will discuss how an agent can be constructed to enable access from applications residing in remote JVMs.

MBean Servers

As discussed in Chapter 1, an *MBean server* is an object defined by the javax.management.MBeanServer interface and/or the javax.management.MBeanServerConnection interface and acts as a registry and repository for MBeans contained by an agent. An MBean server performs all life cycle operations on an MBean such as creation, registration, and deletion. An MBean server also performs query operations that find and retrieve registered MBeans.

The MBeanServer interface extends the javax.management.MBeanServerConnection interface. The MBeanServerConnection interface defines methods that can be called on an MBean server regardless of whether the MBean server is remote or local. The MBeanServer interface extends the MBeanServerConnection interface to define methods that can only be called on a local MBean server.

All interaction with MBeans must be directed through an agent, and thus the agent acts as a proxy for the MBean server that it contains.

Figure 3-1 illustrates the relationships between an agent, its agent services, and an MBean server.

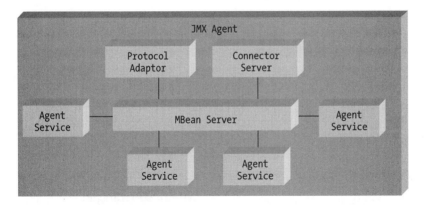

Figure 3-1. A JMX agent with its agent services and MBean server

An agent typically does not have prior knowledge of the details of the resources that it contains or the client applications that will use the resources. It simply relies on the standard generic instrumentation functionality of the JMX framework in order to discover the resources' capabilities and to act on them accordingly.

Recall how earlier I demonstrated a service agent that registered and exposed one MBean, the DateTimeService MBean:

```
MBeanServer mbServer =
    MBeanServerFactory.createMBeanServer();

ObjectName oName =
    new ObjectName("services:name=DateTime,type=information");

mbServer.registerMBean(new DateTimeService(), oName);
```

This type of agent implies that you know beforehand the exact type and number of MBeans that your agent will contain. Most situations do not afford an agent the luxury of knowing beforehand the number and types of MBeans that it will contain. This makes it very important that agents have a mechanism for dynamically adding, removing, and maintaining their list of registered MBeans.

Let's take a look at how you might refactor your service agent to handle adding MBeans dynamically.

Opening Up the ServiceAgent

The first thing you need to do is move the declaration for your MBean server instance out of the main method and declare it as a global, private field of your ServiceAgent class.

```
    private MBeanServer mbServer = null;

    public static void main(String[] args)
    {
        ServiceAgent agent = new ServiceAgent();
    }
```

Declaring an Effective Constructor

Next, explicitly declare a no-arg constructor that will serve to create your MBean server instance and to create and register the HtmlAdaptorServer instance.

```
    public ServiceAgent()
    {
        try
        {
            mbServer = MBeanServerFactory.createMBeanServer();

            ObjectName adaptorOName =
                new ObjectName("adaptors:protocol=HTTP");

            HtmlAdaptorServer htmlAdaptor = new HtmlAdaptorServer();
            mbServer.registerMBean(htmlAdaptor, adaptorOName);
            htmlAdaptor.start();
        }
        catch(MBeanRegistrationException e) {}
        catch(NotCompliantMBeanException e) { }
        catch(MalformedObjectNameException e) {}
        catch(InstanceAlreadyExistsException e) {}
    }
```

Adding the addResource Method

Notice that the lines of code that instantiate and register your DateTimeService MBean have been removed. In their place you include a method named addResource, which allows MBeans to be added dynamically. The addResource method takes as parameters the desired name for the MBean, the property list for the MBean, and the class name of the MBean. The property list is passed in as a Hashtable. The addResource method throws a generic ServiceException that you define in order to encapsulate any exception that is caught within the method.

The first thing you need to do is add an import for the Hashtable class, as follows:

```
import java.util.Hashtable;
```

Now add your implementation for the addResource method as shown here:

```java
public void addResource(String name, Hashtable properties, String className)
    throws ServiceAgentException
{
    try
    {
        Class cls = Class.forName(className);
        Object obj = cls.newInstance();
        Hashtable allProps = new Hashtable();
        allProps.put("name", name);
        properties.putAll(allProps);
        ObjectName oName = new ObjectName("services", allProps);
        mbServer.registerMBean(obj, oName);
    }
    catch (IllegalAccessException e)
    {
        throw new ServiceAgentException(e.getMessage());
    }
    catch (InstantiationException e)
    {
        throw new ServiceAgentException("Unable to create instance of MBean: "
                                    + e.getMessage());
    }
    catch (ClassNotFoundException e)
    {
        throw new ServiceAgentException("Unable to find class for MBean: "
                                    + e.getMessage());
    }
    catch (MalformedObjectNameException e)
    {
        throw new ServiceAgentException("Invalid object name: "
                                    + e.getMessage());
    }
    catch (InstanceAlreadyExistsException e)
    {
        throw new ServiceAgentException("The MBean already exists: "
                                    + e.getMessage());
    }
    catch (MBeanRegistrationException e)
    {
        throw new ServiceAgentException("General registration exception: "
                                    + e.getMessage());
```

```
        }
        catch (NotCompliantMBeanException e)
        {
            throw new ServiceAgentException("The class is not MBean compliant: "
                                        + e.getMessage());
        }
    }
```

Now, you add your ServiceAgentException class. For the time being, keep it very simple, as follows:

```
public class ServiceAgentException extends Exception
{
    public ServiceAgentException()
    {
        super();
    }

    public ServiceAgentException(String message)
    {
        super(message);
    }
}
```

Adding the getResources Method

Next, you add a method, getResources, to facilitate the retrieval of previously registered MBeans from the MBean server within the agent. For now, you will only retrieve MBeans by name. Later, you will add the ability to query for MBeans based on parts of a name, property list fragments, and wildcards.

The first thing you need to do is add an import statement for the Set class, as follows:

```
import java.util.Set;
```

Now you add your implementation for the getResources method:

```
public Set getResources(String name)
    throws ServiceAgentException
{
```

```
    try
    {
        Hashtable allProps = new Hashtable();
        allProps.put("name", name);
        ObjectName oName = new ObjectName("services", allProps);
        Set resultSet = mbServer.queryMBeans(oName, null);
        return resultSet;
    }
    catch (MalformedObjectNameException e)
    {
        throw new ServiceAgentException("Invalid object name: "
                                    + e.getMessage());
    }
}
```

Categorizing Resource Groups Using Domains

JMX categorizes resource groups within a *domain*. A domain is a namespace for a specific set of information and resources within an agent, management system, or application.

Let's look at some of the details and uses for domains and the JMX domain naming conventions.

Domain Names

A JMX domain name is an application-independent, case-sensitive string that labels the namespace defined by an agent, management system, or application. A JMX domain name may be constructed of any string of characters excluding those characters that are used as separators or wildcards for the ObjectName class. The excluded characters include the colon (:), comma (,), equal sign (=), asterisk (*), and question mark (?).

Uniquely Naming MBeans Using Key Properties

The ObjectName class comprises two elements: the domain name and a key property list. The key property list allows MBeans to be given a unique name within the realm of a domain. Key properties are arbitrary property-value pairs, for example, type=service.

The key property list of an ObjectName can contain any number of key properties, but must contain at least one key property. The following examples define valid ObjectName instances for a domain named MyDomain:

```
ObjectName oName = new ObjectName("MyDomain:type=service");
ObjectName oName = new ObjectName("MyDomain:type=service,persistence=transient");
```

Extending an Agent with Agent Services

JMX agents must supply a set of predefined services for operating on MBeans that are registered with the agent's MBean server. These mandatory services are referred to as *agent services* and are usually implemented as MBeans themselves.

Implementing the agent services as MBeans enables an agent to operate on the services in the same manner that it would for an ordinary managed resource. The set of mandatory agent services include the following:

- *Dynamic class loading:* This service is exposed using a technology referred to as the management applet (M-Let). The M-Let technology allows an agent to load classes from arbitrary remote hosts defined by URLs. The classes can then be created and registered as MBeans in the same manner as local MBeans.

- *Monitor:* Monitors observe the value for a given MBean's attribute or attributes and notify listening objects of changes that occur on the value.

- *Timer:* Timers allow notifications to be scheduled as a one-time-only event or as a repeated, periodic event.

- *Relation:* This service defines predefined relation types for associations between MBeans.

Let's look at each of these agent services in more detail.

Dynamic MBean Loading

The dynamic MBean loading service is defined by classes, interfaces, and MBeans within the `javax.management.loading` package. The dynamic MBean loading service enables an agent to retrieve, create, and register MBeans from a remote host.

Dynamic MBean loading is enabled using a compact framework known as a management applet or M-Let. The M-Let framework facilitates loading MBeans specified by an arbitrary URL from a remote host.

The management applet framework is a compact framework that defines the following:

- An XML-like tag, called `MLET`, which describes the information for each MBean, as the following example illustrates:

```
<MLET
    CODE = com.jeffhanson.mlets.MyMLET
    CODEBASE = http://myhost/mlets
    ARCHIVE = "MyMLET.jar"
    NAME = MyMLET>
</MLET>
```

- A URL-locatable text file that contains `MLET`-tagged elements defining MBeans. When an M-Let text file is located, all of the classes specified by its `MLET` tags are downloaded. The classes are then instantiated as MBeans and registered with the MBean server.

- A class loader for retrieving and loading MBean classes from a remote host.

- An MBean that encapsulates the M-Let service itself. The M-Let MBean is registered in the MBean server.

The relationships between components defined by the M-Let framework are illustrated in Figure 3-2.

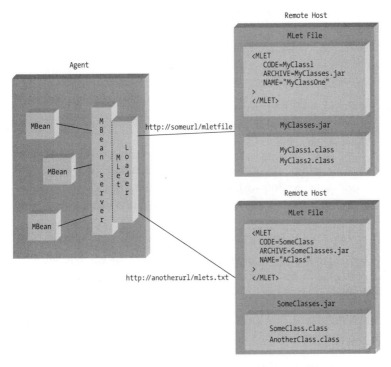

Figure 3-2. A JMX agent, an MLet class loader, and remote hosts

Now, let's look at how the JMX monitor service allows you to observe over time the variations of attribute values in MBeans and to emit notification events based on configurable thresholds.

Using Monitors to Track Changes

Monitors are a set of MBeans defined by classes and interfaces within the `javax.management.monitor` package that define components which allow interested listeners to observe, over a period of time, the value of a given attribute or the changes that occur in the values of a given attribute for a particular MBean. A monitor can transmit notification events for changes that occur within the observed attribute's values at given thresholds.

All monitors implement an MBean interface that extends a common interface, `MonitorMBean`. The `MonitorMBean` interface defines the following attributes and operations:

- `observedAttribute`: This flags the attribute as able to be observed.

- `granularityPeriod`: This attribute defines the granularity period in milliseconds over which to observe.

- `active`: An attribute that tests whether or not a monitor is active. This attribute is set to `true` when the `start` operation is invoked. It is set to `false` when the `stop` operation is called.

- `start`: This operation starts the monitor.

- `stop`: This operation stops the monitor.

Predefined Monitor Types

Three predefined monitors, implemented as MBeans, are provided by a JMX implementation: counter, gauge, and string. The class for each of these extends an abstract class, `Monitor`. The three predefined monitor types are detailed as follows:

- `CounterMonitor`: Monitors attributes that have the characteristics of a counter. These characteristics include the following: The value is always greater than or equal to zero, the value can only be incremented, and the value may roll over.

- `GaugeMonitor`: Monitors attributes that have characteristics of a gauge. This means that the attribute's value may randomly increase or decrease.

- `StringMonitor`: Monitors an attribute that returns a value of type `String`.

Because monitors are interested in the value of an attribute and not the attribute itself, they can monitor any attribute that returns a value with the data type that the monitor recognizes. This allows the StringMonitor, for example, to monitor a given attribute so long as the attribute returns a String as its value.

Types of Monitor Notifications

A monitor allows the value of an attribute for a particular MBean to be observed for certain thresholds. The value is monitored at intervals specified by a granularity period. Thresholds can be either an exact value or the difference derived from two given observation points. The threshold is known as a *derived gauge*.

When a condition for a derived gauge has been satisfied or when an error condition is encountered, a specific notification type is sent by the monitor. The specific conditions are defined by the monitor's management interface. The predefined notification types are as follows:

- jmx.monitor.error.mbean: This notification type is fired by all monitor types and indicates that the observed MBean is not registered with the MBean server.

- jmx.monitor.error.attribute: This notification type is fired by all monitor types and indicates that the observed attribute is not found.

- jmx.monitor.error.type: This notification type is fired by all monitor types and indicates that the observed attribute type is incorrect.

- jmx.monitor.error.threshold: This notification type is only fired by counter and gauge monitors and indicates that a characteristic of the threshold is incorrect.

- jmx.monitor.error.runtime: This notification type is fired by all monitor types and indicates that an unknown error has occurred when accessing the value of the observed attribute.

- jmx.monitor.counter.threshold: This notification type is only fired by counter monitors and indicates that the threshold has been reached for the observed attribute's value.

- jmx.monitor.gauge.high: This notification type is only fired by gauge monitors and indicates that the threshold's upper limit has been reached or exceeded for the observed attribute's value.

- jmx.monitor.gauge.low: This notification type is only fired by gauge monitors and indicates that the threshold's lower limit has been reached or exceeded for the observed attribute's value.

- jmx.monitor.string.matches: This notification type is only fired by string monitors and indicates that the monitor's comparison string has been matched.

- jmx.monitor.string.differs: This notification type is only fired by string monitors and indicates that the monitor's comparison string has been compared against an unequal value.

Supporting Monitor Listeners

Let's see how you would modify your service agent to expose a method that will accept a notification listener and set the listener as the listener to a simple CounterMonitor:

```
 import javax.management.monitor.*;
public class ServiceAgent
{
    static String counterMonitorClass =
        "javax.management.monitor.CounterMonitor";

    private MBeanServer mbServer = null;
    private ObjectName counterMonitorName = null;
    private CounterMonitor counterMonitor = null;

    public ServiceAgent()
    {
        mbServer = MBeanServerFactory.createMBeanServer();

        initializeCounterMonitor();

        // Existing code omitted here for sake of brevity.
    }
```

Adding a CounterMonitor

Now, create and register the CounterMonitor in your service agent. You register it under the MBean server's default domain.

```
protected void initializeCounterMonitor()
{
    ObjectName counterMonitorName = null;
    counterMonitor = new CounterMonitor();

    // Get the domain name from the MBeanServer.
    //
    String domain = mbServer.getDefaultDomain();

    // Create a new CounterMonitor MBean and add it to the MBeanServer.
    //
    try
    {
        counterMonitorName = new ObjectName(domain + ":name="
                                        + counterMonitorClass);
    }
    catch (MalformedObjectNameException e)
    {
        e.printStackTrace();
        return;
    }

    try
    {
        mbServer.registerMBean(counterMonitor, counterMonitorName);
    }
    catch (Exception e)
    {
        e.printStackTrace();
    }
}
```

Registering a CounterMonitor Listener

Now, add a method to set an object as a listener to the CounterMonitor. The
threshold value, the offset value, and the granularity period can all be modified
for your particular needs.

```
public void setCounterMonitorListener(ObjectName observedObjName,
                                    NotificationListener listener,
                                    String attrName)
{
    // Register a notification listener
    // with the CounterMonitor MBean, enabling the listener to receive
```

```
// notifications transmitted by the CounterMonitor.
//
try
{
    Integer threshold = new Integer(1);
    Integer offset  = new Integer(1);
    counterMonitor.setObservedObject(observedObjName);
    counterMonitor.setObservedAttribute(attrName);
    counterMonitor.setNotify(true);
    counterMonitor.setThreshold(threshold);
    counterMonitor.setOffset(offset);
    counterMonitor.setGranularityPeriod(1000);

    NotificationFilter filter = null;
    Object handback = null;
    counterMonitor.addNotificationListener(listener, filter, handback);
    if (counterMonitor.isActive() == false)
        counterMonitor.start();
}
catch (Exception e)
{
    e.printStackTrace();
}
}
```

Testing the CounterMonitor

You can now test your CounterMonitor and listener with the following code. First, set the listener as the listener to the CounterMonitor.

```
ObjectInstance objInst = serviceAgent.addResource("DateTime",
                                                      properties,
                                                      mbeanClassName);
serviceAgent.setCounterMonitorListener(objInst.getObjectName(),
                                                      this,
                                                      "Second");
```

Handling CounterMonitor Notification Events

Any object that is used as a CounterMonitor listener must implement the NotificationListener interface and the handleNotification method defined in the NotificationListener interface to handle notifications sent from the CounterMonitor.

```java
public void handleNotification(Notification notification, Object handback)
    {
        if (notification instanceof MonitorNotification)
        {
            MonitorNotification notif = (MonitorNotification) notification;

            // Get monitor responsible for the notification.
            //
            Monitor monitor = (Monitor) notif.getSource();

            // Test the notification types transmitted by the monitor.
            String t = notif.getType();
            Object observedObj = notif.getObservedObject();
            String observedAttr = notif.getObservedAttribute();

            try
            {
                if (t.equals(MonitorNotification.OBSERVED_OBJECT_ERROR))
                {
                    System.out.println(observedObj.getClass().getName()
                                    + " is not registered in the server");
                }
                else if (t.equals(MonitorNotification.OBSERVED_ATTRIBUTE_ERROR))
                {
                    System.out.println(observedAttr + " is not contained in " +
                                    observedObj.getClass().getName());
                }
                else if (t.equals(MonitorNotification.OBSERVED_ATTRIBUTE_TYPE_ERROR))
                {
                    System.out.println(observedAttr + " type is not correct");
                }
                else if (t.equals(MonitorNotification.THRESHOLD_ERROR))
                {
                    System.out.println("Threshold type is incorrect");
                }
                else if (t.equals(MonitorNotification.RUNTIME_ERROR))
                {
                    System.out.println("Unknown runtime error");
                }
                else if (t.equals(MonitorNotification.THRESHOLD_VALUE_EXCEEDED))
                {
                    System.out.println("observedAttr"
                                    + " has reached the threshold\n");
                }
```

```
        else
        {
            System.out.println("Unknown event type");
        }
    }
    catch (Exception e)
    {
        e.printStackTrace();
    }
  }
}
```

Scheduling Notifications Using Timers

The timer service is a set of classes, interfaces, and MBeans located in the javax.management.timer package, which transmits notifications according to scheduled times. The timer service may repeat the notifications at equal intervals called *periods,* and the notifications can be repeated for a number of given *occurrences.* As with all notifications, the timer notifications will be transmitted to all objects registered with the timer. It is then up to the listener to filter the notifications.

When an object adds a notification to a timer, the caller supplies the notification type and the date the notification is to be sent, or, if the notification is to be sent more than once, the period and the number of occurrences.

Figure 3-3 shows the relationships and concepts of periods and occurrences for timer notifications. The timeline demonstrates three occurrences for illustration purposes only.

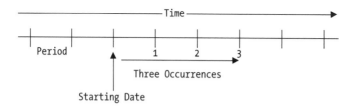

Figure 3-3. Timeline with periods and occurrences

Adding Notifications to a Timer

Notifications are added to a timer using one of the overloaded addNotification methods. The timer adds the notification to an internal list and transmits the notification depending on the parameters that are passed to the addNotification method. The parameters for all addNotification methods are defined as follows:

- type: The dot-delimited notification type.

- message: The notification message.

- userData: Optional user data.

- date: The date when the notification will occur. If the period and occurrences are greater than zero, the date will serve as the starting date for a number of notification events. If the date is prior to the current date, an attempt is made to create the notification by adding the period to the date until it is greater than the current date. If the period is not specified, or if date + (period * occurrences) is earlier than the current date, an exception is thrown.

- period: The interval in milliseconds between notification occurrences. Repeating notifications are not enabled if this parameter is zero or null.

- occurrences: The total number of times that the notification will occur. If the value of this parameter is zero or is not defined (null), and if the period is not zero or null, then the notification will repeat indefinitely.

Figure 3-4 illustrates a notification with three occurrences that is added with a date prior to the current date. Notice that the end result is a notification with two occurrences.

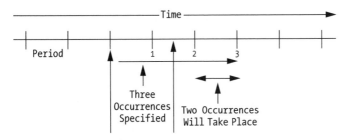

Figure 3-4. Notification added with a date prior to the current date

The addNotification method returns an Integer identifying the notification. This identifier is subsequently passed to the timer to retrieve information about the notification or to remove the notification from the timer.

Receiving Timer Events

The timer MBean extends the `javax.management.NotificationBroadcasterSupport` class and is thus a valid notification broadcaster. This implies, as with all notifications, that a listener to a timer will receive all notifications that the timer transmits. It is up to the listener to pass in an appropriate filter and handback object, when it registers, in order to filter the notification events as needed.

Each time a timer transmits a notification event and the number of occurrences for the notification is greater than zero, the number of occurrences is decremented by one. Thus, when the `getNbOccurrences(Integer notificationID)` method is called, the number returned will reflect the decremented amount.

When a timer has transmitted a notification the total number of times specified, the notification is removed from the timer. At this point, any subsequent attempts to retrieve information from the timer about the notification will result in an error or a null return value.

Starting and Stopping a Timer

The `javax.management.timer.TimerMBean` interface specifies a `start` operation and a `stop` operation for starting/activating and stopping/deactivating a timer. Once a timer is started, it is considered to be active. When a timer is stopped, it is considered to be inactive. The `isActive` operation, specified in the `javax.management.timer.TimerMBean` interface, can be called to determine the active state of a timer.

A timer maintains its list of notifications when it is stopped, and therefore must process its list of notifications when it is restarted. How a timer processes its list of notifications depends on the value of its `sendPastNotifications` flag. The `sendPastNotifications` flag is set to false by default. If it is set to true, the timer will attempt to send notifications from its list when it is restarted from a stopped/inactive state. When the timer is restarted, it checks its list of notifications to see if it is empty. If the list is not empty, the timer will process the notifications in the list as follows:

- If the `sendPastNotifications` flag of the timer is set to true, the timer will iterate over the list of notifications, transmit each notification, and increment the date for each notification according to the `period` and `occurrences` properties of each notification. If after incrementing a notification's date it is still less than the current date, the notification will be sent again and the date will be incremented again according to its `period` and `occurrences` properties. This is repeated until the notification's date is greater than or equal to the current date or the number of occurrences has been exhausted. If the number of occurrences is exhausted, the notification is removed from the timer's list.

- If the sendPastNotifications flag of the timer is set to false, the timer will iterate over the list of notifications and increment the date for each notification according to the period and occurrences properties of each notification. This is repeated until the notification's date is greater than or equal to the current date or the number of occurrences has been exhausted. If the number of occurrences is exhausted, the notification is removed from the timer's list.

Let's see how you can include a simple timer in your service agent and methods to add and remove listeners.

Adding a Timer to the ServiceAgent

The first thing you need to do is add an import statement for your timer, as follows:

```
import javax.management.timer.Timer;
```

The next thing you do is add a member field to the service agent class to hold the ObjectName of the timer.

```
private ObjectName timerOName = null;
```

Now, add methods to start and stop the timer. Notice that for this example you create the timer on the first invocation of the startTimer method.

```
public void startTimer()
    throws ServiceAgentException
{
    if (timerOName == null)
    {
        try
        {
            timerOName = new ObjectName("TimerServices:name=SimpleTimer");
            mbServer.registerMBean(new Timer(), timerOName);
            mbServer.invoke(timerOName, "start", null, null);
        }
        catch (Exception e)
        {
            throw new ServiceAgentException("Error starting timer: "
                                        + e.toString());
        }
    }
```

```
            else
            {
                try
                {
                    if (((Boolean)mbServer.invoke(timerOName, "isActive",
                                            null, null)).booleanValue() == false)
                    {
                        mbServer.invoke(timerOName, "start", null, null);
                    }
                }
                catch (Exception e)
                {
                    throw new ServiceAgentException("Error starting timer: "
                                            + e.toString());
                }
            }
        }

        public void stopTimer()
            throws ServiceAgentException
        {
            if (timerOName != null)
            {
                try
                {
                    if (((Boolean)mbServer.invoke(timerOName, "isActive",
                                            null, null)).booleanValue() == true)
                    {
                        mbServer.invoke(timerOName, "stop", null, null);
                    }
                }
                catch (Exception e)
                {
                    throw new ServiceAgentException("Error starting timer: "
                                            + e.toString());
                }
            }
        }
```

The addTimerNotification Method

Now, you add methods that facilitate adding and removing notifications to the timer. For the sake of brevity, funnel all exceptions to a generic Exception block and wrap them in a ServiceAgentException instance:

```java
public Integer addTimerNotification(String type,
                                    String message,
                                    Object userData,
                                    java.util.Date startDate,
                                    long period,
                                    long occurrences)
    throws ServiceAgentException
{
    Object[] param = new Object[]
    {
        type,
        message,
        userData,
        startDate,
        new Long(period),
        new Long(occurrences)
    };

    String[] signature = new String[]
    {
        String.class.getName(),
        String.class.getName(),
        Object.class.getName(),
        Date.class.getName(),
        long.class.getName(),
        long.class.getName()
    };

    try
    {
        Object retVal = mbServer.invoke(timerOName, "addNotification",
                                        param, signature);
        return (Integer)retVal;
    }
    catch (Exception e)
    {
        throw new ServiceAgentException("Error adding notification: "
                                        + e.toString());
    }
}

public void removeTimerNotification(Integer id)
    throws ServiceAgentException
```

```
{
    Object[] param = new Object[]
    {
        id
    };

    String[] signature = new String[]
    {
        Integer.class.getName()
    };

    try
    {
        mbServer.invoke(timerOName, "removeNotification", param, signature);
    }
    catch (Exception e)
    {
        throw new ServiceAgentException("Error removing notification: "
                                       + e.toString());
    }
}
```

Adding Timer Notification Listener Methods

Finally, you add methods as shown in the following code block that facilitate adding notification listeners to the timer and removing notification listeners from the timer:

```
public void addTimerListener(NotificationListener listener,
                             NotificationFilter filter,
                             Object handback)
    throws ServiceAgentException
{
    try
    {
        mbServer.addNotificationListener(timerOName, listener,
                                         filter, handback);
    }
    catch (Exception e)
    {
        throw new ServiceAgentException("Error adding timer listener: "
                                        + e.toString());
    }
}
```

```
public void removeTimerListener(NotificationListener listener)
   throws ServiceAgentException
{
   try
   {
      mbServer.removeNotificationListener(timerOName, listener);
   }
   catch (Exception e)
   {
      throw new ServiceAgentException("Error removing timer listener: "
                                       + e.toString());
   }
}
```

The Relation Service

The relation service is a framework of classes, interfaces, and MBeans, located in the javax.management.relation package, that outlines logical relations between MBeans. The relation service has a number of responsibilities. For example, the relation service

- Creates and deletes relation types and relations

- Maintains consistency between relations

- Provides a query mechanism for finding relations and MBeans that are referenced in relations

- Transmits notifications to all registered listeners when a relation is added, updated, or removed

- Registers as an MBean registration listener in order to maintain consistency between relations as MBeans are deregistered

Relationship Roles

Roles are represented by instances of the javax.management.relation.Role class. This class encapsulates a *role name* and a list of ObjectNames of MBeans that are referenced by the role. The list of ObjectNames is referred to as the *role value*.

Relations

MBean relations are expressed as n-ary associations between MBeans using named roles. Relations are objects that implement the `javax.management.relation.Relation` interface and represent logical associations between MBeans. They are defined by named relation types embodied in instances of objects that implement the `javax.management.relation.RelationType` interface. Relation types provide information about the named roles that they contain. Role information is encapsulated within `javax.management.relation.RoleInfo` objects that define

- The name of the role

- Whether or not the role is readable or writable

- The description of the role

- The minimum number of referenced MBeans in the role

- The maximum number of referenced MBeans in the role

- The name of the Java class that MBeans must be an instance of or extend in order to be associated with the role

Internal Relations

Relation types can be created internally to the relation service or externally. The relation service then exposes the list of previously defined relation types to objects interested in defining new relations.

Internal relations are created and maintained by the relation service. All objects of an internal relationship are inaccessible to outside objects. Thus, any object wishing to operate on an internal relation must do so by calling an operation on the relation service.

External Relations

External relations are objects created outside of the relation service. External relations must implement the `Relation` interface and be manually added to the relation service as MBeans. External relation MBeans can therefore be accessed in the same manner as any ordinary MBean.

Figure 3-5 illustrates the conceptual associations between the objects participating in the relation service.

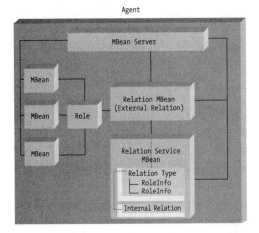

Figure 3-5. Conceptual associations between objects of the relation service

Creating and Starting the Relation Service

The relation service is created in the same manner as a standard MBean. That is, you supply one `ObjectName` for the `javax.management.relation.RelationService` MBean and register it with an MBean server. Thus, you might create and register the relation service MBean as follows:

```
public void initializeRelationService()
{
    try
    {
        Object[] params = new Object[1];
        params[0] = new Boolean(true);  // purge invalid relations immediately
        String[] signature = new String[1];
        signature[0] = "boolean";

        MBeanServer mbServer = MBeanServerFactory.createMBeanServer();

        ObjectName relationServiceOName =
            new ObjectName (mbServer.getDefaultDomain()
                        + ":name=relationService");

        mbServer.createMBean("javax.management.relation.RelationService",
                            relationServiceOName, params, signature);
    }
    catch(Exception e)
    {
        System.out.println(e.toString());
    }
}
```

Using the Relation Service

Let's look at how you might use the relation service. A simple relationship exists between an employee/worker, the employee's supervisor, and the employee's work location. When an employee changes location or positions, the employee's records need to reflect the changes. For example, when an employee changes positions, the employee's supervisor usually changes and sometimes the employee's work location.

You can easily model your employee MBean, your supervisor MBean, and your work location MBean, but modeling the relationships between them and maintaining those relationships can be daunting. Therefore, you will leave the task up to the relation service. You will add to your design the concept of a human resources (HR) relation that will use the relation service framework to handle the employee's associations. Figure 3-6 illustrates the conceptual associations between the objects participating in the HR relation.

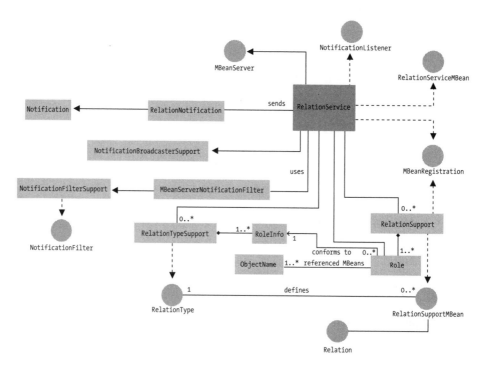

Figure 3-6. The static associations participating in the HR relation

Adding the Relation Service to the ServiceAgent

The first thing you need to do is import the relation classes as follows:

```
import javax.management.relation.*;
```

Now, let's add a convenience method for retrieving your relation-service domain name. You will simply use the default domain for now.

```
public String getRelationServiceDomain()
{
    return mbServer.getDefaultDomain();
}
```

The next thing you will do is create and register the relation service in your service agent. Notice that you create and register the relation service in the same manner as a standard MBean. You pass one parameter, a Boolean, that specifies if you want each relation purged immediately when the relation becomes invalid.

```
public void initializeRelationService()
{
    try
    {
        relationServiceOName = new ObjectName(getRelationServiceDomain()
                                            + ":name=relationService");
        // Check to see if the relation service is already running.
        Set names = mbServer.queryNames(relationServiceOName, null);
        if (names != null && names.isEmpty() == false)
            return;

        Object[] params = new Object[1];
        params[0] = new Boolean(true);  // Purge invalid relations immediately.
        String[] signature = new String[1];
        signature[0] = "boolean";
        MBeanServer mbServer = MBeanServerFactory.createMBeanServer();
        mbServer.createMBean("javax.management.relation.RelationService",
                            relationServiceOName, params, signature);
    }
    catch(Exception e)
    {
        System.out.println(e.toString());
    }
}
```

I won't go into detail about each of the MBeans that are part of the relation, because their behavior is rather mundane; however, I want to point out to you the main points of each as follows:

- The WorkerMBean exposes attributes and operations to allow a worker's supervisor, salary, position, work location, etc., to be modified and retrieved.

- The SupervisorMBean exposes the same attributes and operations as the WorkerMBean, and exposes attributes and operations to add and remove team members and retrieve the size of the supervisor's team.

- The WorkLocationMBean exposes attributes and operations to retrieve the building name, the name of the administrative assistant, and the mail stop, and to add and remove employees.

- The HRRelationMBean exposes operations to modify an employee's supervisor, work location, and position while keeping relationships intact.

Now, let's look at the some of the details of the HRRelationMBean. The class declaration shows that you extend the RelationSupport class to benefit from the built-in features that it provides:

```
public class HRRelation extends RelationSupport
    implements HRRelationMBean, MBeanRegistration
```

You define four operations in your HRRelationMBean interface. The implementations of these operations use invocations on the MBean server to perform operations on the specific Worker, Supervisor, and WorkLocation MBeans. The four operations are as follows:

1. define: Creates all role objects, role information objects, and the actual relation objects

2. transferEmployee: Transfers an employee to a new work location and updates the employee's supervisor as needed

3. changeEmployeePosition: Changes an employee's position and updates the employee's work location and supervisor as needed

4. replaceSupervisor: Changes an employee's supervisor

Defining the HRRelation

The define method calls private methods on the HRRelation class that create the role information object, the role objects, and the relation object.

```
public void define()
    throws MBeanException
{
    createMBeans();
    RoleInfo[] roleInfo = createRoleInfos();
    ArrayList roleList = createRoles();
    createRelationType(roleInfo);
    createRelation(roleList);
}
```

The remainder of the methods implemented by the HRRelation MBean comprises either utility methods or the following methods that create the role objects, role information objects, and the actual relation.

Creating the MBeans for the HRRelation

The createMBeans method creates and registers the MBeans that will participate in the relation. You create a static list of MBeans for the sake of this example. In a production setting, the MBeans should be created dynamically as needed.

```
public void createMBeans()
    throws MBeanException
{
    try
    {
        // Register the worker.
        Object[] params = new Object[3];
        params[0] = new String("John');
        params[1] = new String("Doe");
        params[2] = new Integer(1); // Employee number
        String[] signature = new String[3];
        signature[0] = String.class.getName();
        signature[1] = String.class.getName();
        signature[2] = int.class.getName();

        ObjectName workerOName =
            new ObjectName(GetRelationServiceDomain()
                            + ":type=worker,empNum=1");
```

```
            mbServer.createMBean("com.apress.jhanson.hr.Worker",
                              workerOName, params, signature);


        // Register the supervisor.
        Object[] params1 = new Object[3];
        params1[0] = new String("Jane");
        params1[1] = new String("Smith");
        params1[2] = new Integer(2); // Employee number
        String[] signature1 = new String[3];
        signature1[0] = String.class.getName();
        signature1[1] = String.class.getName();
        signature1[2] = int.class.getName();

        ObjectName supervisorOName =
            new ObjectName(getRelationServiceDomain()
                            + ":type=supervisor,empNum=2");

        mbServer.createMBean("com.apress.jhanson.hr.Supervisor",
                              supervisorOName, params1, signature1);


        // Register the work location.
        Object[] params2 = new Object[3];
        params2[0] = new String("D");    // Building name
        params2[1] = new String("D100"); // Mail stop
        String[] signature2 = new String[3];
        signature2[0] = String.class.getName();
        signature2[1] = String.class.getName();

        ObjectName workLocationOName =
            new ObjectName(getRelationServiceDomain()
                            + ":type=worklocation");

        mbServer.createMBean("com.apress.jhanson.hr.WorkLocation',
                              workLocationOName, params2, signature2);

    }
    catch (Exception e)
    {
        throw new MBeanException(e);
    }
}
```

Creating the RoleInfo Objects for the HRRelation

The createRoleInfos method creates the RoleInfo objects that define each role and the constraints for each role. You create RoleInfo objects for three roles: *Worker, Supervisor,* and *WorkLocation.*

```
public RoleInfo[] createRoleInfos()
    throws MBeanException
{
    RoleInfo[] roleInfos = new RoleInfo[3];

    try
    {
        roleInfos[0] = new RoleInfo("Worker",
                                    "com.apress.jhanson.hr.Worker",
                                    true, // Readable
                                    true, // Writable
                                    1, // Must have at least one
                                    100, // Can have 100, max
                                    "Worker role");

        roleInfos[1] = new RoleInfo("Supervisor",
                                    "com.apress.jhanson.hr.Supervisor",
                                    true, // Readable
                                    true, // Writable
                                    1, // Must have at least one
                                    1, // Can have 1, max
                                    "Supervisor role");

        roleInfos[2] = new RoleInfo("WorkLocation",
                                    "com.apress.jhanson.hr.WorkLocation",
                                    true, // Readable
                                    true, // Writable
                                    1, // Must have at least one
                                    1, // Can have 1, max
                                    "WorkLocation role");
    }
    catch (Exception e)
    {
        throw new MBeanException(e);
    }

    return roleInfos;
}
```

Creating the Relation Types for the HRRelation

The createRelationType method takes the array of RoleInfo objects created in the createRoleInfos method and forwards it to the createRelationType operation on the relation service to create the relation type. Give your relation type the name of HRRelationType.

```
public void createRelationType(RoleInfo[] roleInfos)
    throws MBeanException
{
    try
    {
        Object[] params = new Object[2];
        params[0] = "HRRelationType";
        params[1] = roleInfos;
        String[] signature = new String[2];
        signature[0] = "java.lang.String";
        signature[1] = (roleInfos.getClass()).getName();

        mbServer.invoke(relationServiceOName,
                        "createRelationType", params, signature);
    }
    catch (Exception e)
    {
        throw new MBeanException(e);
    }
}
```

Creating the Roles for the HRRelation

The createRoles method creates the roles that participate in your HR relation using the same names that you specified in the createRoleInfos method. The createRoles method also adds the names of the worker, supervisor, and location MBeans that participate in the relation.

```
public ArrayList createRoles()
    throws MBeanException
{
    try
    {
        ArrayList employeeRoleValue = new ArrayList();
        employeeRoleValue.add(new ObjectName(relationServiceDomain
                                    + ":name=worker,empNum=1"));
```

```
        employeeRoleValue.add(new ObjectName(relationServiceDomain
                                    + ":name=worker,empNum=2"));
        employeeRoleValue.add(new ObjectName(relationServiceDomain
                                    + ":name=worker,empNum=3"));
        Role employeeRole = new Role("Worker", employeeRoleValue);

        ArrayList supervisorRoleValue = new ArrayList();
        supervisorRoleValue.add(new ObjectName(relationServiceDomain
                                    + ":name=supervisor"));
        Role managerRole = new Role("Supervisor", supervisorRoleValue);

        ArrayList workLocationRoleValue = new ArrayList();
        workLocationRoleValue.add(new ObjectName(relationServiceDomain
                                    + ":name=worklocation"));

        Role physLocationRole = new Role("WorkLocation",
                                    workLocationRoleValue);

        ArrayList roleList = new ArrayList();
        roleList.add(employeeRole);
        roleList.add(managerRole);
        roleList.add(physLocationRole);

        return roleList;
    }
    catch (Exception e)
    {
        throw new MBeanException(e);
    }
}
```

Creating the Actual HRRelation

The createRelation method creates and registers your HRRelation MBean with
the relation type you created earlier. The HRRelation MBean is then added to the
relation service using the addRelation operation of the relation service MBean.

```
public void createRelation(ArrayList roleList)
    throws MBeanException
{
    try
    {
        Object[] params = new Object[4];
        params[0] = "HRRelation";
```

```
            params[1] = relationServiceOName;
            params[2] = "HRRelationType";
            params[3] = roleList;

            String[] signature = new String[4];
            signature[0] = "java.lang.String";
            signature[1] = relationServiceOName.getClass().getName();
            signature[2] = "java.lang.String";
            signature[3] = roleList.getClass().getName();

            ObjectName relationMBeanName =
                    new ObjectName(relationServiceDomain + ":type=RelationMBean");

            mbServer.createMBean("com.apress.jhanson.hr.HRRelation",
                                    relationMBeanName,
                                    params, signature);

            // Add the relation.
            params = new Object[1];
            signature = new String[1];
            params[0] = relationMBeanName;
            signature[0] = "javax.management.ObjectName";

            mbServer.invoke(relationServiceOName,
                            "addRelation", params, signature);
        }
        catch (Exception e)
        {
            throw new MBeanException(e);
        }
    }
```

Summary

The agent level defined by the JMX specification targets the management solutions development community by providing a comprehensive and flexible framework for building management agents. Agents expose instrumented resources in a manner that allows management applications to discover them and invoke operations on them in a standard fashion. An agent can reside in a local JVM or in a remote JVM. This makes it possible to build management applications that interact with agents and resources in a generic way, thus allowing management applications the ability to administrate any system that adheres to this framework.

In addition to facilitating access to instrumented resources, an agent broadcasts notifications to interested notification receivers that have previously registered with it. An agent exposes an MBean server, at least one protocol adaptor or connector, and several mandatory services, known as *agent services*. The mandatory agent services are registered as MBeans and include a monitoring service, a timer service, a relation service, and a dynamic class-loading service.

CHAPTER 4

MBean Servers

THE PRIMARY COMPONENT of the JMX agent layer is the managed bean (MBean) server. The MBean server acts as a registry and repository for all MBeans. It also exposes functionality that allows queries to be applied against it in order to discover the MBeans that are registered with it.

An MBean server functions as an abstraction layer between managed resources and management applications. Instances of MBeans are never directly accessed by management applications; instead, the MBean server acts as a proxy object between MBeans and the outside world. When an object is registered as an MBean with an MBean server, all requests to the MBean must go through the MBean server. Likewise, all operations that retrieve a reference to an MBean return only a proxy object or name representing the MBean. This ensures that a loose coupling exists between any application or service and the MBeans. This loose coupling allows modifications to be made on the resources that MBeans represent without altering the components and applications that access them.

Creating an MBean Server

An MBean server is created by invoking one of the static createMBeanServer methods or newMBeanServer methods on the javax.management.MBeanServerFactory class. The MBeanServerFactory maintains a reference to each MBean server created by the createMBeanServer methods, but does not keep a reference to an MBean server created by the newMBeanServer methods. The releaseMBeanServer(MBeanServer mBeanServer) method can be called to release any references that the MBeanServerFactory might be maintaining.

When creating an MBean server, a name for the default domain of the agent must be assigned to it. If the create method not requiring a domain name is used, a domain name will be assigned to the MBean server by the JMX implementation. If the create method requiring a domain name is used, the caller of the method must supply the default domain name.

Finding an MBean Server

The MBeanServerFactory class exposes a static method, findMBeanServer(String mBeanServerId), that can be used to find previously created MBean servers. The ID of the MBean server is the only parameter that needs to be passed to the

method. The `findMBeanServer` method returns a `java.util.ArrayList` object
containing all MBean servers that match the `mBeanServerId` parameter. If the
`mBeanServerId` parameter is null, all MBean servers the `MBeanServerFactory` class
has a reference to will be returned.

The MBean server ID parameter that is passed to `findMBeanServer()` is
documented in most implementations of JMX 1.x as the `AgentID`. However, the
parameter is actually compared against the `MBeanServerId` attribute of the delegate object for each MBean server instance to which the `MBeanServerFactory`
instance has a reference. This is not so confusing, because the MBean server
and agent are so closely coupled; however, this is only the start of a complicated process.

The `createMBeanServer` methods exposed by the `MBeanServerFactory` class do
not allow the MBean server to be named by the caller. Hence, the `MBeanServerId`
attribute is assigned a name by the JMX implementation. This currently ends up
being set to something like the name of the local host with a sequence number
or a timestamp appended on the end, as follows:

```
private String getMBeanServerID()
{
    String host = "localhost";
    try
    {
        host = InetAddress.getLocalHost().getHostName();
    }
    catch (UnknownHostException ignored)
    {
    }
    ++m_mbeanServerCount;
    return host + "_" + m_mbeanServerCount;
}
```

So how do you find an MBean server? The facts as they have been discussed
so far tell you that you must have a reference to the MBean server, returned from
the `createMBeanServer` method, in order to query for the `MBeanServerId` attribute
of its delegate object. Once you have the `MBeanServerId` attribute value, you can
ask the `MBeanServerFactory` class to find the MBean server that you already have
a reference to!

The implication here is that the component that creates the MBean server
must save the reference to the MBean server returned from the `createMBeanServer`
methods. Then the component can be asked for the MBean server reference. In
this case, the `ServiceAgent` object creates the MBean server, so it must retain a reference to the MBean server and expose a method that returns the reference.

Once you have modified the ServiceAgent class to retain the reference to the MBean server, you can add a method that will return the MBean server:

```
public MBeanServer getMBeanServer()
{
    return mbServer;
}
```

Since the agent has a reference to the MBean server, it can get the MBean server's ID. For the sake of curiosity, add a method that will do this and return it to the caller:

```
public String getMBeanServerID()
{
    try
    {
        ObjectName delegateOName =
            new ObjectName("JMImplementation:type=MBeanServerDelegate");
        return (String)mbServer.getAttribute(delegateOName, "MBeanServerId");
    }
    catch (Exception e)
    {
        e.printStackTrace();
    }

    return "";
}
```

From this method, you can see that you must get the MBeanServerId from an object defined with a type of MBeanServerDelegate. Let's discuss the details of this object.

MBean Server Delegate

Each MBean server must define and reserve a domain called JMImplementation in which to register one MBean of type javax.management.MBeanServerDelegate. The MBeanServerDelegate MBean is automatically created and registered when an MBean server is started. The purpose of this object is to identify and describe the MBean server, in terms of its management interface, with which it is registered. The MBeanServerDelegate object also implements the NotificationEmitter and serves to transmit MBeanServerNotification events for its MBean server when an MBean is registered in or deregistered from the MBean server.

Objects wishing to receive `MBeanServerNotification` events from an MBean server must register as a notification listener with the `MBeanServerDelegate` object. This is achieved indirectly through the MBean server, as follows:

```
ObjectName delegateOName =
    new ObjectName("JMImplementation:type=MBeanServerDelegate");
NotificationFilter filter = null;
NotificationListener listener = this;
Object handbackObj = new String("MyHandback object");
mbServer.addNotificationListener(delegateOName, listener,
                                    filter, handbackObj);
```

In this example, assume that the `addNotificationListener` method is being called by an object that implements the `NotificationListener` interface. You also see an object named `handbackObj` that is passed to the `addNotificationListener` method. A *handback object* is used in the JMX notification system to allow notification listeners to resolve the actual target for a particular notification event. Later, I will show you how this works in detail.

The `MBeanServerDelegate` object also exposes read-only information on behalf of the MBean server such as the JMX specification name, vendor, and version number. The complete `ObjectName` of `MBeanServerDelegate`, as specified by JMX, is `JMImplementation:type=MBeanServerDelegate`.

Modifying the Default MBean Server Implementation

It is possible to replace the default implementation of the `MBeanServer` interface with a completely different implementation. When the `createMBeanServer` or `newMBeanServer` method of the `MBeanServerFactory` class is called, it checks to see if the `javax.management.builder.initial` system property exists. If it does exist, the `MBeanServerFactory` assumes that it names a public class that extends `javax.management.MBeanServerBuilder`. The `MBeanServerFactory` will then instantiate an object of this new class and return it as the `MBeanServer` instance.

An `MBeanServerBuilder` must be able to create an instance of `MBeanServer` and an instance of `MBeanServerDelegate` or a subclass of `MBeanServerDelegate`. The MBean server can be a complete reimplementation of the `MBeanServer` interface or an aggregate of the default implementation and a new object.

Naming and Registering MBeans

All management operations performed on MBeans are made through an agent that proxies the operations to its MBean server. When an MBean registers with an MBean server, the server will add it to its current set of MBeans.

The MBeanServer interface specifies methods for creating and registering new MBeans and a method for creating and registering MBeans that already exist. The methods for creating and registering new MBeans are defined as follows:

- ObjectInstance createMBean(String className, ObjectName name)

- ObjectInstance createMBean(String className, ObjectName name, ObjectName loaderName)

- ObjectInstance createMBean(String className, ObjectName name, Object params[], String signature[])

- ObjectInstance createMBean(String className, ObjectName name, ObjectName loaderName, Object params[], String signature[])

The parameters for the preceding methods are defined as follows:

- className: The class name of the MBean to create and register.

- name: The ObjectName of the MBean to create and register. This parameter may be null. If this parameter is null, the object must implement the MBeanRegistration interface and return the name from the preRegister method of this interface.

- loaderName: The ObjectName of the class loader to use to create and register the MBean.

- params: An array containing the parameters of the MBean's constructor to call during the creation process.

- signature: An array containing the class names of the parameters of the MBean's constructor that will be called.

The method for registering MBeans that already exist is defined as follows:

- ObjectInstance registerMBean(Object object, ObjectName name)

The parameters for the preceding method are defined as follows:

- object: The object that will be registered as an MBean.

- name: The ObjectName of the MBean to register. This parameter may be null. If this parameter is null, the object must implement the MBeanRegistration interface and return the name from the preRegister method of this interface.

Note that all of the methods that create an MBean or register an MBean return an object of type `javax.management.ObjectInstance`. The `ObjectInstance` class exposes only the `ObjectName` and class name of the object that it represents. The reason for this resides in the fact that an agent proxies all operation and attribute calls to its MBeans and never gives out the actual reference to the MBeans. This provides a level of abstraction away from the MBeans, allowing transparent remote communications, swapping of MBean instances, and other actions at runtime.

Controlling MBean Registration

JMX affords a certain amount of control to an MBean when it is registered or deregistered with an MBean server. This is facilitated by the use of callback methods defined in the `MBeanRegistration` interface.

If an MBean implements the `MBeanRegistration` interface, an MBean server will call the methods of this interface at appropriate times during the registration or deregistration process of the MBean. The methods for this interface are listed here:

- `ObjectName preRegister(MBeanServer server, ObjectName name)`: This method is called just before the MBean is registered. An MBean may throw an exception from this method to cancel the registration process for itself. The MBean server parameter passed to this method allows the MBean to know with which MBean server the MBean is registered. The return value for this method is of type `ObjectName`. This allows the MBean to return a name under which it will be registered. However, this only applies if the `ObjectName` parameter is null.

- `void postRegister(Boolean registrationDone)`: This method is called just after the MBean is registered. The only parameter passed to this method is a Boolean, signifying whether or not the registration process succeeded.

- `void preDeregister()`: This method is called just before an MBean is deregistered. An MBean may throw an exception from this method to cancel the deregistration process for itself.

- `void postDeregister()`: This method is called just after an MBean is deregistered.

Figure 4-1 illustrates the interactions during MBean registration between an agent, an MBean server, and an MBean that implements the `MBeanRegistration` interface.

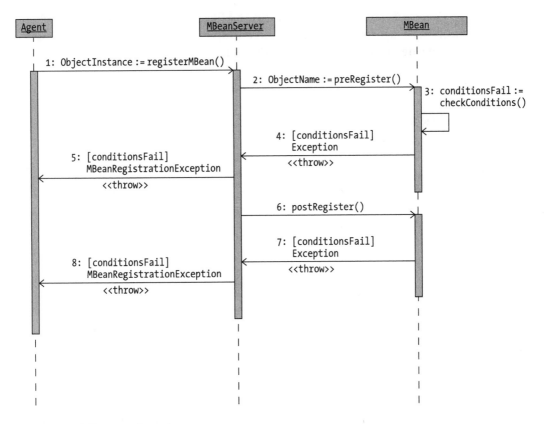

Figure 4-1. MBean registration sequence

MBean Registration Notifications

Interested components can register as a NotificationListener object with an
MBean server in order to be notified when any MBean is registered or deregistered.
All components registered as listeners will receive a REGISTRATION_NOTIFICATION
event from the MBean server whenever an MBean is registered and an
UNREGISTRATION_NOTIFICATION event when an MBean is deregistered. Both event
types are defined by the MBeanServerNotification class and are wrapped in an
MBeanServerNotification object to be thrown by the MBean server.

An interested listener calls the addNotificationListener method on an MBean
server in order to add itself as a NotificationListener object to the MBean server.
The addNotificationListener method actually adds a listener to a specified MBean
designated by the ObjectName parameter. Therefore, to register with an MBean
server, a listener must add itself as a listener to the MBean server's delegate object.

Once a listener has been added to an MBean server, it will be notified when any MBean is registered or deregistered with the MBean server. The following example demonstrates a listener adding itself to an MBean server:

```
try
{
    ObjectName oName =
        new ObjectName("JMImplementation:type=MBeanServerDelegate");
    NotificationFilter filter = null;
    Object handback = new String("Handback object 1");
    mbServer.addNotificationListener(oName, this, filter, handback);
}
catch (MalformedObjectNameException e)
{
        e.printStackTrace();
}
catch (InstanceNotFoundException e)
{
        e.printStackTrace();
}
```

As the example demonstrates, a listener actually adds itself as a listener to the `MBeanServerDelegate` object by specifying the delegate's `ObjectName`. Since a listener registers only once for all notifications, the handback object and the filter object are required in order to allow the listener to recognize and filter notifications.

MBean Server Queries

MBean servers can be queried for the presence of one or more registered MBeans using the `queryMBeans` method or the `queryNames` method. MBeans can be searched for by object name, attribute values, or both.

Query methods provided by an MBean server take *query expression objects,* which are used to construct query expressions, as parameters. The query expression objects are then passed as parameters to the following MBean server's query methods as follows:

- Set `queryMBeans(ObjectName oName, QueryExp queryExp)`: This method retrieves a `java.util.Set` of `ObjectInstance` objects representing the MBeans that match the query's criteria.

- Set `queryNames(ObjectName oName, QueryExp queryExp)`: This method retrieves a `java.util.Set` of `ObjectName` objects representing the MBeans that match the query's criteria.

Both methods use their parameters in the same way to perform a query. The only difference between the two methods is the Set of retrieved objects. The queryMBeans method retrieves a Set of ObjectInstance objects and the queryNames method retrieves a Set of ObjectName objects.

The ObjectName parameter for both methods is used as a pattern to match when the query is performed. The Set of MBeans with object names that match the pattern defined by the ObjectName parameter is referred to as the *scope* of the query.

If the ObjectName parameter is null, the scope is considered to be all MBeans registered with the MBean server. If the query expression is null, no filtering is performed on the MBeans, and the resulting Set is filled with all MBeans in the scope. When both parameters are null, the result is the set of all MBeans registered in the MBean server. Execution time for a query can be powerfully optimized if the caller supplies an ObjectName parameter that is specific enough to retrieve only the MBeans desired. If the ObjectName parameter contains the entire name of an MBean, only that MBean will be returned. The query expression can be used to test the attribute values of the MBean to determine whether or not to return the MBean.

The QueryExp parameter for both methods contains filtering criteria defined by the caller. The criteria defined by the query expression are used to filter the MBeans that fall within the scope of the query. Criteria are matched against the attribute values of the MBeans. An empty Set is returned by both methods in the event that no MBeans are found that match the criteria.

Query Expressions

Queries are applied to an MBean server by passing query expression objects as parameters to one of the query methods of the MBean server. A query expression object is an instance of a class that represents a relational expression. A *relational expression* is an expression that forms a possibility for a logical set of MBeans. For example, consider the following expression:

Find all MBeans in which the printer type equals *color* or the printer model is *Acme* and the printer location equals *building B*.

The preceding expression can be considered to have a logical possibility of finding all color printers and Acme printers that reside in building B. You can divide the preceding expression into three logical subexpressions as follows:

- Printer type equals color.

- Printer model is Acme.

- Printer location equals building B.

The subexpressions of the preceding example consist of values (*printer type, printer location, color*, etc.) that are connected by Boolean or relational operators (*or* and *and*). By applying the preceding logical expression to the entire set of printers available within a campus, you should be able to filter the set of printers that the query will find in order to return the printers you desire. Keeping this in mind, let's take a look at how JMX enables an MBean server to solve the same problem.

In JMX, MBean server query expressions are embodied within instances of classes that implement the QueryExp interface. JMX supplies a number of classes that fit this definition, as you see in the class hierarchy illustrated in Figure 4-2.

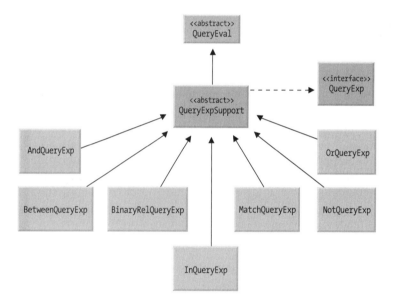

Figure 4-2. Query expression class hierarchy

JMX also supplies a number of classes that represent values for a query expression. These classes implement the ValueExp interface and are illustrated in Figure 4-3.

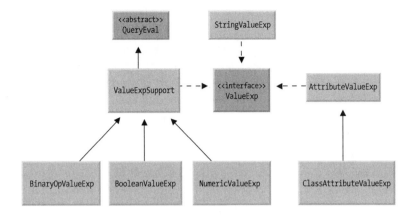

Figure 4-3. Query expression value class hierarchy

As these illustrations show, JMX supplies classes and interfaces for building query expressions. The javax.management.Query class exposes static methods that are used to build query expression objects and value expression objects.

Objects that represent complete query expressions are identified by instances of classes that implement the javax.management.QueryExp interface. The javax.management.ValueExp interface is implemented by classes that represent values, such as strings, numbers, and attributes, that can be passed as arguments to relational expressions.

Applying Query Expressions

Using the query expression objects and value objects supplied by JMX, you are able to construct a set of objects that represents your printer query. You can then pass the final query expression object to one of the query methods on an MBean server to find the printers you desire. This is illustrated in the printer query in the following example:

```
try
{
    MBeanServer mbServer = serviceAgent.getMBeanServer();

    // Register printer A.
    String mbeanClassName1 = "com.apress.jhanson.resources.Printer";
    Hashtable properties1 = new Hashtable();
    properties1.put("type", "printer");
    ObjectInstance objInst1 = serviceAgent.addResource("PrinterA",
                                                       properties1,
                                                       mbeanClassName1);
```

```
// Set attributes for printer A.
mbServer.setAttribute(objInst1.getObjectName(),
                         new Attribute("Type", "BlackAndWhite"));
mbServer.setAttribute(objInst1.getObjectName(),
                         new Attribute("Model", "HP"));
mbServer.setAttribute(objInst1.getObjectName(),
                         new Attribute("Location", "Building A"));

// Register printer B.
String mbeanClassName2 = "com.apress.jhanson.resources.Printer";
Hashtable properties2 = new Hashtable();
properties2.put("type", "printer");
   ObjectInstance objInst2 = serviceAgent.addResource("PrinterB",
                                               properties2,
                                               mbeanClassName2);
// Set attributes for printer B.
mbServer.setAttribute(objInst2.getObjectName(),
                         new Attribute("Type", "Color"));
mbServer.setAttribute(objInst2.getObjectName(),
                         new Attribute("Model", "Canon"));
mbServer.setAttribute(objInst2.getObjectName(),
                         new Attribute("Location", "Building B"));

// Register printer C.
String mbeanClassName3 = "com.apress.jhanson.resources.Printer";
Hashtable properties3 = new Hashtable();
properties3.put("type", "printer");
ObjectInstance objInst3 = serviceAgent.addResource("PrinterC",
                                               properties3,
                                               mbeanClassName3);
// Set attributes for printer C.
mbServer.setAttribute(objInst3.getObjectName(),
                         new Attribute("Type", "BlackAndWhite"));
mbServer.setAttribute(objInst3.getObjectName(),
                         new Attribute("Model", "Acme"));
mbServer.setAttribute(objInst3.getObjectName(),
                         new Attribute("Location", "Building B"));

...
```

Using a Match Constraint

String-matching constraint methods are used to test attribute values for character string patterns. Here a string-matching constraint is used to match printers that have a Type of Color, a Model of Acme, and a Location of Building B.

...

```
        // Create a query expression for attribute "Type"
        // with a value of "Color".
        AttributeValueExp printerTypeAttr = Query.attr("Type");
        StringValueExp type = Query.value("Color");
        QueryExp queryExp1 = Query.match(printerTypeAttr, type);

        // Create a query expression for attribute "Model"
        // with a value of "Acme".
        AttributeValueExp printerModelAttr = Query.attr("Model");
        StringValueExp model = Query.value("Acme");
        QueryExp queryExp2 = Query.match(printerModelAttr, model);

        // Create a query expression for attribute "Location"
        // with a value of "Building B".
        AttributeValueExp printerLocationAttr = Query.attr("Location");
        StringValueExp location = Query.value("Building B");
        QueryExp queryExp3 = Query.match(printerLocationAttr, location);

        // Use the static methods of the Query class to build
        // objects to form conjunctions and disjunctions.
        QueryExp queryExp4 = Query.or(queryExp1, queryExp3);
        QueryExp queryExp5 = Query.or(queryExp2, queryExp3);
        QueryExp queryExp6 = Query.and(queryExp4, queryExp5);
```

...

Setting the Query Scope

Query scope is defined by object names that match a given pattern. You are interested in all printers that match your query, so you define the scope for your query to return all printers that match as demonstrated here:

...

```
        // Create the ObjectName that specifies the scope
        // of our query.
        ObjectName queryScope = new ObjectName("*:*");
```

```
// Execute the query.
Set result = mbServer.queryNames(queryScope, queryExp6);

// Now, iterate over the results of the query.
Iterator iter = result.iterator();
while (iter.hasNext())
{
    Object obj = iter.next();
    System.out.println("Query found: " + obj.toString());
}
}
catch (Exception e)
{
    System.out.println("Error: " + e.toString());
}
```

Since `PrinterB` has a type equal to `Color` and `PrinterC` has a model of `Acme` and they both have a `Location` of `Building B`, the example will yield the following results:

```
Query found: services:name=PrinterB
Query found: services:name=PrinterC
```

Using Wildcards in Query Expressions

It is also possible to pass wildcards as values to a query expression when using the `match` method of the `Query` class. For example, let's assume that you want to find all color printers that have a model name that begins with *Ca*. Using the set of MBeans registered in the previous example, you can structure a query expression that demonstrates the use of a wildcard, as follows:

```
// Create the ObjectName that specifies the scope
// of our query.
ObjectName queryScope = new ObjectName("*:*");

// Execute the query.
QueryExp exp = Query.and(Query.geq(Query.attr("Type"),
                            Query.value("Color")),
                            Query.match(Query.attr("Model"),
                            Query.value("Ca*")));
```

```
Set result = mbServer.queryNames(queryScope, exp);

// Now, iterate over the results of the query.
Iterator iter = result.iterator();
while (iter.hasNext())
{
    Object obj = iter.next();
    System.out.println("Query found: " + obj.toString());
}
```

Notice from this example how you are able to use an asterisk as a wildcard when passing "Ca*" as a value expression. Wildcards can also be used in the ObjectName to define the scope of the query. Legal wildcards include the asterisk (*) and the question mark (?). Since PrinterB has a type equal to Color and a model of Canon, the example will yield the following results:

```
Query found: services:name=PrinterB
```

Methods for Defining Query Expressions

The javax.management.Query class provides a comprehensive set of static methods that can be used to construct value expressions, query expressions, and query constraints, as described in the following sections.

Boolean Constraint Methods

Boolean constraint methods, which appear in the following list, are used to apply Boolean operations on one or more QueryExp arguments. The returned query expressions may be passed to additional query methods or may be used for listing and enumerating MBeans.

- QueryExp and(QueryExp q1, QueryExp q2): Returns a query expression that is the conjunction of two other query expressions

- QueryExp or(QueryExp q1, QueryExp q2): Returns a query expression that is the disjunction of two other query expressions

- QueryExp not(QueryExp q1): Returns a constraint that is the negation of its single argument

Equality Constraint Methods

Equality constraint methods are used to test one or more QueryExp arguments for equality or inequality. The returned query expressions may be passed to additional query methods or may be used for listing and enumerating MBeans. Following is a list of these methods:

- QueryExp gt(ValueExp v1, ValueExp v2): Returns a query expression that represents a "greater than" constraint on two values

- QueryExp geq(ValueExp v1, ValueExp v2): Returns a query expression that represents a "greater than or equal to" constraint on two values

- QueryExp leq(ValueExp v1, ValueExp v2): Returns a query expression that represents a "less than or equal to" constraint on two values

- QueryExp lt(ValueExp v1, ValueExp v2): Returns a query expression that represents a "less than" constraint on two values

- QueryExp eq(ValueExp v1, ValueExp v2): Returns a query expression that represents an equality constraint on two values

- QueryExp between(ValueExp v1, ValueExp v2, ValueExp v3): Returns a query expression that represents the constraint that one value (v1) is between two other values

String Matching Constraint Methods

String matching constraint methods, listed here, are used to test AttributeValueExp arguments for patterns specified by StringValueExp arguments. The returned query expressions may be passed to additional query methods or may be used for listing and enumerating MBeans.

- QueryExp match(AttributeValueExp a, StringValueExp s): Returns a query expression where a specified AttributeValueExp matches a file globbing-style pattern specified by a StringValueExp. Globbing characters *, ?, and [may be escaped with \. Character classes can use ! for negation and - for character ranges. Wildcard searches can be performed by using the * for any character sequence and ? for a single character. The pattern [...] may be used for a sequence of characters.

- QueryExp initialSubString(AttributeValueExp a, StringValueExp s): Returns a query expression where a specified AttributeValueExp begins with a pattern specified by a StringValueExp.

- QueryExp anySubString(AttributeValueExp a, StringValueExp s): Returns a query expression where a specified AttributeValueExp contains a pattern specified by a StringValueExp.

- QueryExp finalSubString(AttributeValueExp a, StringValueExp s): Returns a query expression where a specified AttributeValueExp ends with a pattern specified by a StringValueExp.

Value Expression Creation Methods

Value expression methods are used to create instances of the ValueExp class or instances of subclasses of the ValueExp class. The type of parameter that is passed to each method determines the exact object that is returned. The returned query expressions may be passed to additional query methods. The value expression methods are as follows:

- StringValueExp value(String val): Returns a new string expression representing its single argument

- ValueExp value(Number val): Returns a numeric value expression for its single argument that can be used in any Query call that expects a ValueExp

- ValueExp value(int val): Returns a numeric value expression for its single int argument that can be used in any Query call that expects a ValueExp

- ValueExp value(long val): Returns a numeric value expression for its single long argument that can be used in any Query call that expects a ValueExp

- ValueExp value(float val): Returns a numeric value expression for its single float argument that can be used in any Query call that expects a ValueExp

- ValueExp value(double val): Returns a numeric value expression for its double argument that can be used in any Query call that expects a ValueExp

- ValueExp value(boolean val): Returns a Boolean value expression for its single argument that can be used in any Query call that expects a ValueExp

Attribute Value Expression Creation Methods

Attribute value expression methods, shown in the following list, are used to create instances of the `AttributeValueExp` class. The returned query expressions may be passed to additional query methods.

- `AttributeValueExp attr(String name)`: Returns a new attribute expression for the attribute named by the single parameter

- `AttributeValueExp attr(String className, String name)`: Returns a new qualified attribute expression for an attribute of a class

- `AttributeValueExp classattr()`: Returns a new class attribute expression that can be used in any `Query` call that expects a `ValueExp`

Binary Expression Methods

Binary expression methods are used to perform mathematical operations on a pair of numeric parameters passed in as `ValueExp` objects. The returned value expressions may be passed to additional query methods. Following is a list of these methods:

- `ValueExp plus(ValueExp value1, ValueExp value2)`: Returns a binary expression representing the sum of two numeric values, or the concatenation of two string values

- `ValueExp times(ValueExp value1,ValueExp value2)`: Returns a binary expression representing the product of two numeric values

- `ValueExp minus(ValueExp value1, ValueExp value2)`: Returns a binary expression representing the difference between two numeric values

- `ValueExp div(ValueExp value1, ValueExp value2)`: Returns a binary expression representing the quotient value1 divided by value2

Miscellaneous Methods

The following method is very useful for discovering a value in a list:

- `QueryExp in(ValueExp val, ValueExp valueList[])`: Returns an expression constraining a value (`val` parameter) to be one of an explicit list (`valueList` parameter)

MBean Proxies

All calls on an MBean must go through an MBean server. This makes for a somewhat clumsy mechanism for invoking operations and for retrieving and setting attributes. As an alternative, a proxy for an MBean can be created and calls can be made directly on the proxy object itself rather than on the MBean server. The calls are still routed through the MBean server, but the syntax is friendlier and less error prone.

Proxies are constructed using the javax.management.MBeanServerInvocationHandler class. For example, let's assume that you want to instrument the following class as a standard MBean:

```
public class User
{
    private String name = "John Doe";

    public String getName()
    {
      return name;
    }

    public void setName(String newValue)
    {
        name = newValue
    }

    public void sendEMail(String subject, String message)
    {
        // Do the work.
    }
}
```

In order to instrument the User class, you might define an interface that follows the naming conventions for a standard MBean as follows:

```
public interface UserMBean
{
    public String getName();
    public void setName(String newValue);
    public void sendEMail(String subject, String message);
}
```

With the class and the interface in place, an instance of the class could be registered with an MBean server and clients could make calls on the MBean server to set attributes of the MBean, as follows:

```
mbServer.setAttribute(objName, new Attribute("Name", "Jim Doe"));
```

This will work just fine, assuming that you name the attribute correctly, create a new `Attribute` object, and pass the `Attribute` object to the MBean server to do the work for you. A cleaner and safer mechanism can be put into place using a proxy constructed by the `MBeanServerInvocationHandler` class, as follows:

```
UserMBean user =
      (UserMBean)MBeanServerInvocationHandler.
         newProxyInstance(mbServer,
                                   objName,
                                   UserMBean.class,
                                   false);
```

Now, you can make calls in a more natural manner on the proxy object itself:

```
String oldName = user.getName();
user.setName("Jim Doe");
```

MBean Server Remote Communications

Any application or service that is operating outside of an MBean server's VM must have a mechanism for accessing the MBean server remotely. To facilitate this, an MBean server's agent relies on *protocol adaptors* and *connectors* to make it and the MBean server's registered MBeans accessible from remote applications and services. Each adaptor supports a specific protocol for communications between the agent and the remote client. No client-side component is needed when using an adaptor, because the adaptor relies on existing tools and protocols for communication. Many JMX implementations provide an HTML/HTTP adaptor to display agent and MBean information using a Web browser.

Connectors provide a client-side component to assist with the communication responsibilities between the client and an agent. Connectors provide a consistent interface across protocols in order to enable a remote application or service with the ability to connect to an agent without regard to the protocol used.

Figure 4-4 shows how operation invocations can be made from an application or service to a remote agent. The example shows how an MBean proxy is used locally to propagate MBean invocations through the connector client and how invocations on an MBean server are made directly on the connector client.

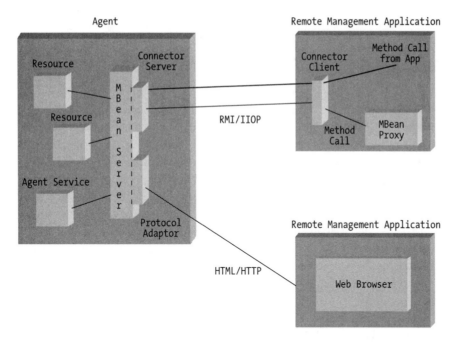

Figure 4-4. Operation invocations on a remote agent and its MBean server

Summary

The MBean server is the primary component of the JMX agent layer and acts as a registry and repository for all MBeans. An MBean server provides an abstraction layer between managed resources and management applications, and acts as a proxy object between MBeans and the outside world.

An MBean server is created by invoking one of the static createMBeanServer methods or newMBeanServer methods on the MBeanServerFactory class.

Each MBean server must define and reserve a domain called JMImplementation in which to register one MBean of type javax.management.MBeanServerDelegate. The MBeanServerDelegate MBean is automatically created and registered when an MBean server is started. The purpose of this object is to identify and describe the MBean server, in terms of its management interface, that it is registered with.

The MBeanServer interface specifies methods for creating and registering new MBeans and a method for creating and registering MBeans that already exist. When an object is registered as an MBean with an MBean server, all requests to the MBean must go through the MBean server. Likewise, all operations that retrieve a reference to an MBean return only a proxy object or name representing the MBean. This ensures that there is a loose coupling between any application or service and the MBeans. This loose coupling allows modifications to be made on the resources that MBeans represent without altering the components and applications that access them.

An MBean server uses callback methods, defined in the MBeanRegistration interface, to allow an MBean a certain amount of control when it is registered or deregistered with the MBean server.

Interested components can register as a NotificationListener object with an MBean server in order to be notified when any MBean is registered or deregistered. All components registered as listeners will receive a REGISTRATION_NOTIFICATION event from the MBean server whenever an MBean is registered and an UNREGISTRATION_NOTIFICATION event when an MBean is deregistered.

MBean servers can be queried for the presence of one or more registered MBeans using the queryMBeans method or the queryNames method. MBeans can be searched for by object name, attribute values, or both.

Query methods provided by an MBean server take query expression objects as parameters. Query expression objects are used to construct query expressions. The query expression objects are then passed as parameters to the MBean server's query methods.

All calls on an MBean must go through an MBean server. This makes for a somewhat clumsy mechanism for invoking operations and for retrieving and setting attributes. As an alternative, a proxy for an MBean can be created and calls can be made directly on the proxy object itself rather than on the MBean server. The calls are still routed through the MBean server, but the syntax is friendlier and less error prone.

CHAPTER 5

Distributed Management System Design

A MANAGEMENT SYSTEM serves many purposes. These include discovering and disseminating information about specific resources, modifying information about specific resources, and returning the results of modifications to users and devices. Modifications to information can take the form of computations on data, data mediation, or conversion of data from one format to another.

A management system must also meet a number of different challenges, including the following:

- Controlling, monitoring, updating, and reporting the state of devices, applications, and services

- Converting management data into readable form

- Providing Quality of Service (QoS) and repairing errors to minimize system downtime

- Providing accounting and auditing services of resources and users

The purposes and challenges of management systems have changed over the years. The following section presents a brief overview of how these changes have been brought about.

Management System Evolution

The evolution of large, complex software systems has presented systems managers with a higher risk of errors and system failures. Also, the demand for new management system services and features has increased over the years almost in parallel with the increase in management system complexity. Increased bandwidth, transmission quality, and more sophisticated equipment have all helped to fuel this demand.

Management system providers have scrambled to retrofit and redesign their products with increased complexity to meet these demands. Also, many equipment manufacturers are installing their own management tools in their hardware to manage hardware configurations and faults. These sophisticated machines are being integrated with advanced software systems in order to provide a centralized and integrated solution for handling management needs.

The increased complexity of management systems, the increased risks of errors and failures, and the diversity of hardware and software solutions has led to changes in standards and initiatives, as outlined in the following sections.

History of Management Standards and Initiatives

System management standards and initiatives have evolved from their modest beginnings into more intricate principles to meet the needs of complex and advanced distributed management systems. The following is a brief historical look at the evolution of management standards and initiatives.

OSI Management Framework

Around 1986, the ISO/IEC Joint Technical Committee introduced the Open Systems Interconnection (OSI) management framework. This framework defined five management functions that made up the OSI network management framework, usually designated as FCAPS:

- Fault management

- Configuration management

- Accounting management

- Performance management

- Security management

The OSI management framework is detailed at http://rfc-1095.rfc-list.com/rfc-1095-7.htm.

Common Management Information Services/Common Management Information Protocol

Around 1987, Common Management Information Services (CMIS) and Common Management Information Protocol (CMIP) became part of the group of OSI standards. CMIP was chartered with transporting management information between systems and devices. Within CMIS, peer processes used a small set of messages to exchange information. CMIP is still used in telecommunications systems. In 1989, CMIP was ported to TCP/IP and named the Common Management Information Protocol over TCP/IP (CMOT). More information about these standards can be found at http://www.faqs.org/rfcs/rfc1189.html.

Guidelines for Definition of Managed Objects

Later in 1987, the Guidelines for Definition of Managed Objects (GDMO) standard was introduced as a way to define managed objects in a standard fashion. This consistency for describing managed objects allows workstations, servers, devices, and software applications to be monitored and controlled in a consistent manner provided that the device or software manufacturer described their product accordingly. GDMO uses Abstract Syntax Notation One (ASN.1) as the syntax and encoding for defining objects. Details about GDMO can be found at http://www.cellsoft.de/telecom/gdmo.htm.

Simple Gateway Monitoring Protocol

The Simple Gateway Monitoring Protocol (SGMP) was also issued in late 1987 to provide a platform-neutral standard by which the variables of a gateway's configuration could be inspected or altered by remote users. SGMP information can be found at http://www.faqs.org/rfcs/rfc1028.html.

High-Level Entity Management System

Also introduced in 1987 was an effort to define a management standard for all devices known as the High-Level Entity Management System (HEMS). HEMS is made up of three parts: a query processor, an event generator, and applications that know how to send requests to the query processor and interpret the replies using High-Level Entity Management Protocol (HEMP). HEMP is an application protocol that runs on existing transport protocols to provide the formatting rules for HEMS queries and replies. HEMS is detailed at http://community.roxen.com/developers/idocs/rfc/rfc1021.html.

Management Information Base

In 1988, RFC 1066 defined the concept of a management information base (MIB). A MIB represents a virtual information store of managed resource information. RFC 1066, along with other documents, outlines an architecture and system for monitoring and control of components on TCP/IP-based internets. The documents also define formal descriptions of object information models for network management along with a set of generic types using Abstract Syntax Notation One (ASN.1).

Simple Network Management Protocol

In 1988, the Simple Network Management Protocol (SNMP) was recommended by the Internet Activities Board (IAB) as the foundation for network management. SNMP is a protocol designed for TCP/IP network management. Details about SNMP can be found at `http://www.snmplink.org/`.

Telecommunications Management Network

With the backing of the International Telecommunication Union (ITU-TS), the Telecommunications Management Network (TMN) was formally defined in 1988 to create a standard that would allow network elements to be consistently managed.

Using the OSI management framework as its model, TMN defines how resources, referred to as network elements (NEs), are managed by entities such as operating support systems (OSSs).

TMN describes telecom network management from four viewpoints:

1. A *functional architecture*

2. A *physical architecture*

3. An *information architecture*

4. A *logical layered architecture* (LLA), which outlines different responsibilities for management entities

TMN uses an object-oriented approach to define information in NEs modeled as attributes in managed objects. Management functions are carried out by operations consisting of CMIS primitives.

The telecommunications industry has recently coined the term *operating support systems* to generically refer to systems that perform management functions, inventory controls, status monitoring, and more for telecommunications networks. Additional information on TMN can be found at `http://www.iec.org/online/tutorials/tmn/`.

Remote Network Monitoring

Remote Network Monitoring (RMON) was introduced in 1991 as a technology for monitoring subnetworks remotely as a whole using the concept of probes. *Probes* are devices that monitor network traffic and report errors, in the form of alarms, to a management application. For additional information about RMON, see `http://www.simpleweb.org/ietf/rfcs/complete/rfc3273.txt`.

Object Management Group and CORBA

In the early 1990s, the Object Management Group (OMG) published a specification defining the Common Object Request Broker Architecture (CORBA) Object model, the Interface Definition Language (IDL), and a set of application programming interfaces (APIs) for dynamic request management and invocation (DII) and an Interface Repository. Later, OMG CORBA emerged to the forefront to define MIBs, instrument resources, and provide generic management services. For more information about OMG, see `http://www.omg.org`.

Distributed Management Task Force

In 1992, the Distributed Management Task Force (DMTF) was created to work with leading industry vendors in an attempt to spearhead the development of management standards for distributed desktop, network, enterprise, and Internet environments. See `http://www.dmtf.org/` for more information about the DMTF.

Desktop Management Interface

In 1994, the DMTF defined the Desktop Management Interface (DMI) to form a layer of abstraction between management software and a desktop system's components. DMI consists of interfaces that are designed to be accessed remotely using remote procedure calls (RPCs). DMI has focused on ease of use and has been designed to be

- Independent of a specific computer, OS, or protocol

- Used with or without a network

- Used remotely through DCE/RPC, ONC/RPC, or TI/RPC

- Easily mapped to existing management protocols

A complete description of DMI can be found at `http://www.dmtf.org/standards/standard_dmi.php`.

Web-Based Enterprise Management

DMTF began a process in 1996 to define the meaning of management data. This work resulted in the Common Information Model (CIM). The Common

Information Model is a common data model of an implementation-neutral schema for describing overall management information in a network/enterprise environment. CIM is composed of a specification and a schema. The specification defines the details for integration with other management models, whereas the schema provides the actual model descriptions.

It's important to understand that CIM is a definition, not an implementation. It can map to Common Management Information Protocol, Component Object Model (COM), Common Object Request Broker Architecture, Desktop Management Interface, High-Level Entity Management System, Java, Simple Network Management Protocol, a proprietary standard, or any other three-letter acronym (TLA) data-storage method/map. CIM is a translator or provider of data. It normalizes data and could be stored in a Sybase database by a CORBA ORB running as a result of a network asset process. It could provide data to a Java network-management application that makes a query using CIM-defined data (schema). Of course, this would have to happen via a process (or processes) that could map from a proprietary format to CIM to any other data format. Developers of a Java network-management application could create logic once to determine CPU utilization, rather than requiring a different method for every management agent and operating system they needed to manage.

CIM soon blossomed into the full-blown Web-Based Enterprise Management (WBEM) architecture. WBEM is an initiative based on a set of management and Internet standard technologies developed to unify the management of enterprise computing environments. WBEM provides the ability for the industry to deliver a well-integrated set of standard-based management tools leveraging the emerging technologies such as CIM and XML.

Also under the WBEM umbrella is the Directory Enabled Network (DEN) initiative. DEN was designed to provide the building blocks for more intelligent management by mapping concepts from CIM (such as systems, services, and policies) to a directory, and integrating this information with other WBEM elements in the management infrastructure. This utilizes existing user and enterprise-wide data already present in a company's directory, empowers end-to-end services, and supports distributed network-wide service creation, provisioning, and management. For additional information about WBEM, see `http://www.dmtf.org/standards/standard_wbem.php`.

Java Management API

In 1996, the Java Management API (JMAPI) was proposed by Sun and some of its partners to define a Java-based programming framework and environment for building Web-based network and systems management tools.

JMAPI offered services for developing SNMP agents, managers, and proxies, thereby providing an easy integration mechanism between SNMP and Java.

Open Management Interface

In 2002, HP OpenView formed a strategic partnership with webMethods to bring about the Open Management Interface (OMI) specification. OMI defines APIs and technologies that EAI vendors support to manipulate objects, expose attributes and relationships, monitor status information, and represent real-time management information about their environment within an enterprise management platform.

The OMI specification defines a SOAP API to access management information generated by an application environment and to execute management commands. The benefit of the OMI specification is that it uses XML-over-HTTP to simplify complex, real-time interactions made between management platforms and enterprise applications. For a detailed description of OMI, refer to http://www.webmethods.com/PDF/OMI_Spec.pdf.

Java Management Extensions

In 1999, JMAPI was renamed as Java Management Extensions (JMX). JMX defines the means for instrumenting resources as Java-manageable objects for controlling and monitoring by agents.

History of Management Designs

System management designs have evolved along with the changes in standards from simple hardware configurations into decentralized distributed system configurations. The following looks at the history of some of the more notable configuration designs.

Terminal-Configurable Devices

Early network management configurations consisted of simple dedicated hardware devices typically configured from a terminal connected directly to a serial port on the device itself. The command sets for these devices consisted of a limited group of commands typically used to enable or disable ports or change attributes of device protocols. Figure 5-1 illustrates this configuration.

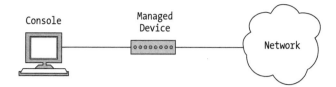

Figure 5-1. A simple terminal-configurable device

In-Band and Out-of-Band Network Management

As the number of these devices multiplied, out-of-band mechanisms were employed by applying concentrator network techniques such as utilizing a serial communication cable attached to the RS-232 console port of the managed device, as shown in Figure 5-2.

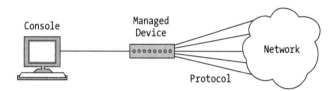

Figure 5-2. Out-of-band device management configuration

In-band mechanisms were also employed by transmitting the management information along the same network as the managed device, as shown in Figure 5-3.

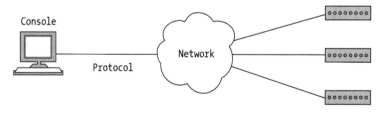

Figure 5-3. In-band device management configuration

Policy-Based Network Management

In the early 1990s, policy-based network management was introduced. In policy-based system management, policies are simple rules that grant access to resources if certain conditions are met. For example, a user with an ID of jdoe can be granted access to a virtual private network (VPN) during certain times of the day.

Policy-based network management made significant advances to promote the automation of meeting and maintaining management goals over a broad category of managed devices and applications across large distributed systems.

Enterprise Management Systems

As the Internet became a driving force and TCP/IP became the standard protocol for business, more and more devices were suddenly available for use. This escalated the problems that management systems were facing. Managing and controlling systems that were adorned with workstations, printers, peripheral devices, and so on was swiftly becoming a monumental task. As a result, businesses began to flood the corporate network environment with many different management systems for each new database product, application, and the like. The concept of enterprise management systems (EMS), illustrated in Figure 5-4, was introduced to macro-manage the entire gamut of applications, servers, databases, and other resources existing across the enterprise.

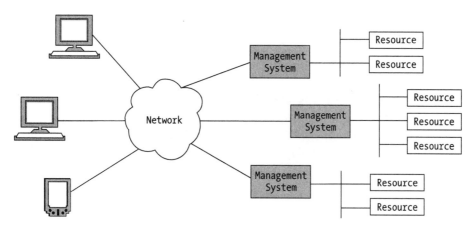

Figure 5-4. Enterprise network management configuration

Distributed Object Computing

The deregulation of telecommunications and flooding of networks with an ever-increasing wave of devices, workstations, and mainframes exposed a compelling need for improved resource management and information sharing.

Distributed systems tend to be large, diverse, dynamic, and lacking a common governing authority, thus making them very difficult to manage. To address this, management systems started to move away from management-specific protocols and embraced more pervasive protocols, platforms, and technologies.

Distributed Object Computing (DOC) was introduced to solve the problems associated with this dynamic new state of affairs. Distributed Object Computing uses object-oriented techniques and methodologies to provide services and tools for building distributed applications. Platforms like OMG's Common Object Request Broker Architecture, Distributed Component Object Model (DCOM), and Distributed Computing Environment (DCE) are some of the more well-known implementations of DOC.

Eventually, DOC was tailored to integrate with legacy network management products to address management challenges for distributed systems. As a result, management applications and services could be distributed throughout a network instead of restricted to one centralized location.

Although DOC addressed heterogeneous distributed domains, it still relied on some form of static proprietary runtime environment. As the popularity of the Web increased, Web-based protocols such as HTTP became the desired transport to overcome proprietary restrictions and to enable a more pervasive presence for all types of applications, including network management and resource management.

Web-Based Management

The current state of reliance on Web protocols by applications and services creates a natural path for management platforms to take as well. XML, HTTP, and HTTPS are some of the more widely used protocols today. Management platforms are exploiting these technologies to create management systems that can be accessed from virtually anywhere at any time. Figure 5-5 illustrates how the use of Web technologies can create a world-wide presence for management systems.

Using Web technologies for management removes the dependence on proprietary runtime environments and management consoles. Web browsers, XML, HTTP, and HTML are quickly replacing the static proprietary tools and technologies used in legacy management systems.

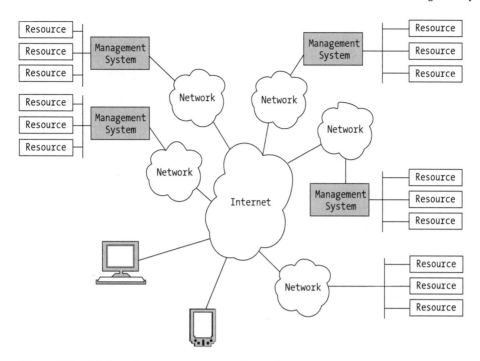

Figure 5-5. Web-based management configuration

Management Framework Patterns

System management frameworks tend to follow four different architectural patterns. The following is a brief discussion of these.

Specialized/Detached

Early management systems were built around a simple detached pattern that monitored and managed devices themselves using a proprietary command point. This involved controlling devices with specialized management clients, as illustrated in Figure 5-6.

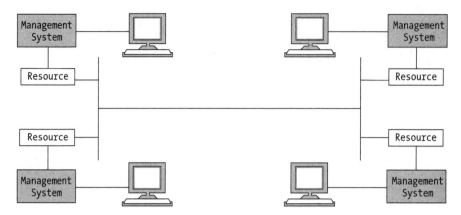

Figure 5-6. Specialized/Detached framework configuration

Centralized

Management systems evolved to the point where a centralized command center could be employed. Frameworks using this type of pattern typically rely on a model that uses polling techniques to monitor network status and device status and to update console applications. This pattern is illustrated in Figure 5-7.

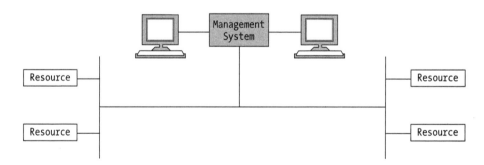

Figure 5-7. Centralized framework configuration

Hierarchical

The hierarchical pattern that the OSI model introduced has been employed by a number of different management frameworks. The hierarchical pattern allows an abstraction of management control for multiple management command points. This provides a central management point for all devices and resources within a given network. Techniques such as partitioning and replication are used in a hierarchical model to provide a level of failover for a management system. The hierarchical pattern is illustrated in Figure 5-8.

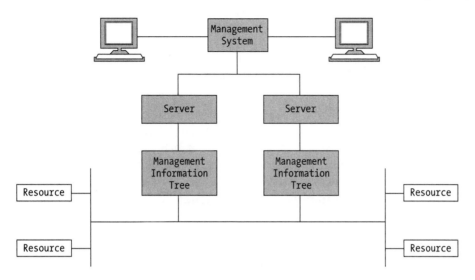

Figure 5-8. Hierarchical framework configuration

Distributed/Cooperative

This pattern, illustrated in Figure 5-9, defines a model for building management systems that can transmit messages and notifications to remote management clients. Diverse management systems in a distributed management system can cooperate with each other in order to share information and maintain accurate records.

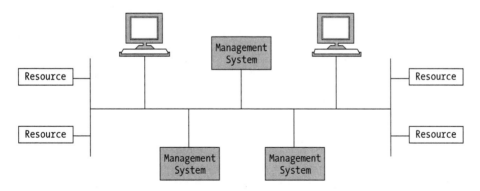

Figure 5-9. Distributed/Cooperative framework configuration

Let's take a look at how techniques and principles from the hierarchical management pattern and the distributed/cooperative management pattern can be combined and applied within a manager/agent system.

Manager/Agent Frameworks

Management design has brought about a management framework that defines a manager/agent concept. Managers and agents share status and control information about resources in order to build a unified management view of a network.

Within a manager/agent framework, managed resources are controlled and manipulated in order to maintain and modify management structure. The interaction between a manager and an agent usually involves the manager directing the agent to manipulate its managed resources using operations on attributes of the managed resource. An agent responds to a manager with managed resource attribute values and transmits notifications pertaining to events that affect managed resource attribute values. The interaction between a manager and an agent is illustrated in Figure 5-10.

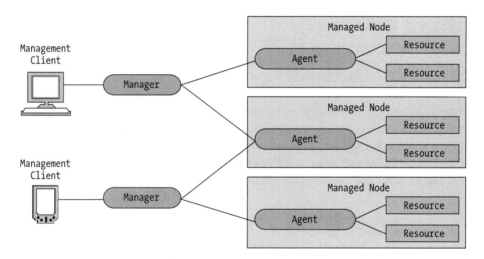

Figure 5-10. Manager/Agent interaction

Managers

A *manager* is an application or service that acts on behalf of a client in order to connect with and use an agent to perform operations on managed resources. A manager invokes operations on an agent with the aim of gathering information about the agent's managed resources or manipulating the resources. A manager receives information from an agent in response to operation invocations and as event notifications from an agent.

Management clients interact with managers in order to access and manipulate managed resources. Management clients rely on managers to shield them from complex details about agent structures and protocols. Management clients also rely on managers to interact with agents to perform such operations as configuring connection parameters, upgrading resources, securing resources, distributing processes, and balancing loads.

Managers typically perform some standard operations. These include

- Taking client requests and returning responses

- Notifying clients of exceptional events that occur

- Locating agents for clients

- Returning to clients the status of managed resources

Managers typically communicate with agents by sending requests to the agents and then either blocking the response or employing an asynchronous mechanism, such as polling or registering as an event listener, in order to receive the response later.

Agents

A *management agent* is a software entity that accepts management requests from managers or management clients, services the requests, and then waits for the next request. Management agents are responsible for exposing, to managers or management clients, information associated with a managed resource exposed as attributes of the resource. An agent invokes operations that are received from a manager and returns responses to the manager. An agent can also notify a manager in the event that attributes of a managed resource changes or in the event that an error or exception has occurred. An agent can service requests from multiple managers.

Agents typically perform some standard operations. These include

- Returning to managers or clients information retrieved as the result of queries performed against a collection of managed resources

- Returning to managers or clients event notifications generated by the agent or by the agent's managed resources

- Registering managed resources provided by clients, managers, applications, or services

- Controlling access to managed resources based on a client's or manager's identity or location

Manager and Agent Models and Roles

Applications or services that expose management interfaces are typically thought of as operating in an agent role, and applications or services that employ those interfaces are typically thought of as operating in a manager role.

Managers and agents can take on similar roles, depending on the circumstances. For example, agents and managers can interact in a peer-to-peer model; agents may operate in a hierarchical model; and managers may interact with each other on a peer-to-peer basis. Even though many different types of manager-agent models are possible, four typically occur: horizontal, centralized, hierarchical, and distributed. Let's take a quick look at each of these models.

Horizontal

Systems where managers operate in a peer-to-peer relationship are sometimes referred to as belonging to a horizontal model, which is illustrated in Figure 5-11.

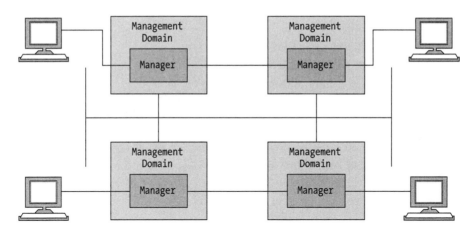

Figure 5-11. Horizontal manager model

Centralized

Systems where managers are embodied as central controlling hubs, such as is found in management operation centers, are often referred to as belonging to a centralized model, as shown in Figure 5-12.

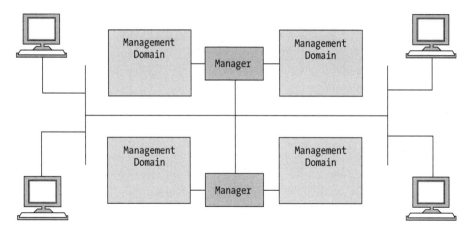

Figure 5-12. Centralized manager model

Hierarchical

Systems where managers and/or agents exist in a hierarchical relationship, such as is found in an agent/subagent model, are often referred to as belonging to a hierarchical model. This model is illustrated in Figure 5-13.

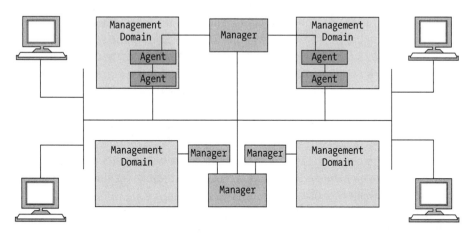

Figure 5-13. Hierarchical manager model

Distributed

Systems where managers and/or agents exist in a networked relationship are often referred to as belonging to a distributed model, which is illustrated in Figure 5-14.

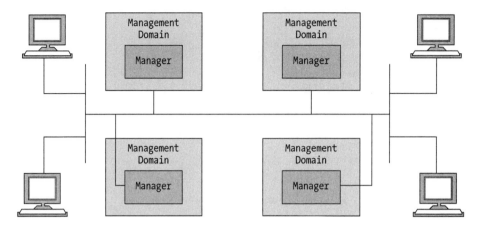

Figure 5-14. Distributed manager model

Master Agents and Subagents

Management systems maintaining a large network of agents can be optimized using a hierarchy of agents and subagents that are controlled by a master agent. Within this structure, the master agents act as liaisons between managers and subagents. Managers are shielded from the details of the agent hierarchy by the master agents. Managers connect and communicate only with the master agents.

The encapsulation of subagents by a master agent allows the subagent hierarchy to appear as a single agent to a manager. This abstraction permits dynamic modifications to be made to the subagent structure without altering the public interface seen by a manager. Figure 5-15 illustrates the relationship between managers, master agents, and subagents.

Master agents are responsible for propagating information exposed by their subagents. Master agents can also expose information for their own managed resources and services. Managers connect and interact with master agents, and not the subagents, in a master-agent/subagent framework. In fact, managers know nothing about subagents and assume they are communicating with one agent.

As the previous figure points out, subagents can span master-agent domains and have multiple master agents. Also noticeable is the fact that a subagent can initiate notifications that are relayed to the manager by the master agent.

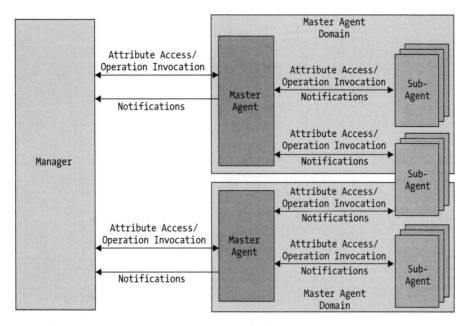

Figure 5-15. Manager, master agent, and subagent interaction

Manager Domains

For large distributed systems to be managed efficiently, they often need to be partitioned into multiple logical segments that are controlled by individual managers. These segments are often referred to as *manager domains*.

Interdomain communication between multiple managers typically occurs on a peer-to-peer basis. Information is passed back and forth between managers responsible for each domain.

Domains can be determined by evaluating logical functionality or characteristics of certain elements such as

- Quality of service

- Service or application types

- Fault tolerance

- User types

- Security policies

- Geographical locations

- Protocol types

- Resource types

- Device types

Figure 5-16 illustrates a system of managed resources, agents, and managers that have been partitioned into different domains.

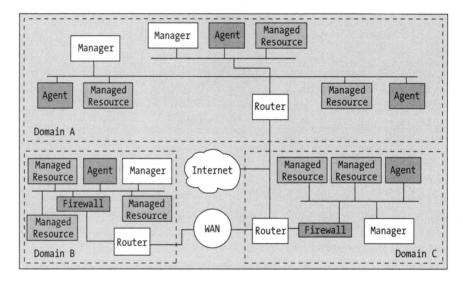

Figure 5-16. Example of manager/agent domains

Manager of Managers (MoMs)

When a system becomes too complex, it is often necessary to introduce a manager that is responsible for coordinating and administrating the managers of each domain. This manager is referred to as *manager of managers* (MoM). In a MoM-administrated environment, domain managers rely on the MoM to communicate with other managers.

In addition to coordinating managers, MoMs are responsible for diagnosing the overall health and status of the aggregate of all domains. This is a result of gathering and monitoring global events and attributes retrieved from each domain manager, and it allows MoMs to effectively evaluate how a domain is performing in relation to other domains. Figure 5-17 illustrates a system of managed resources, agents, and managers that have been partitioned into different domains that are managed by a MoM.

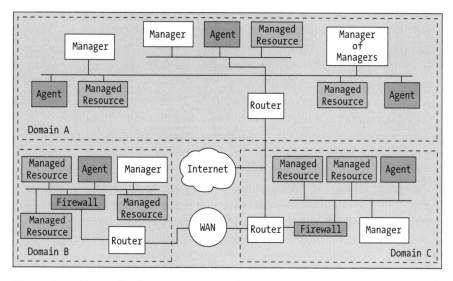

Figure 5-17. Example of manager/agent domains with MoM

Managers and JMX

Managers that are developed using the Java programming language request information from other managers and agents. Agents in turn retrieve the information from MBeans. Figure 5-18 illustrates the relationships between management clients, managers, agents, and MBeans in a simple JMX model.

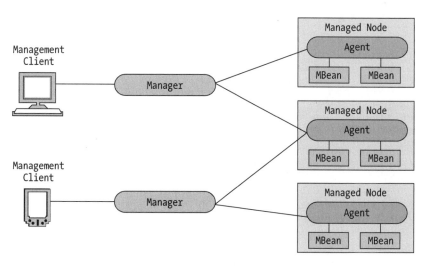

Figure 5-18. Manager/Agent model using JMX

The JMX Remoting specification defines a remote communication entity known as a *connector*. A connector is used by an agent to publicize its MBean server to remote managers and management clients. A connector consists of a *connector client* and a *connector server.*

A connector client is essentially the remote publication of an agent's management interface. Connector clients are responsible for finding a connector server and establishing a connection with it. A connector client and a connector server have a one-to-one physical relationship; however, more than one logical connection may exist between a connector client and a connector server. A client application or manager also may contain many connector clients connected to different connector servers.

A connector server is implemented and exposed by an agent in order to allow the agent to listen for requests from remote connector clients. Connector servers may handle many connections with different remote clients. Figure 5-19 illustrates an example of some common remote manager/agent configurations using connector clients and connector servers.

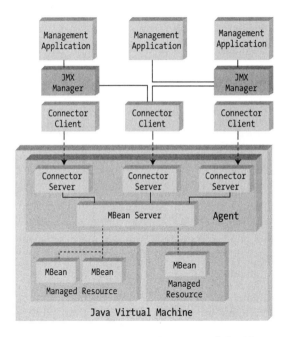

Figure 5-19. JMX manager/agent model with remote clients

Summary

A management system serves many purposes, including discovering and disseminating information about specific resources, modifying information about specific resources, and returning the results of modifications to users and devices. Modifications to information can take the form of computations on data, data mediation, or conversion of data from one format to another.

A management system must also meet a number of different challenges such as controlling, monitoring, updating, and reporting the state of devices, applications, and services.

The evolution of large, complex software systems has presented systems managers with a higher risk of errors and system failure. Also, the demand for new management system services and features has increased over the years almost in parallel with the increase in management system complexity. Increased bandwidth, transmission quality, and more sophisticated equipment have all helped to fuel this demand.

Management system providers have scrambled to retrofit and redesign their products with increased complexity to meet these demands. Also, many equipment manufacturers are installing their own management tools into their hardware to manage hardware configurations and faults. These sophisticated machines are being integrated with advanced software systems in order to provide a centralized and integrated solution for handling management needs.

The increased complexity of management systems, the increased risks of errors and failures, and the diversity of hardware and software solutions has led to the following approximate history of standards and initiatives.

System management standards and initiatives have evolved from modest beginnings into complex and advanced distributed management systems. This evolution of management standards and initiatives has included the OSI Management Framework, CMIS/CMIP, the Guidelines for Definition of Managed Objects, and others.

System management designs have evolved along with the changes in standards from simple hardware configurations into decentralized distributed system configurations. This evolution has included many different configuration designs such as terminal-configurable devices, in-band and out-of-band network management, policy-based network management, to name a few.

System management frameworks tend to follow four different architectural patterns:

- Specialized/Detached

- Centralized

- Hierarchical

- Distributed/Cooperative

Management design has brought about a management framework that defines a manager/agent concept. Managers and agents share status and control information about resources in order to build a unified management view of a network.

Within a manager/agent framework, managed resources are controlled and manipulated in order to maintain and modify management structure. The interaction between a manager and an agent usually involves the manager directing the agent to manipulate its managed resources using operations on attributes of the managed resource. An agent responds to a manager with managed resource attribute values and transmits notifications pertaining to events that affect managed resource attribute values.

A manager is an application or service that acts on behalf of a client in order to connect with and use an agent to perform operations on managed resources. A manager invokes operations on an agent with the aim of gathering information about the agent's managed resources or manipulating the resources. A manager receives information from an agent in response to operation invocations and as event notifications from an agent.

A management agent is a software entity that accepts management requests from managers or management clients, services the requests, and then waits for the next request. Management agents are responsible for exposing, to managers or management clients, information associated with a managed resource exposed as attributes of the resource. An agent invokes operations that are received from a manager and returns responses to the manager, and can also notify a manager in the event that attributes of a managed resource changes or in the event that an error or exception has occurred. An agent can service requests from multiple managers.

Applications or services that expose management interfaces are typically thought of as operating in an agent role and applications or services that employ those interfaces are typically thought of as operating in a manager role.

Managers and agents can take on similar roles, depending on the circumstances. For example, agents and managers can interact in a peer-to-peer model; agents may operate in a hierarchical model; managers may interact with each other on a peer-to-peer basis. Even though many different types of manager-agent models are possible, four typically occur:

- Horizontal

- Centralized

- Hierarchical

- Distributed

Management systems maintaining a large network of agents can be optimized using a hierarchy of agents and subagents that are controlled by a master agent. Within this structure, the master agents act as liaisons between managers and subagents. Managers are shielded from the details of the agent hierarchy by the master agents. Managers connect and communicate only with the master agents.

Large distributed systems often need to be partitioned into multiple logical segments that are controlled by individual managers, to be managed efficiently. These segments are often referred to as manager domains.

When a system becomes too complex, it is often necessary to introduce a manager that is responsible for coordinating and administrating the managers of each domain. This manager is referred to as manager-of-managers, or MoM. In a MoM-administrated environment, domain managers rely on the MoM to communicate with other managers.

Managers that are developed using the Java programming language request information from other managers and agents. Agents in turn retrieve the information from MBeans.

The JMX-Remoting specification defines a remote communication entity known as a connector, which is used by an agent to publicize its MBean server to remote managers and management clients. A connector consists of a connector client and a connector server.

A connector client is essentially the remote publication of an agent's management interface, and it is responsible for finding a connector server and establishing a connection with it. A connector client and a connector server have a one-to-one physical relationship; however, more than one logical connection may exist between a connector client and a connector server. A client application or manager also may contain many connector clients connected to different connector servers.

CHAPTER 6

The Three-Level Model and Distributed Services

DISTRIBUTED MANAGEMENT applications are composed of components that cooperate together across a network to publish and consume management functions. The JMX distributed services level exposes components in an effort to provide an environment and framework for exposing JMX agents, resources, and services to remote clients. The distributed services level, combined with the agent level and instrumentation level, provides an inclusive platform for implementing complete, robust management applications and services.

The JMX distributed services level facilitates management solutions that are interoperable, flexible, secure, and portable. Management solutions constructed within the technological sphere of the JMX distributed services level can benefit from its communication standards, protocol flexibility and transparency, location transparency, and standard security mechanisms.

The JMX distributed services level defines management components and frameworks that provide scalable operations to operate on agents and MBeans in a distributed environment. These components and frameworks expose interfaces for management applications to interact securely in a location-transparent manner with agents and their manageable resources. Figure 6-1 illustrates the relationship between the JMX distributed services level and the other JMX levels.

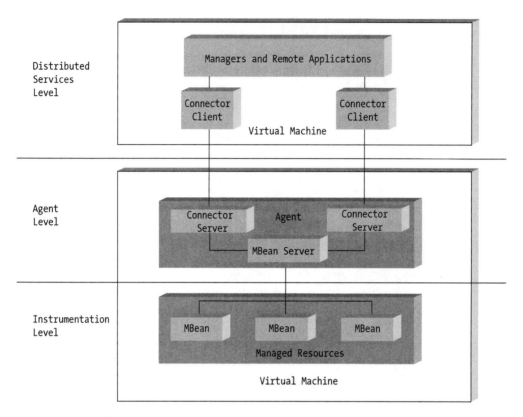

Figure 6-1. The three levels of JMX

In this chapter, I will introduce you to the JMX distributed services level and show how it is used along with other JMX technologies. First, we will look at how JMX defines the concept of *connectors* in order to join client and server components.

Clients and Servers Unite with Connectors

The JMX distributed services specification defines a concept for software components that make MBean servers accessible to remote Java clients. These components are known as *connectors*. Connectors encompass the client end (*connector client*) and server end (*connector server*) of a communication link between a management application or manager and an MBean server. Connectors can be adapted for any standard protocol accessible from Java; however, the distributed JMX specification mandates that only an RMI protocol adaptation be supported by a compliant implementation. The specification does define an optional connector adaptation called the *JMX Messaging Protocol,* or *JMXMP,* which is based on TCP sockets. Since all connectors expose the same Java interface, management applications can select a connector client that more closely matches their environment and needs. Since connectors provide a level of indirection between applications and MBean servers, applications can transparently replace connectors as needed.

A connector client exports an interface that emulates a remote MBean server. Connectors provide continuous communications with an MBean server over a given protocol. A connector client is responsible for locating a connector server with which it establishes a connection.

Although each connector client can be connected to exactly one connector server, each client application may contain multiple connector clients connected to different connector servers.

A connector server exposes an MBean server and listens for client connection requests with which it can create a connection. A given connector server may establish many concurrent connections with different clients.

Clients wanting to interact with an MBean server remotely retrieve an object that implements the MBeanServerConnection interface. This interface is the parent of the MBeanServer interface that clients use to interact with an MBean server when running in the same virtual machine. Since both interfaces are similar, a client can use the same code to transparently access local and remote MBean servers. The main differences between the two interfaces are a few methods that are only relevant when accessing an MBean server locally. Also, only the methods of the MBeanServerConnection interface declare that they throw IOException.

Creating Connector Servers

A connector server is encapsulated by an object that extends the javax.management.remote.JMXConnectorServer class. For example, an RMI connector server is embodied in the javax.management.remote.rmi.RMIConnectorServer class. The javax.management.remote.generic.GenericConnectorServer class can be extended to encapsulate nonstandard connector servers. To create a connector server, you must instantiate such a subclass.

A connector server and an MBean server are associated in one of the following two ways:

1. An MBean server can be associated with the connector server when the connector server is constructed, as follows:

    ```
    MBeanServer mBeanServer =
      MBeanServerFactory.createMBeanServer();
    JMXServiceURL url =
      new JMXServiceURL("service:jmx:rmi:///jndi/rmi://myhost:9999/server");
    ```

```
JMXConnectorServer connectorServer =
  JMXConnectorServerFactory.newJMXConnectorServer(url,

                                                  null,
                                                  mBeanServer);
connectorServer.start();
JMXServiceURL serverAddress =
  connectorServer.getAddress();
```

2. The connector server can be registered as an MBean in the MBean server for which it is associated, as the following example illustrates:

```
MBeanServer mBeanServer =
  MBeanServerFactory.createMBeanServer();
JMXServiceURL url =
  new JMXServiceURL("service:jmx:rmi:///jndi/rmi://myhost:9999/server");
JMXConnectorServer connectorServer =
  JMXConnectorServerFactory.newJMXConnectorServer(url,

                                                  null,
                                                  mBeanServer);
// Note that starting ObjectNames with a colon,
// as in the following statement,implies the default domain
ObjectName serverName =
  new ObjectName(":type=connectorserver,name=myconnectorserver");
mBeanServer.registerMBean(connectorServer, serverName);
connectorServer.start();
```

Publishing a Connector Server with Existing Infrastructures

As mentioned previously, in the distributed services level of JMX, a connector consists of a connector client and a connector server. A connector server is attached to an MBean server and listens for connection requests from clients. A connector server can be published with existing infrastructures, including the following:

- *Service Location Protocol (SLP):* The JMXServiceURL of a connector server is registered with SLP.

- *Jini Network Technology:* The JMXConnector stub of a connector server is registered with the Jini Lookup Service.

- *Java Naming and Directory Interface (JNDI):* The JMXServiceURL of a connector server is registered with an LDAP directory.

Creating Connector Clients

Connector clients are encapsulated by objects that implement the JMXConnector interface. There are primarily two ways in which a connector client is created: using a JMXConnectorFactory or using connection stubs. The method to use depends on the underlying infrastructure that is used to locate the connector server. I discuss some of the possibilities in the following sections.

Using a JMXConnectorFactory to Create a Connector Client

If the address of a connector server is known to the client, the client can use the connect method or the newConnector method of the JMXConnectorFactory class to make a connection. This is often used when the server address is published statically from an SLP-enabled directory or SLP service agent.

The following example illustrates this process:

```
// Create the connector server.
MBeanServer mBeanServer = MBeanServerFactory.createMBeanServer();
JMXMPConnectorServer connectorServer = new JMXMPConnectorServer(mBeanServer);
connectorServer.start();
// Retrieve the server's address using the getAddress method.
JMXServiceURL serverAddress = connectorServer.getAddress();
// Publish the server's address using an SLP-enabled component.
mySLPServerComponent.publish(serverAddress);
```

A management application can then connect to the server as follows:

```
// Retrieve the connector server address using an SLP-enabled component.
JMXServiceURL serverAddress = mySLPClientComponent.getServerAddress();
// Connect to the server using this address.
JMXConnector connectorClient = JMXConnectorFactory.connect(serverAddress)
```

Using a Connection Stub to Create a Connector Client

If the address of a connector server is not known to the client, the client can use the connector server's *connector stub* to connect with it. A connector stub is an object implementing the JMXConnector class and is generated by a connector server. A connector stub is serializable so that it might be transmitted to a remote client. Once a client has access to a connector stub, the client can call the stub's connect method to connect to the connector server.

The following example illustrates how an MBean server can export that server to remote managers as follows:

```
// Create the connector server.
MBeanServer mBeanServer = MBeanServerFactory.createMBeanServer();
JMXMPConnectorServer connectorServer = new JMXMPConnectorServer(mBeanServer);
connectorServer.start();
// Obtain the connector stub.
JMXConnector connectorStub = connectorServer.getStub(properties);
// Store the stub somewhere in a directory, lookup service, HTTP server, etc.
myJNDIComponent.store(connectorStub, properties);
```

A management application can then connect to the server as follows:

```
// Retrieve stub from storage.
JMXConnector connectorClient = myJNDIComponent.retrieve(properties);
// Call the stub's connect method.
connectorClient.connect();
```

Finding a Connector Server

In order to connect with a connector server, a management client can retrieve the address or stub of a connector server that has been registered with existing infrastructures, including the following:

- *Service Location Protocol:* The JMXServiceURL of a connector server is retrieved.

- *Jini Network Technology:* The JMXConnector stub of a connector server is retrieved.

- *Java Naming and Directory Interface:* The JMXServiceURL of a connector server is retrieved.

Finding Servers Using Connector Server Addresses

Connections are established using addresses or connection stubs. A connector server address is encapsulated by the immutable JMXServiceURL class. A JMXServiceURL address is an embodiment of the *Abstract Service URL for SLP,* as defined in RFC 2609 and amended by RFC 3111. It must take the following form:

```
service:jmx:protocol:sap
```

All connector server addresses begin with "service:jmx:". The remaining sections of a connector server address are defined as follows:

- protocol: The transport protocol to be used to make the connection. It consists of a string of one or more letters, digits, +, or -.

- sap: Short for service access point, this represents the IP-based address at which the connector server is found, according to the syntax defined by RFC 2609.

Here's an example of a connector server address:

```
service:jmx:jmxmp://myhost:1234
```

The preceding example demonstrates a connector server address that uses the JMXMP connector to find a server at host: myhost, port: 1234.

Terminating Connections Between Clients and Servers

A connection can be terminated by the client connector or by the server connector as they wish. IOExceptions are thrown if operations are attempted when the connection has been terminated.

The RMI Connector

The RMI connector is the only connector that must be present in all implementations of the distributed JMX specification. The RMI connector uses the RMI infrastructure to communicate between client and server. Java Remote Method Protocol (JRMP) and Internet Inter-ORB Protocol (IIOP) are the two transport protocols used by RMI. The RMI connector supports both transport types.

Mechanics of the RMI Connector

For every RMIConnectorServer object, there is a remotely exported object that implements the remote interface RMIServer. A client that wants to communicate with the connector server retrieves the remote object's stub. Any method called on the stub is forwarded to the remote object. So a client that has a stub for the RMIServer object can call a method on it, and expect the same results as if the method were called on the RMIConnectorServer object itself.

JMX and Distributed Notification Events

The distributed JMX specification defines a model for transmitting notification events remotely. This model is based on the standard Java event model. As with the local notification event model, remote notification events can be transmitted by MBean instances and by an MBean server.

A JMX implementation may provide services that allow distribution of this notification event model, thus allowing a management application to listen to MBean events and MBean server events remotely.

In Figure 6-2, a connector client calls the addNotificationListener method of the MBeanServerConnection interface, supplying one NotificationListener parameter. As illustrated, a client connector notifies a server connector of a new listener request, at which point the server responds by calling addNotificationListener on the local MBean server.

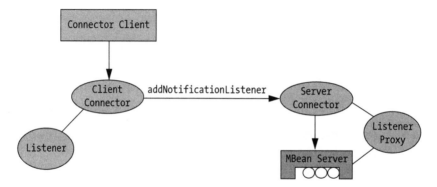

Figure 6-2. A client can add a remote listener using a client connector.

Figure 6-3 shows how a remote listener receives notification events from a remote MBean server. When an MBean transmits a notification event, the MBean server calls its listener proxy's handleNotification method, which causes the proxy to forward the notification event to the server connector, which, in turn, forwards the notification event to the client listener.

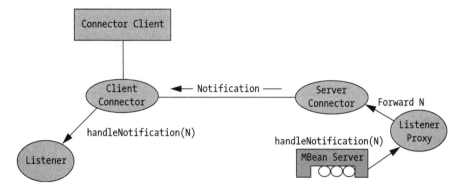

Figure 6-3. A remote client is notified by a remote MBean server.

RMIConnector Notification Events

When a user of the JMXConnector interface for an RMIConnector client adds a listener, the addNotificationListener method in the MBeanServerConnection interface is used to add a listener proxy to the server. This listener proxy queues up notification events at the server. When the client calls the remote fetchNotifications method, any queued up notification events are returned to it. If there are no queued notification events when fetchNotifications is called, it blocks until at least one notification event is available.

The connector client continually repeats the following two actions:

1. Call fetchNotifications.

2. Dispatch the received notification events to the appropriate listeners.

During an idle period when there are no notification events, this loop is blocked in the fetchNotifications call. Essentially, this means that there is always at least one remote method call in progress on an RMIMBeanServerConnection object at any given time, and as a consequence

- At least one thread per connection exists on the client end and one on the server end.

- At least one network connection is open between client and server.

- RMI's distributed garbage collection will not remove the server object even if the client dies, because the fetchNotifications method will still be in progress on it.

To avoid the last problem, a client may pass a timeout to the fetchNotifications method. The fetchNotifications method will block until there is at least one notification or until the specified timeout is reached.

Pluggable Object Wrapping

The distributed JMX API offers an interface that defines how to wrap parameters that use a nondefault class loader to handle cases in which the arguments to an MBean method called through MBeanServer.invoke and the attribute values supplied to setAttribute or setAttributes may be Java classes that are known to the target MBean but not to the connector server. If these objects were treated like any other, the connector server would get a ClassNotFoundException when it tries to deserialize a request containing them. Object wrapping solves this problem by encoding an attribute value inside an object of a type that is known to the connector server, such as byte[] or String.

To avoid this problem, deserialization at the server end of a connection proceeds in two stages as follows:

1. The objects that are necessarily of classes known to the connector server are deserialized. This is enough to determine what kind of request has been received, which MBean it is destined for, and what class loader is appropriate to use.

2. The remaining values can be deserialized using this class loader.

The ObjectWrapping interface allows customization of the way object wrapping is done. By default, it constructs a byte array containing the output of ObjectOutputStream.writeObject on the object or objects to be wrapped. But this would be unsuitable if, for example, the transport is using XML. So in such a case, an ObjectWrapping object could be plugged into the connector that wraps the objects in XML. This XML can then be included in the larger XML text constructed by the transport.

The Generic Connector

The distributed JMX specification defines a generic connector that is designed to be configurable by plugging in modules to define the following:

- The transport protocol used to transmit requests from a client to a server and to transmit responses and notification events from the server to clients

- The object wrapping for objects sent from a client to a server whose class loader may depend on the target MBean

The JMXMPConnector is a configuration of the generic connector in which the transport protocol is based on TCP and the object wrapping is native Java serialization. Security is based on Java Secure Socket Extension (JSSE), Java Authentication and Authorization Service (JAAS), and Simple Authentication and Security Layer (SASL).

The generic connector and its JMXMP configuration are optional; therefore an implementation may choose not to include them.

The Generic Connector Protocol

The generic connector protocol defines a set of protocol messages that are exchanged between the client connector and the server connector, and the sequence these message exchanges must follow. Implementations of the distributed JMX specification must exchange these messages in the defined sequence so that they can interoperate with other implementations. Figure 6-4 depicts the class diagram of all the messages defined by the generic connector protocol.

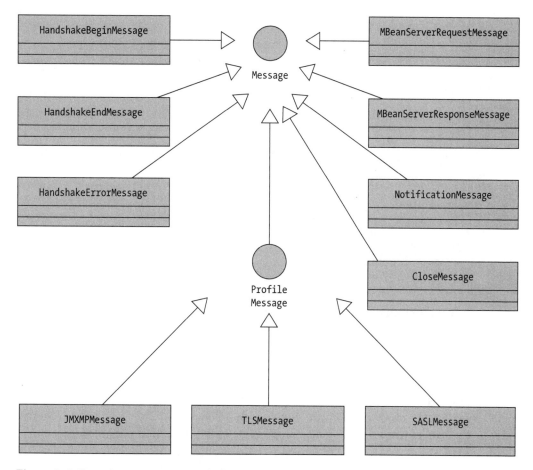

Figure 6-4. Generic connector protocol messages

The generic connector protocol messages are generally divided into four categories:

Handshake messages:

- HandshakeBeginMessage

- HandshakeEndMessage

- HandshakeErrorMessage

Profile messages:

- JMXMPMessage

- TLSMessage (JMXMP Connector only)

- SASLMessage (JMXMP Connector only)

MBean server operation messages:

- MBeanServerRequestMessage

- MBeanServerResponseMessage

- NotificationMessage

Connection message:

- CloseMessage

Handshake and Profile Message Exchanges

The handshake message exchanges are started by a connector server as soon as the connect method on the JMXConnector class is called by the client and the connection between the client and the server is established.

The connector server transmits to the client a HandshakeBeginMessage with the server's supported profiles. These profiles are retrieved from the environment map through the jmx.remote.profiles property. The client then starts the profile message exchanges for the profiles chosen from the server's supported profiles.

The JMXMP profile is used to negotiate the version of JMXMP to use. This profile is always implicitly enabled, but is only negotiated if the client and server differ in their default versions.

For the other profiles, the client will first check that all of the profiles asked for in its environment map are supported by the server. If not, it will transmit a HandshakeErrorMessage to the server and close the connection.

A client will negotiate for each profile asked for in its environment map. The order in which profiles are negotiated is the order they appear in the client's environment map. This order may be important. For example, if the client negotiates the SASL/PLAIN profile before the TLS profile, it will transmit a password in clear text over the connection.

If it negotiates TLS first, the connection will become encrypted before the password is sent. It is unspecified how the server accepts or denies the sequence of profiles executed by the client. However, it is recommended that if the profiles in the server's environment map imply a certain level of security, the server should reject a connection whose negotiated profiles do not ensure that level of security. For example, if the server is configured with only the TLS profile, then it should reject connections that do not negotiate TLS. If the server is configured with the TLS profile and with the SASL/DIGEST-MD5 profile specifying the same level of security with regard to authentication and encryption, then it should reject connections that do not negotiate either profile.

The profile exchanges are performed one at a time and always started by the client. Once the profile exchanges are completed, the client transmits a HandshakeEndMessage to the server. No further profile exchanges are then possible. The server replies either with the same HandshakeEndMessage if it accepts the profiles that have been negotiated or with a HandshakeErrorMessage if it does not. In the latter case, the connection is closed.

After the handshake phase has been completed, the client can get a reference to the remote MBean server, transmit MBean server requests, and register listeners for receiving notification events.

The server will transmit responses to the client MBean server requests and will forward notification events to the interested clients. Figure 6-5 depicts the initial handshake and profile message exchanges.

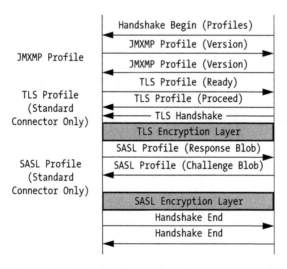

Figure 6-5. Handshake and profile message exchanges

The only messages that are mandatory are HandshakeBeginMessage and HandshakeEndMessage. The profile message exchanges depend on the configuration of the server and the client by means of the jmx.remote.profiles property in the environment map passed in at the creation of the JMXConnector and JMXConnectorServer.

At any time during the handshake phase, if either the client or server encounters an error, the client or server must transmit a HandshakeErrorMessage defining why the operation failed. The end of the connection that encountered the problem will transmit the error message to the other end of the connection and immediately close the connection. The end of the connection that receives the message will also close the connection immediately on reception of the handshake error message. Figure 6-6 depicts how an error is indicated by either a client or a server to the other peer during the initial handshake message exchanges.

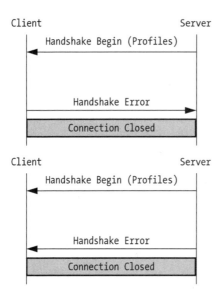

Figure 6-6. Handshake error message exchanges

Bindings to Lookup Services

The distributed JMX specification does not provide any specific API that would make it possible for a client to find the address of a connector server attached to a JMX agent it knows about, or to discover which JMX agents are running, or the addresses of the connector servers that make it possible to connect to them. Rather, the distributed JMX specification details how to advertise and find JMX agents using existing discovery and lookup infrastructures.

This specification discusses three such infrastructures:

1. The Service Location Protocol, as defined by RFC 2608 and RFC 2609

2. The Jini Network Technology

3. The Java Naming and Directory Interface with an LDAP back end

The following describes how a JMX agent may register its connector servers with these infrastructures, and how a JMX client may query these infrastructures in order to find and connect to the advertised servers.

Lookup Attributes

All three infrastructures (SLP, Jini, and JNDI) considered in the distributed JMX specification encompass the notion of *lookup attributes*. These attributes are properties that qualify the registered services. They are passed to the infrastructure when the service is registered and can be used as filters when performing a lookup.

A client can then query the lookup service in order to find all the connectors registered by a JMX agent that match one or more attributes. A client that obtains several services as a result of a lookup query can also further inquire about the lookup attributes registered for those services in order to determine which of these returned matching services it wants to use.

In order for a JMX client to be able to format a query to the lookup service independently of the JMX Remote API implementation used on the JMX agent side, and to understand the meaning of the retrieved attributes, the distributed JMX specification identifies a common set of JMX lookup attributes whose semantics will be known by all JMX agents and JMX clients.

When registering a connector server with a lookup service a JMX agent will

1. Build the `JMXServiceURL` describing its connector server or obtain a `JMXConnector` stub from that server.

2. Register that URL or `JMXConnector` stub with the lookup service.

3. Provide any additional lookup attributes that may help a client locate the server.

Summary of Environment Parameters

The string jmx.remote. precedes all environment parameters defined by the distributed JMX specification. Implementations that define further parameters must not use this namespace. It is recommended that they follow the reverse domain name convention used by Java packages—for example, com.sun.jmx.remote.something.

In Table 6-1, each parameter is defined by the following characteristics:

- The name after the initial "jmx.remote." string

- The type that the associated value must have

- Whether the parameter applies to connector clients, to connector servers, or both

- For server parameters, whether the parameter is visible, that is whether it appears in the Map returned by JMXConnectorServerMBean.getAttributes()

Table 6-1. Environment Parameter Definitions

Name jmx.remote. +	Type	Client/Server	Visible	Meaning
context	Object	Both	No	Context transmitted during handshake.
default.class.loader	ClassLoader	Both	No	Default class loader to deserialize objects received from the other end of a connection.
default.class.loader.name	ObjectName	Server	Yes	Name of class loader. MBean that will be used to deserialize objects received from the client.
profiles	String	Both	Yes	List of profiles proposed (server) or required (client) by the connector.
protocol.provider.class.loader	ClassLoader	Client	N/A	See JMXConnectorFactory documentation.
protocol.provider.pkgs	String	Client	N/A	See JMXConnectorFactory documentation.

Table 6-1. Environment Parameter Definitions (continued)

Name jmx.remote. +	Type	Client/Server	Visible	Meaning
rmi.authenticator	RMIAuthenticator	Server	No	Object to authenticate incoming connections to the RMI connector.
rmi.client.socket. factory	RMIClient Socket Factory	Server	No	Client socket factory for connections to the RMI connector.
rmi.credentials	Object	Client	N/A	Client credentials to authenticate to the RMI connector server.
rmi.server.socket. factory	RMIServer Socket Factory	Server	No	Server socket factory for connections to the RMI connector.
rmi.port	String	Server	Yes	Port to use to export the RMI objects created by an RMI connector. See RMIConnectorServer documentation.
sasl.authorization.id	String	Client	N/A	Authorization ID when this is different from the authentication ID.
sasl.callback.handler	CallbackHandler	Both	No	Callback handler for SASL mechanism.
server.address. wildcard	String	Server	Yes	"true" or "false" accordingly, as the connector server should listen on all local network interfaces or just one. See JMXMPConnectorServer documentation.
tls.enabled.cipher. suites	String	Both	Yes	TLS cipher suites to enable.
tls.enabled.protocols	String	Both	Yes	TLS protocols to enable.
tls.need.client. authentication	String	Server	Yes	"true" or "false" accordingly, as the connector server requires client authentication.

Table 6-1. Environment Parameter Definitions (continued)

Name jmx.remote. +	Type	Client/Server	Visible	Meaning
tls.socket.factory	SSLSocketFactory	Both	No	TLS socket factory for this connector.
tls.want.client. authentication	String	Server	Yes	"true" or "false" accordingly, as the connector server requires client authentication if supported by the negotiated cipher suite.

Service Templates

Formal descriptions of SLP bindings and JMX connectors are embodied within service templates. Service templates describing the service:jmx services in conformance to RFC 2609 are as follows.

The following is the service template for the service:jmx service type:

- *Template filename:* jmx.0.0.en

- *Name of submitter:* JSR-160 Expert Group <JSR-160-EG@JCP.ORG>

- *Language of service template:* en

- *Security considerations:*

  Security is defined by each of the concrete service types.
  See these templates for further details.

- *Template text:*

```
template-type=jmx
template-version=0.0
template-description=
      This is an abstract service type. The purpose of the jmx service
      type is to organize in a single category all JMX Connectors that
      makes it possible to remotely access JMX Agents.
      JMX Connectors are defined by the Java Specification Request 160
      (JSR 160). More information on JSR 160 can be obtained from the
      Java Community Process Home page at:
         http://www.jcp.org/en/jsr/detail?id=160
```

```
Template-url-syntax=
     url-path= ; Depends on the concrete service type.
                    ; See these templates


AgentName= string L
#The name of the JMX Agent - see JSR 160 sepcification


ProtocolType= string O L
#The type of the protocol supported by the JMX Connector
#Currently only two protocols are mandatory in the specification;
#"rmi" and "rmi=iiop". A third optional protocol is also being
standardized; "jmxmp".
#However this could be extended in the future to support other types
#of protocols, e.g. "http", "https", "soap", "beep", etc...


AgentHost= string O M L
#The host name or IP address of the host on which
the JMX Agent is running.
#If multiple values are given they must be aliases to the same host.


Property=string O M L
#Additional properties qualifying the agent, in the form of Java-like
#properties, e.g. " .sun.jmx.remote.connect.timeout=200"
```

The following is the service template for the service:jmx:jmxmp service type:

- *Template filename:* jmx:jmxmp.0.0.en

- *Name of submitter:* JSR-160 Expert Group <JSR-160-EG@JCP.ORG>

- *Language of service template:* en

- *Security considerations:*

  Security for the JMXMP connector is defined by the JSR 160 specification and is based on SASL mechanisms.

- *Template text:*

```
template-type=jmx:jmxmp
template-version=0.0
template-description=
     This template describes the JMXMP Connector defined by JSR 160.
     More information on this connector can be obtained from the
```

```
JSR 160 specification available from the JCP Home Page at:
    http://www.jcp.org/en/jsr/detail?id=160
```

```
Template-url-syntax=
    url-path= ; There is no URL path defined for a jmx:jmxmp URL.
```

The following is the service template for the service:jmx:rmi service type:

- *Template filename:* jmx:rmi.0.0.en

- *Name of submitter:* JSR-160 Expert Group <JSR-160-EG@JCP.ORG>

- *Language of service template:* en

- *Security considerations:*

  There is no special security defined for the jmx:rmi connector, besides
  the mechanisms provided by RMI itself (e.g., socket factory). In its default
  configuration, the jmx:rmi connector is not secure. Applications that are
  concerned with security should therefore not advertise their jmx:rmi connectors through this template, unless they have taken the appropriate
  steps to make it secure.

- *Template text:*

```
template-type=jmx:rmi
template-version=0.0
template-description=
    This template describes the RMI Connector defined by JSR 160.
    More information on this connector can be obtained from the
    JSR 160 specification available from the JCP Home Page at:
        http://www.jcp.org/en/jsr/detail?id=160
```

```
template-url-syntax=
    url-path = jndi-path / stub-path / ior-path
    stub-path = "/stub/" *xchar
        ; serialized RMI stub encoded as BASE64 without newlines
    jndi-path = "/jndi/" *xchar
        ; name understood by JNDI API, shows were RMI stub is stored
    ior-path = "/ior/IOR:" *HEXDIG
        ; CORBA IOR
```

```
        ; The following rules are extracted from RFC 2609
safe = "$" / "-" / "_" / "." / "~"
    extra = "!" / "*" / "'" / "(" / ")" / "," / "+"
    uchar = unreserved / escaped
    xchar = unreserved / reserved / escaped
    escaped = 1*('" HEXDIG HEXDIG)
    reserved = ";" / "/" / "?" / ":" / "@" / "&" / "=" / "+"
    unreserved = ALPHA / DIGIT / safe / extra
```

The following is the service template for the service:jmx:rmi-iiop concrete service type:

- *Template filename:* jmx:rmi-iiop.0.0.en

- *Name of submitter:* JSR-160 Expert Group <JSR-160-EG@JCP.ORG>

- *Language of service template:* en

- *Security considerations:*

There is no special security defined for the jmx:rmi-iiop connector, besides the mechanisms provided by RMI over IIOP itself (e.g., socket factory). In its default configuration, the jmx:rmi-iiop connector is not secure. Applications that are concerned with security should therefore not advertise their jmx:rmi-iiop connectors through this template, unless they have taken the appropriate steps to make it secure.

- *Template text:*

```
template-type=jmx:iiop
template-version=0.0
template-description=
    This template describes the RMI Connector defined by JSR 160.
    More information on this connector can be obtained from the
    JSR 160 specification available from the JCP Home Page at:
        http://www.jcp.org/en/jsr/detail?id=160

template-url-syntax=
    url-path = jndi-path / stub-path / ior-path
    stub-path = "/stub/" *xchar
        ; serialized RMI stub encoded as BASE64 without newlines
    jndi-path = "/jndi/" *xchar
        ; name understood by JNDI API, shows were RMI stub is stored
    ior-path = "/ior/IOR:" *HEXDIG
        ; CORBA IOR
```

```
; The following rules are extracted from RFC 2609
safe = "$" / "-" / "_" / "." / "~"
    extra = "!" / "*" / "'" / "(" / ")" / "," / "+"
    uchar = unreserved / escaped
    xchar = unreserved / reserved / escaped
    escaped = 1*('" HEXDIG HEXDIG)
    reserved = ";" / "/" / "?" / ":" / "@" / "&" / "=" / "+"
    unreserved = ALPHA / DIGIT / safe / extra
```

Summary

In this chapter, I introduced the JMX distributed services level and demonstrated how it is used along with other JMX technologies. I showed you how JMX defines the concept of client connectors and server connectors and how they are united by lookup servers using connector server addresses.

Using the distributed services framework of JMX allows client and server components to easily connect with each other to conduct management sessions and to promote distributed service use with existing or proprietary lookup services. The JMX distributed services level facilitates management solutions that are interoperable, flexible, secure, and portable. Management solutions constructed within the technological sphere of the JMX distributed services level can benefit from its communication standards, protocol flexibility and transparency, location transparency, and standard security mechanisms.

The RMI connector is the only connector that must be present in all implementations of the distributed JMX specification. The RMI connector uses the RMI infrastructure to communicate between client and server. JRMP and IIOP are the two transport protocols used by RMI. The RMI connector supports both transport types.

The distributed JMX specification defines a model, based on the standard Java event model, for transmitting notification events remotely. As with the local notification event model, remote notification events can be transmitted by MBean instances and by an MBean server.

A JMX implementation may provide services that allow distribution of this notification event model, thus allowing a management application to listen to MBean events and MBean server events remotely.

The distributed JMX specification defines a generic connector that is designed to be configurable by plugging in modules to define two things: the transport protocol used to transmit requests from a client to a server and to transmit responses and notification events from the server to clients, and the object wrapping for objects sent from a client to a server whose class loader may depend on the target MBean.

The generic connector protocol defines a set of protocol messages that are exchanged between the client connector and the server connector, and the sequence these message exchanges must follow. Implementations of the distributed JMX specification must exchange these messages in the defined sequence so that they can interoperate with other implementations.

The distributed JMX specification does not provide any specific API that would make it possible for a client to find the address of a connector server attached to a JMX agent it knows about, or to discover which JMX agents are running, or the addresses of the connector servers that make it possible to connect to them. Rather, the distributed JMX specification details how to advertise and find JMX agents using existing discovery and lookup infrastructures.

This specification discusses three such infrastructures: the Service Location Protocol, as defined by RFC 2608 and RFC 2609; the Jini Network Technology; and the Java Naming and Directory Interface with an LDAP back end.

All three infrastructures considered in the distributed JMX specification use lookup attributes, which are properties that qualify the registered services. They are passed to the infrastructure when the service is registered, and can be used as filters when performing a lookup.

CHAPTER 7

JMX Connectors

THE JMX STANDARD DEFINES the notion of *connectors*. A connector is attached to a JMX MBean server and makes it accessible to remote Java clients. The client end of a connector exports essentially the same interface as the MBean server. Connectors include a remote component that provides end-to-end communications with the agent over a variety of protocols (for example, HTTP, HTTPS, IIOP). Since all connectors have the same Java technology–based interface, management applications use the connector most suited to their networking environment and even change connectors transparently as needs evolve.

A connector consists of a *connector client* and a *connector server* as follows:

- A connector server is attached to an MBean server and listens for connection requests from clients. A given connector server may establish many concurrent connections with different clients.

- A connector client takes care of finding the server and establishing a connection with it. A connector client will usually be in a different Java Virtual Machine (JVM) from the connector server, and will often be running on a different machine. A given connector client is connected to exactly one connector server. A client application may contain many connector clients connected to different connector servers. Also, more than one connection may exist between a given client and a given server.

Many different implementations of connectors are possible. In particular, there are many possibilities for the protocol used to communicate over a connection between client and server. The JMX Remoting specification defines a standard protocol based on RMI that must be supported by every conformant implementation. It also defines an optional protocol based directly on TCP sockets, called JMXMP. An implementation of the JMX Remoting specification may omit the JMXMP connector.

Establishing a JMX Remote Connection

In Figure 7-1, a connector client connects a connector server with the address service:jmx:jmxmp://host1:9876. A successful connection request returns the client end of the connection to the connector client.

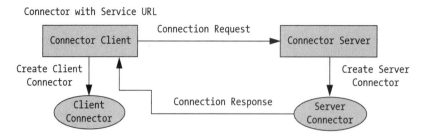

Figure 7-1. Connector client and server communicate to make a connection.

In Figure 7-2, the operation getMBeanInfo("a:b=c") on the MBeanServerConnection in a remote client is translated into a getMBeanInfo request that is sent to the server end of the connection via the connector protocol. The server reacts to this request by performing the corresponding operation on the local MBean server, and sends the results back to the client. If the operation succeeds, the client's getMBeanInfo call returns normally. If the operation produces an exception, the connector arranges for the client's getMBeanInfo call to receive the same exception. If a problem occurs in the communication of the request, the client's getMBeanInfo call will get an IOException.

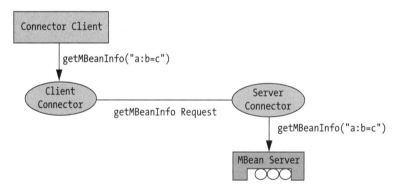

Figure 7-2. An operation on the client results in the same operation on the MBean server.

MBean Server Operations Through a Connection

From the client end of a connection, user code can obtain an object that implements the MBeanServerConnection interface. This interface is very similar to the MBeanServer interface that user code would use to interact with the MBean server if it were running in the same JVM.

MBeanServerConnection is the parent interface of MBeanServer. It contains all of the same methods except for a small number of methods only appropriate for local access to the MBean server. All of the methods in MBeanServerConnection declare IOException in their "throws" clause in addition to the exceptions declared in MBeanServer.

Because MBeanServer extends MBeanServerConnection, client code can be written that works identically whether it is operating on a local MBean server or on a remote one through a connector.

Terminating a Connection

Either end of a connection may terminate the connection at any time. If the client terminates a connection, the server will clean up any state relative to that client, such as listener proxies. If client operations are in progress when the client terminates the connection, then the threads that invoked them will receive an IOException.

If the server terminates a connection, the client will get an IOException for any remote operations that were in progress and any remote operations subsequently attempted.

Connecting to Connector Servers Using Connector Server Addresses

A connector server usually has an address that clients can use to establish connections to it. Some connectors may provide alternative ways to establish connections, such as through connection stubs.

When a connector server has an address, this address is typically described by the JMXServiceURL class. A user-defined connector may choose to use another address format, but it is recommended to use JMXServiceURL where possible.

All JMXServiceURL addresses begin with service:jmx:. The appended jmxmp indicates the connector to use, in this case the JMXMP connector. host1 and 9876 are respectively the host and the port on which the connector server is listening.

The immutable class javax.management.remote.JMXServiceURL extends java.lang.Object and implements the java.io.Serializable interface to represent the address of a JMX connector server.

The address is an Abstract Service URL for SLP, as defined in RFC 2609 and amended by RFC 3111. It must look like this:

```
service:jmx:protocol:address
```

Here, *protocol* is the transport protocol to be used to connect to the connector server. It is a string of one or more ASCII characters, each of which is a letter, a digit, or one of the characters + or -. The first character must be a letter.

The *address* is the address at which the connector server is found. Its supported syntax is

```
//host[:port][url-path]
```

An example of a connector server address is this:

```
service:jmx:jmxmp://host1:9876
```

The *host* is a host name, an IPv4 numeric host address, or an IPv6 numeric address enclosed in square brackets. The *port*, if any, is a decimal port number. 0 means a default or anonymous port, depending on the protocol. The *url-path*, if any, begins with a slash (/) or a semicolon (;) and continues to the end of the address. It can contain attributes using the semicolon syntax specified in RFC 2609. Those attributes are not parsed by the JMXServiceURL class, and incorrect attribute syntax is not detected. Although it is legal according to RFC 2609 to have a *url-path* that begins with a semicolon, not all implementations of SLP allow it, so it is recommended to avoid that syntax.

Case is not significant in the initial service:jmx:protocol string or in the host part of the address. Depending on the protocol, case can be significant in the *url-path*.

Creating a Connector Server

A connector server is represented by an object of a subclass of JMXConnectorServer. To create a connector server, you must instantiate such a subclass. The connector server for the JMXMP connector is represented by the JMXMPConnectorServer class. The GenericConnectorServer class can be used to create nonstandard connectors. To be useful, a connector server must be attached to an MBean server, and it must be active.

A connector server can be attached to an MBean server in one of two ways. Either the MBean server it is attached to is specified when the connector server is constructed, or the connector server is registered as an MBean in the MBean server it is attached to.

A connector server does not have to be registered in an MBean server. It is even possible, though unusual, for a connector server to be registered in an MBean server different from the one it is attached to.

The abstract class JMXConnectorServer extends the javax.management.NotificationBroadcasterSupport class and implements the JMXConnectorServerMBean interface and the MBeanRegistration interface. JMXConnectorServer is the superclass of every connector server. As mentioned earlier, connector server is attached to an MBean server. It listens for client connection requests and creates a connection for each one.

A connector server is associated with an MBean server either by registering it in that MBean server, or by passing the MBean server to its constructor. A connector server is inactive when created. It only starts listening for client connections when the `JMXConnectorServerMBean.start()` method is called. A connector server stops listening for client connections when the `JMXConnectorServerMBean.stop()` method is called or when the connector server is unregistered from its MBean server.

Stopping a connector server does not unregister it from its MBean server. A connector server once stopped cannot be restarted.

Each time a client connection is made or broken, a notification of class `JMXConnectionNotification` is emitted.

The following code extract shows how to create a connector server that listens on an unspecified port on the local host. It is attached to the MBean server mbs but not registered in it.

```
MBeanServer mbs = MBeanServerFactory.createMBeanServer();
JMXServiceURL addr = new JMXServiceURL("jmxmp", null, 0);
JMXConnectorServer cs = new JMXMPConnectorServer(addr, null, mbs);
cs.start();
```

The address that the connector server is actually listening on, including the port number that was allocated, can be obtained by calling `cs.getAddress()`.

The following code extract shows how to do the same thing, but with a connector server that is registered as an MBean in the MBean server it is attached to:

```
MBeanServer mbs = MBeanServerFactory.createMBeanServer();
JMXServiceURL addr = new JMXServiceURL("jmxmp", null, 0);
JMXConnectorServer cs = new JMXMPConnectorServer(addr, null);
ObjectName csName = new ObjectName(":type=cserver,name=mycserver");
mbs.registerMBean(cs, csName);
cs.start();
```

The RMI Connector

The RMI connector is the only connector that must be present in all implementations of the JMX Remoting specification. It uses the RMI infrastructure to communicate between client and server.

The `javax.management.remote.rmi.RMIConnector` class extends `java.lang.Object` and implements the `javax.management.remote.JMXConnector` interface and the `java.io.Serializable` interface.

An instance of the `RMIConnector` class represents a connection to a remote RMI connector. Usually, such connections are made using `javax.management.remote.JMXConnectorFactory`. However, specialized applications can use this class directly, for example, with a `javax.management.remote.rmi.RMIServer` stub obtained without going through JNDI.

Using RMI Transports

RMI defines two standard transports, JRMP and IIOP. JRMP, or Java Remote Method Protocol, is the default transport. This is the transport you get if you use only the java.rmi.* classes from J2SE. IIOP, or Internet Inter-ORB Protocol, is a protocol defined by CORBA. Using RMI over IIOP allows for interoperability with other programming languages. It is covered by the javax.rmi.* and org.omg.* classes from J2SE. RMI over these two transports is referred to as *RMI/JRMP* and *RMI/IIOP.* The RMI connector supports both transports.

Mechanics of the RMI Connector

For every RMI connector server, there is a remotely exported object that implements the remote interface RMIServer. A client that wants to communicate with the connector server needs to obtain a remote reference, or stub, that is connected to this remote object. RMI arranges that any method called on the stub is forwarded to the remote object. So a client that has a stub for the RMIServer object can call a method on it, and the result will be that the same method will be called in the server's object.

Figure 7-3 shows two clients that both have stubs for the same server object. The server object is labeled impl because it is the object that implements the functionality of the RMIServer interface.

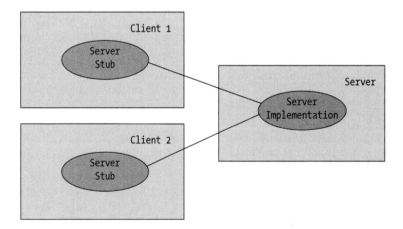

Figure 7-3. Several clients can have stubs connected to the same server object.

In addition to the remote object representing the connector server, one remote object exists for every client connection through the connector to the MBean server. When a client wants to invoke methods on the remote MBean server, it invokes the `newClient` method in its server stub. This causes the `newClient` method in the remote server object to be invoked. This method creates a new remote object that implements the remote interface `RMIMBeanServerConnection`, as shown in Figure 7-4. This interface contains all the remotely accessible methods of the MBean server. The value returned from the client's `newClient` method is a stub that is connected to this new object. When the client calls an MBean server method such as `getAttribute`, this produces a call to the corresponding method in the `RMIMBeanServerConnection` stub, and hence a remote call to the corresponding implementation object in the server.

1. Client calls newClient method on server stub.

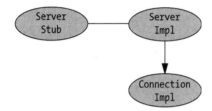

2. Server creates new RMI connection object.

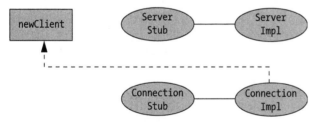

3. Stub for new object is result of newClient method.

Figure 7-4. A new client connection is a new remote object on the server.

Wrapping RMI Objects

User code does not usually interact directly with the `RMIServer` and `RMIMBeanServerConnection` objects. On the server side, the `RMIServer` object is created and exported by an `RMIConnectorServer`. `RMIConnectorServer` is a subclass of `JMXConnectorServer`, and as such is a connector server in the sense of the JMX Remoting specification. `RMIMBeanServerConnection` objects are related internally by the `RMIServer` implementation, but user code in the server never sees them.

On the client side, an RMIServer stub may be explicitly obtained from somewhere. More usually, it is obtained as part of the process of looking up a URL for the RMI connector, but is wrapped in an RMIConnector object. User code usually only deals with this RMIConnector object. RMIConnector implements the JMXConnector interface, and it is through this interface that it is usually accessed.

In normal use, user code never invokes any methods from RMIServer, and never sees any objects of type RMIMBeanServerConnection. These objects are hidden by the RMIConnector class.

The RMIMBeanServerConnection Interface

The RMIMBeanServerConnection interface is similar to the MBeanServerConnection interface defined by JMX, but has some important differences as follows:

- Parameters that are subject to class loading rules are wrapped inside a MarshalledObject so that they can be unwrapped by the server, after the server has determined the appropriate class loader to use.

- The addNotificationListener and removeNotificationListener methods use listener IDs instead of listeners.

- Additional methods are available to get the connection ID and to close the connection.

- An additional method obtains outstanding notifications.

Registering for and Retrieving Remote Notifications

When a user of the JMXConnector interface for an RMI connector client adds a listener, the listener proxy queues notifications at the server end of the connection. When the client calls the remote fetchNotifications method, any queued up notifications are returned to it. If there are no queued notifications when fetchNotifications is called, it blocks until at least one arrives.

The connector client continually repeats these two actions:

1. Call fetchNotifications.

2. Dispatch the received notifications to the appropriate listeners.

During an idle period when there are no notifications, this loop is blocked in the fetchNotifications call. This means that, essentially, there is always at least one remote method call in progress on an `RMIMBeanServerConnection` object at any given time. Consequently

- At least one thread exists per connection on the client end and one on the server end.

- At least one network connection is open between client and server. (RMI is able to close idle connections, but the connection is never idle.)

- RMI's distributed garbage collection will not remove the server object even if the client dies, because the `fetchNotifications` method will still be in progress on it.

To avoid the last problem, an implementation may pass a timeout to the `fetchNotifications` method in its loop. The specification does not define any standard way to control the length of such a timeout.

An alternative approach would have been for the server to call a method in a remote object exported by the client to deliver notifications. This approach was not adopted because it is often not possible to open connections in the reverse direction, because of firewalls for example.

Connecting to an RMI Connector Server

Broadly, you have three ways to connect to an RMI connector server:

1. Supply a `JMXServiceURL` to the `JMXConnectorFactory` that specifies the RMI or RMI-IIOP protocol. This is the most usual way to connect. The `JMXServiceURL` indicates a directory entry in which an `RMIServer` stub can be found, as described in the API specification of the `javax.management.remote.rmi` package. The details of looking up this directory entry and creating a `JMXConnector` from it are hidden from the caller.

2. Obtain a `JMXConnector` stub from somewhere, for example, a directory such as LDAP, the Jini Lookup Service, or the returned value of an RMI method call. This stub is an object generated by `RMIConnectorServer.getStub` of type `JMXConnector`. It is not an RMI stub and should not be confused with the RMI stubs of type `RMIServer` or `RMIMBeanServerConnection`. However, it references an `RMIServer` stub that it uses when its connect method is called.

3. Obtain an `RMIServer` stub from somewhere and use it as a parameter to the constructor of `RMIConnector`.

The Generic Connector

The JMX Remoting API includes a generic connector as an optional part of the API. This connector is designed to be configurable by plugging in modules to define the following:

- The transport protocol used to send requests from the client to the server and to send responses and notifications from the server to the client.

- The object wrapping for objects sent from the client to the server whose class loader may depend on the target MBean.

The JMXMP connector is a configuration of the generic connector where the transport protocol is based on TCP and the object wrapping is native Java serialization (as defined by `java.io.ObjectOutputStream`, etc.). Security is based on Java Secure Socket Extensions (JSSE), the Java Authentication and Authorization Service (JAAS), and the Simple Authentication and Security Layer (SASL).

The generic connector and its JMXMP configuration are optional, which means that an implementation may choose not to include them.

The abstract class `javax.management.generic.GenericConnector` extends `java.lang.Object` and implements the `javax.management.remote.JMXConnector` interface. An instance of this class represents a client connection to a remote JMX server. This class uses a `MessageConnection` object to specify the transport for communicating with the server.

User code does not usually instantiate subclasses of this abstract class. Instead, when this class is subclassed, a `JMXConnectorProvider` should be added to the `JMXConnectorFactory` so that users can instantiate the subclass implicitly through the `JMXServiceURL` provided when connecting.

The Pluggable Transport Protocol

Each configuration of the generic connector includes a transport protocol that is an implementation of the interface `MessageConnection`. Each end of a connection has an instance of this interface. The interface defines three main methods as follows:

- The `writeMessage` method writes a Java object to the other end of the connection. The Java object is of the type `Message` defined by the connector. It may reference other Java objects of arbitrary Java types. For the JMXMP connector, the possible types of messages are contained in the `javax.management.remote.message` package.

- The `readMessage` method reads a Java object from the other end of the connection. The Java object is of type `Message` and again may refer to objects of arbitrary other types.

- The `close` method closes the connection.

The connection is a full-duplex connection between the client and the server, as shown in Figure 7-5. A stream of requests is sent from client to server, and a stream of responses and notifications is sent from server to client.

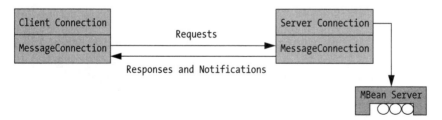

Figure 7-5. MessageConnection defines a full-duplex transport between client and server.

When client code issues an MBeanServerConnection request such as getMBeanInfo, the request is wrapped inside an MBeanServerRequestMessage object and written to the server using MessageConnection.writeMessage. The client code then waits for the corresponding response. Meanwhile, another thread in the client can write another request. When a response arrives, its message ID is used to match it to the request it belongs to, and the thread that issued that request is woken up with the response.

Customizing Serialization Using Pluggable Object Wrapping

The arguments to an MBean method called through MBeanServer.invoke, and the attribute values supplied to setAttribute or setAttributes, may be of Java classes that are known to the target MBean but not to the connector server. If these objects were treated like any other, the connector server would get a ClassNotFoundException when it tries to deserialize a request containing them.

To avoid this problem, deserialization at the server end of a connection proceeds in two stages. First, the objects that are necessarily of classes known to the connector server are deserialized. This is enough to determine what kind of request has been received, which MBean it is destined for (if any), and therefore what class loader is appropriate for use. Then the remaining objects (arguments to invoke or attribute values for setAttribute(s)) can be deserialized using this class loader.

The ObjectWrapping interface allows customization of the way object wrapping is done. By default, it constructs a byte array containing the output of ObjectOutputStream.writeObject on the object or objects to be wrapped. But this would be inappropriate if, for example, the MessageConnection is using XML. So in such a case, an ObjectWrapping object could be plugged into the connector that wraps the objects in XML. This XML can then be included in the larger XML text constructed by the MessageConnection.

Properties Controlling Client and Server

When creating a JMXConnector or a JMXConnectorServer, an environment map can be supplied. One of the functions of this environment is to provide configuration parameters for the underlying profiles. The following sections describe these parameters.

Controlling Connection Aspects Using Global Properties

These properties control global aspects of the connection, which means they are valid regardless of the profiles selected.

- jmx.remote.profiles: A string that is a space-separated list of profile names to be supported by the client and/or the server. Examples of profile names are JMXMP, TLS, SASL/EXTERNAL, SASL/OTP. If this property is unspecified, no profiles will be in used.

- jmx.remote.context: An arbitrary object to be conveyed by the handshake messages from one peer to the other. The object should be serializable and of a class that is known to the other peer. If this property is unspecified, a null context will be conveyed.

The JMXMP connector currently makes no use of this object and does not expose it to user code on the client or server.

TLS Properties

These properties control the TLS profile as follows:

- jmx.remote.tls.socket.factory: An object of type javax.net.ssl.SSLSocketFactory that is an already initialized TLS socket factory. The SSLSocketFactory can be created and initialized through the SSLContext factory. If the value of this property is not specified, the TLS socket factory defaults to SSLSocketFactory.getDefault().

- jmx.remote.tls.enabled.protocols: A string that is a space-separated list of TLS protocols to enable. If the value of this property is not specified, the TLS enabled protocols default to SSLSocket.getEnabledProtocols().

- `jmx.remote.tls.enabled.cipher.suites`: A string that is a space-separated list of TLS cipher suites to enable. If the value of this property is not specified, the TLS-enabled cipher suites default to `SSLSocket.getEnabledCipherSuites()`.

- `jmx.remote.tls.need.client.authentication`: A string that is `true` or `false` according to whether the connector server requires client authentication. If true, a client that does not authenticate during the handshake sequence will be refused.

- `jmx.remote.tls.want.client.authentication`: A string that is `true` or `false` according to whether the connector server requires client authentication if appropriate to the cipher suite negotiated. If true, then if a client negotiates a cipher suite supporting authentication but that client does not authenticate itself, the connection will be refused.

SASL Properties

These properties control the SASL profile as follows:

- `jmx.remote.sasl.authorization.id`: A string that is the connector client's identity for authorization when it is different from the authentication identity. If this property is unspecified, the provider derives an authorization identity from the authentication identity.

- `jmx.remote.sasl.callback.handler`: An object of type `javax.security.auth.callback.CallbackHandler` that is the callback handler to be invoked by the SASL mechanism to retrieve user information. If this property is unspecified, no callback handler will be used.

Defining a New Transport

The standard protocols defined by the JMX Remoting specification may not correspond to all possible environments. Examples of other protocols that could be of interest are

- A protocol that runs over a serial line to manage a JMX agent in a device that is not networked.

- A protocol that uses HTTP/S because it is a familiar protocol that system administrators may be more willing to let through firewalls than RMI or JMXMP.

- A protocol that formats messages in XML (perhaps in an XML-based RPC protocol such as SOAP) to build on an existing XML-based infrastructure. Such a transport could potentially be used by non-Java clients.

There are two ways to implement a user-defined protocol. One is to define a transport for the generic connector using the MessageConnection and MessageConnectionServer classes. The other is to define a new provider for the JMXConnectorFactory.

Defining a transport for the generic connector has the advantage that many of the trickier implementation details, in particular those concerning listeners, are already handled. The transport has to take care of establishing the connection and serializing and deserializing the various Message classes. Potentially, the transport may include other exchanges, for example, to set up a secure connection, that are not the result of a MessageConnection.writeMessage and are never seen by a MessageConnection.readMessage. This is the case for the TLS and SASL exchanges in the JMXMP connector, for example.

Defining a provider for the JMXConnectorFactory is explained in the API documentation for that class. A provider may be based on the generic connector, or it may implement a protocol completely from scratch.

Summary of Environment Parameters

The string jmx.remote. precedes all environment parameters defined by the JMX standard. Implementations that define further parameters must not use this namespace. It is recommended that they follow the reverse domain name convention used by Java packages, for example, com.sun.jmx.remote.something.

In Table 7-1, each parameter is defined by the following characteristics:

- The name after the initial jmx.remote. string

- The type that the associated value must have

- Whether the parameter applies to connector clients, to connector servers, or both

- For server parameters, whether the parameter is visible, that is, whether it appears in the Map returned by JMXConnectorServerMBean.getAttributes()

Table 7-1. Environment Parameter Definitions

Name jmx.remote.+	Type	Client/Server	Visible	Meaning
authenticator	JMXAuthenticator	Server	No	Object to authenticate incoming connections to the connector.
context	Object	Both	No	Context transmitted during handshake.
credentials	Object	Client	N/A	Client credentials to authenticate to the RMI connector server.
default.class.loader	ClassLoader	Both	No	Default class loader to deserialize objects received from the other end of a connection.
default.class.loader.name	ObjectName	Server	Yes	Name of class loader MBean that will be used to deserialize objects received from the client.
jndi.rebind	String	Server	Yes	"true" or "false" according to whether an RMI stub object can overwrite an existing object at the JNDI address specified in a JMXServiceURL.
message.connection	Message Connection	Client	N/A	Object describing the transport used by the generic connector.
message.connection.server	Message Connection Server	Server	No	Object describing the transport used by the generic connector serve.r
object.wrapping	ObjectWrapping	Both	No	Object describing how parameters with nondefault serialization are handled.
profiles	String	Both	Yes	List of profiles proposed (server) or required (client) by the connector.

Table 7-1. Environment Parameter Definitions (continued)

Name jmx.remote.+	Type	Client/Server	Visible	Meaning
protocol.provider. class.loader	ClassLoader	Client	N/A	Name of the attribute that specifies the class loader for loading protocol providers.
protocol.provider.pkgs	String	Client	N/A	Name of the attribute that specifies the provider packages that are consulted when looking for the handler for a protocol.
rmi.client.socket. factory	RMIClientSocket Factory	Server	No	Client socket factory for connections to the RMI connector.
rmi.server.socket. factory	RMIServerSocket Factory	Server	No	Server socket factory for connections to the RMI connector.
sasl.authorization.id	String	Client	N/A	Authorization ID when this is different from the authentication ID.
sasl.callback.handler	CallbackHandler	Both	No	Callback handler for SASL mechanism.
server.address. wildcard	String	Server	Yes	"true" or "false" according to whether connector server should listen on all local network interfaces or just one.
tls.enabled.cipher. suites	String	Both	Yes	TLS cipher suites to enable.
tls.enabled.protocols	String	Both	Yes	TLS protocols to enable.
tls.need.client. authentication	String	Server	Yes	"true" or "false" according to whether connector server requires client authentication.

Table 7-1. Environment Parameter Definitions (continued)

Name jmx.remote.+	Type	Client/Server	Visible	Meaning
tls.socket.factory	SSLSocketFactory	Both	No	TLS socket factory for this connector.
tls.want.client. authentication	String	Server	Yes	"true" or "false" according to whether connector server requires client authentication if supported by the negotiated cipher suite.

Describing JMX Services Using Service Templates

The JMX Remoting specification defines service templates that describe the service:jmx services in conformance to RFC 2609 are a formal description of the bindings between the Service Location Protocol and JMX remote connectors. Please refer to the template definitions in Chapter 6 for further details.

Summary

The JMX standard defines the notion of *connectors,* which attach to a JMX MBean server and make it accessible to remote Java clients. The client end of a connector exports essentially the same interface as the MBean server. Connectors include a remote component that provides end-to-end communications with the agent over a variety of protocols (for example, HTTP, HTTPS, IIOP). Since all connectors have the same Java technology–based interface, management applications use the connector most suited to their networking environment and even change connectors transparently as needs evolve.

A given connector client is connected to exactly one connector server. A client application may contain many connector clients connected to different connector servers. There may be more than one connection between a given client and a given server.

From the client end of a connection, user code can obtain an object that implements the MBeanServerConnection interface. This interface is very similar to the MBeanServer interface that user code would use to interact with the MBean server if it were running in the same JVM.

Either end of a connection may terminate the connection at any time. If the client terminates a connection, the server will clean up any state relative to that client, such as listener proxies. If client operations are in progress when the client terminates the connection, then the threads that invoked them will receive an IOException.

A connector server usually has an address, which clients can use to establish connections to it. Some connectors may provide alternative ways to establish connections, such as through connection stubs.

When a connector server has an address, this address is typically described by the JMXServiceURL class. A user-defined connector may choose to use another address format, but it is recommended to use JMXServiceURL where possible.

A connector server is represented by an object of a subclass of JMXConnectorServer. To create a connector server, you must instantiate such a subclass. The connector server for the JMXMP connector is represented by the JMXMPConnectorServer class. The GenericConnectorServer class can be used to create nonstandard connectors. To be useful, a connector server must be attached to an MBean server, and it must be active.

The RMI connector is the only connector that must be present in all implementations of the JMX Remoting specification. It uses the RMI infrastructure to communicate between client and server.

When a user of the JMXConnector interface for an RMI connector client adds a listener, the listener proxy queues notifications at the server end of the connection. When the client calls the remote fetchNotifications method, any queued up notifications are returned to it. If there are no queued notifications when fetchNotifications is called, it blocks until at least one arrives.

The JMX Remoting API includes a generic connector as an optional part of the API. This connector is designed to be configurable by plugging in modules to define the transport protocol used to send requests from the client to the server and to send responses and notifications from the server to the clients. It is also designed to allow modules to be plugged in to define the object wrapping for objects sent from the client to the server whose class loader may depend on the target MBean.

Each configuration of the generic connector includes a transport protocol, which is an implementation of the interface MessageConnection. Each end of a connection has an instance of this interface.

When creating a JMXConnector or a JMXConnectorServer, an environment map can be supplied. One of the functions of this environment is to provide configuration parameters for the underlying profiles.

The standard protocols defined by the JMX Remoting specification may not correspond to all possible environments. There are two ways to implement a user-defined protocol. One is to define a transport for the generic connector using the MessageConnection and MessageConnectionServer classes. The other is to define a new provider for the JMXConnectorFactory.

CHAPTER 8

Remote Lookup

IN THIS CHAPTER, you will learn how a JMX agent may register its connector servers with its infrastructures, and how a JMX client may query these infrastructures in order to find and connect to the advertised servers.

The JMX Remoting specification describes how you can advertise and find JMX agents by using existing discovery and lookup infrastructures. The specification does not define any discovery and lookup APIs specific to the JMX Remoting technology.

Finding a Server

To use one of the JMX Remoting lookup services, you must implement JMX Remoting agents and JMX Remoting clients. A single JVM can contain many JMX Remoting agents and/or JMX Remoting clients.

A JMX Remoting agent is a logical server application composed of the following features:

- One MBean server

- One or more JMX Remoting connector servers that allow remote clients to access the MBeans contained in the MBean server

A JMX Remoting client is a logical client application that opens a client connection with a JMX Remoting agent.

A JMX Remoting agent can register its JMX connector servers with existing lookup and discovery infrastructures, namely the ones in the following list, so that a JMX client can create or obtain a JMXConnector object to connect to the advertised servers.

- *Service Location Protocol (SLP):* A JMX client can retrieve a JMX service URL from SLP, and use it to connect to the corresponding server.

- *Jini Network Technology:* A JMX client can retrieve a JMX connector stub from the Jini Lookup Service (LUS) and connect to the corresponding server.

- *Lightweight Directory Access Protocol (LDAP):* A JMX client can retrieve a JMX service URL from an LDAP directory using the Java Naming and Directory Interface (JNDI) architecture, and use it to connect to a corresponding JMX connector server. See `ftp://ftp.rfc-editor.org/in-notes/rfc3494.txt` for more information about LDAP.

Publishing a Server

A JMX agent can publish its JMX connector servers with existing lookup and discovery infrastructures, as in the following list, so that a JMX client that does not know about such a server can find it and connect to it.

- *Service Location Protocol:* A JMX agent should register the JMX service URL of a JMX connector server with SLP, so that a JMX client may retrieve it and use it to connect to the server.

- *Jini Network Technology:* A JMX agent should register the JMX connector stub of a JMX connector server with the Jini Lookup Service, so that a JMX client can retrieve this stub and connect to the server.

- *Java Naming and Directory Interface:* A JMX agent should register the JMX service URL of a JMX connector server in an LDAP directory, so that a JMX client can retrieve this URL and use it to connect to the server.

How to Connect to an RMI Connector Server

Broadly, you have three ways to connect to an RMI connector server:

1. Supply a `JMXServiceURL` to the `JMXConnectorFactory` that specifies the RMI or RMI-IIOP protocol. This is the usual way to connect. `JMXServiceURL` indicates a directory entry in which an `RMIServer` stub can be found, as described in the API specification of the `javax.management.remote.rmi` package. The details of looking up this directory entry and creating a `JMXConnector` from it are hidden from the caller.

2. Obtain a `JMXConnector` stub from somewhere, for example, a directory such as LDAP, the Jini Lookup Service, or as the returned value of an RMI method call. This stub is an object generated by `RMIConnectorServer.getStub` of type `JMXConnector`. It is not an RMI stub and should not be confused with the RMI stubs of type `RMIServer` or `RMIMBeanServerConnection`. However, it references an `RMIServer` stub that it uses when its connect method is called.

3. Obtain an `RMIServer` stub from somewhere and use it as a parameter to the constructor of `RMIConnector`.

Bindings to Lookup Services

The JMX Remoting specification specifies JMX connectors that make it possible for a JMX client to access and manage MBeans exposed through a JMX agent (an MBean server) running in a remote JVM. It also defines a `JMXServiceURL` class, which represents the address of a JMX connector server, and makes it possible for a JMX client to obtain a JMX connector connected to that server. However, the JMX Remoting specification does not provide any specific API that would make it possible for a client to find the address of a connector server attached to a JMX agent it knows about, or to discover which JMX agents are running, or the addresses of the connector servers that make it possible to connect to them. Rather than reinventing the wheel, the JMX Remoting specification instead details how to advertise and find JMX agents using existing discovery and lookup infrastructures.

The JMX Remoting specification discusses three such infrastructures as follows:

- The Service Location Protocol, as defined by RFC 2608 and RFC 2609

- The Jini Network Technology

- The Java Naming and Directory Interface with an LDAP back end

General Principles

Although the APIs with which to register and query a server access point with a lookup service vary from one infrastructure to another, the general principles remain the same:

1. The JMX agent creates one or more JMX connector servers.

2. Then for each connector that it wants to expose, it registers the `JMXServiceURL` (SLP, JNDI/LDAP) or the `JMXConnector` stub (Jini) with the lookup service, possibly giving additional attributes that qualify the JMX agent and/or connector.

3. The JMX client queries the lookup service, and retrieves one or more `JMXServiceURL` addresses (or `JMXConnector` stubs) that match the query.

4. It then either uses the `JMXConnectorFactory` in order to obtain a `JMXConnector` connected with the server identified by a retrieved `JMXServiceURL` (SLP, JNDI/LDAP), or it directly connects to the server using the provided `JMXConnector` stub (Jini).

JMXServiceURL vs. JMXConnector Stubs

When using SLP, it is natural to register and retrieve a service URL from the lookup service. However, this procedure is not as natural when using technologies like Jini. In Jini, the `Service` object you register and get from the lookup service is usually a stub that directly implements the interface of the underlying service, and not some object that gives you back some information on how to connect to the service. Therefore the JMX Remoting specification specifies different ways of advertising a JMX connector server, depending on the underlying lookup service that is used as follows:

- *SLP:* Register the URL string representation of the JMX service URL (`JMXServiceURL.toString()`). This is natural as SLP is a URL-based protocol.

- *Jini:* Register a `JMXConnector` stub. The `JMXConnector` interface is the direct interface of the JMX connector service.

- *JNDI/LDAP:* Register the URL string representation of the JMX service URL (`JMXServiceURL.toString()`). The JNDI can be configured on the client side (via `StateFactories` and `ObjectFactories`) to automatically create and return a new `JMXConnector` from the `DirContext` containing the JMX service URL, or simply return the `DirContext` from which that JMX service URL can be extracted.

Lookup Attributes

All three infrastructures considered in the JMX Remoting specification incorporate lookup attributes. These attributes are properties that qualify the registered services. They are passed to the infrastructure when the service is registered, and can be used as filters when performing a lookup.

A client can then query the lookup service in order to find all the connectors registered by a JMX agent matching one or more attributes. A client that obtains several services as a result of a lookup query can also further inquire about the lookup attributes registered for those services in order to determine which of these returned matching services it wants to use.

In order for a JMX client to be able to format a query to the lookup service independently of the JMX Remote API implementation used on the JMX agent side, and to understand the meaning of the retrieved attributes, the JMX Remoting specification specifies a common set of JMX lookup attributes whose semantics will be known by all JMX agents and JMX clients. In the remainder of this chapter, I will use the term *lookup attributes* for these.

Table 8-1 defines the set of common lookup attributes that can be provided at connector registration and that can be used to filter the lookup. Most of these

attributes are optional. A JMX agent may choose whether it wants to specify
them when it registers a JMXServiceURL with the lookup service.

> **NOTE**   *The name format of the lookup attributes is different depending on the*
> *back-end lookup service.*

Table 8-1. Common Lookup Attributes

Name/ID	Type	Multivalued	Optional/Mandatory	Description
AgentName	String	No	Mandatory	AgentName is a simple name used to identify the agent in a common way. It can also be viewed as a logical name for the service implemented by the agent. AgentName makes it possible to search for all connectors registered by a given agent. The JMX Remoting specification does not define the format of an agent name. However, the characters colon (:) and slash (/) are reserved for a future version.
ProtocolType	String	No	Optional	ProtocolType is the protocol type of the registered connector, as returned by JMXServiceURL.getProtocol(). ProtocolType makes it possible to retrieve only the connectors using a given protocol that the client supports.
AgentHost	String	Yes	Optional	AgentHost is the name or IP address of the host on which the agent is running. This attribute is multivalued in order to allow aliasing—namely, whether one single host is known under several names. This attribute is multivalued only if the underlying lookup protocol supports multivalued attributes.

Table 8-1. Common Lookup Attributes (continued

Name/ID	Type	Multivalued	Optional/Mandatory	Description
Property	String	Yes	Optional	Property is a string containing a Java-like property, in the form "`<propertyname>=<value>`"—for example, "`com.sun.jmx.remote.tcp.connect.timeout=200`". This attribute is multivalued so that it can be used to map several properties. It might be used by agents as a means to provide additional information to client applications. For instance, this attribute could be used to hold some of the attributes that were passed to a connector server within the environment map at construction time. However, an agent must not rely on the fact that a client will read these attributes, and a client must not rely on the fact that an agent will provide them. All the information that any client will need to connect to a specific server must be contained in the server's JMX service URL, or in its JMX API connector stub.

When registering a connector server with a lookup service, a JMX agent will

1. Build the `JMXServiceURL` describing its connector server (SLP, JNDI/LDAP), or obtain a `JMXConnector` stub from that server (Jini).

2. Register that URL (SLP, JNDI/LDAP) or `JMXConnector` stub (Jini) with the lookup service.

3. Provide any additional lookup attributes that may help a JMX client to locate the server.

Using the Service Location Protocol

The Service Location Protocol is an IETF standards track protocol (RFC 2608, RFC 2609) that provides a framework to allow networking applications to discover the existence, location, and configuration of networked services in enterprise networks. The SLP white paper provides a concise description of SLP and its positioning with respect to other technologies, like DNSSRV and LDAP.

The following steps summarize the procedure defined in the JMX Remoting specification for using the SLP Lookup Service to advertise and find JMX Remoting agents:

1. The agent creates one or more JMX Remoting connector servers.

2. For each connector to expose, the agent registers the address with the SLP Lookup Service, possibly giving additional attributes that qualify the agent and/or the connector, and can be used as filters.

3. The client queries the SLP Lookup Service, and retrieves one or more addresses that match the query.

4. Finally, the client obtains a connector that is connected with the server identified by a retrieved address.

The JMX Remoting specification defines URL schemes that are compliant with the SLP protocol. The specification also defines mandatory and optional SLP lookup attributes that are provided at registration time.

SLP Service URL

The JMXServiceURL defined by the JMX Remoting specification is directly compliant with RFC 2609. Therefore, there is a direct mapping exists between JMX service URLs and SLP service URLs, since their String representation is identical.

SLP Lookup Attributes

SLP supports multivalued attribute registrations; these attributes are provided at registration time, when registering the service URL of the connector server. The filtering method used for lookup is an LDAPv3 filter string. The attributes that must or may be provided by a JMX agent when registering a connector server URL are those defined in section 6.2.2, "Lookup Attributes," of the JMX Remoting specification.

Discovering the SLP Service

With SLP, discovering the lookup service is transparent to the user; the running SLP daemon is responsible for finding the service agent or directory agent (depending on the configuration of the daemon). The following line demonstrates how to locate the lookup service using the SLP provider for Java found at http://www.openslp.org/:

```
final Locator slpLocator =
    com.solers.slp.ServiceLocationManager.getLocator(Locale.US);
```

Registering a JMX Service URL with SLP

The following code will register a JMX connector URL with the SLP Lookup Service.

The jmxUrl parameter is a JMXConnectorServer URL obtained from JMXConnectorServer.getAddress(). The name parameter is the AgentName with which the URL will be registered in the SLP Lookup Service. The Advertiser class is used to perform the SLP registrations.

```
import com.solers.slp.ServiceLocationException;
import com.solers.slp.ServiceURL;
import com.solers.slp.ServiceLocationManager;
import com.solers.slp.Advertiser;
import com.solers.slp.ServiceLocationAttribute;
import javax.management.remote.JMXServiceURL;
import java.util.Vector;



public class SLPServer
{
    // The Service URL will remain registered for 300 secs.
    //
    public final static int JMX_DEFAULT_LEASE = 300;

    // Default scope.
    //
    public final static String JMX_SCOPE = "DEFAULT";

  public static void register(JMXServiceURL jmxUrl, String name)
      throws ServiceLocationException
```

```
{
    // Create the SLP service URL.
    //
    // Note: It is recommended that the JMX agents make use of the
    // leasing feature of SLP, and periodically renew their lease.
    //
    ServiceURL serviceURL =
            new ServiceURL(jmxUrl.toString(),
                                        JMX_DEFAULT_LEASE);

    // Prepare Lookup Attributes.
    //
    Vector attributes = new Vector();
    Vector attrValues = new Vector();

    // Specify default SLP scope.
    //
    attrValues.add(JMX_SCOPE);
    ServiceLocationAttribute attr1 =
        new ServiceLocationAttribute("SCOPE", attrValues);
    attributes.add(attr1);

    // Specify AgentName attribute (mandatory).
    //
    attrValues.removeAllElements();
    attrValues.add(name);
    ServiceLocationAttribute attr2 =
        new ServiceLocationAttribute("AgentName", attrValues);
    attributes.add(attr2);

    // Get SLP Advertiser.
    //
    final Advertiser slpAdvertiser =
        ServiceLocationManager.getAdvertiser(Locale.US);

    // Register the service: URL.
    //
    slpAdvertiser.register(serviceURL, attributes);
    System.out.println("\nRegistered URL: " + jmxUrl);
    }
}
```

Looking Up a JMX Service URL with SLP

The Locator class is used to perform the SLP lookup.

```java
import com.solers.slp.Locator;
import com.solers.slp.ServiceLocationException;
import com.solers.slp.ServiceLocationManager;
import com.solers.slp.ServiceURL;
import com.solers.slp.ServiceType;
import com.solers.slp.ServiceLocationEnumeration;
import com.solers.slp.ServiceLocationAttribute;

import javax.management.remote.JMXConnectorFactory;
import javax.management.remote.JMXConnector;
import javax.management.remote.JMXServiceURL;
import javax.management.MBeanAttributeInfo;
import javax.management.ObjectName;
import javax.management.MBeanInfo;
import javax.management.MBeanServerConnection;
import java.util.Locale;
import java.util.Vector;
import java.util.ArrayList;
import java.util.List;
import java.util.Iterator;
import java.util.Set;
import java.io.IOException;


public class SLPClient
{
    // Default scope.
    //
    public final static String JMX_SCOPE = "DEFAULT";

    public static List lookup(Locator slpLocator, String name)
        throws IOException, ServiceLocationException
    {
        // Set the query string.
        //
        // Will return only those services for which the AgentName
        // attribute was registered. Since JSR 160 specifies that
        // the AgentName attribute is mandatory, this makes it possible
        // to filter out all the services that do not conform
        // to the spec.
```

```
// If <name> is null, it is replaced by "*", so that all
// services for which the AgentName attribute was specified match,
// regardless of the value of that attribute. Otherwise, only
// those services for which AgentName matches the
// name or pattern specified by <name> will be returned.
//
String query = "(&(AgentName=" + ((name != null)?name:"*") + "))";

// Set the lookup scope.
//
Vector scopes = new Vector();
scopes.add(JMX_SCOPE);

// Lookup the JMX agents....
//
debug("Looking up JMX Agents with filter: " + query);

ServiceLocationEnumeration result =
    slpLocator.findServices(new ServiceType("service:jmx"),
                            scopes, query);

final ArrayList list = new ArrayList();

// Build the JMXConnector list.
//
while (result.hasMoreElements())
{
    final ServiceURL surl = (ServiceURL) result.next();

    if (debug)
    {
        // Retrieve the Lookup Attributes that were registered
        // with this URL.
        //
        debug("Getting attributes...");
        final ServiceLocationEnumeration slpAttributes =
            slpLocator.findAttributes(surl, scopes, new Vector());
        debug("... Got attribute enumeration.");
        while (slpAttributes.hasMoreElements())
        {
            final ServiceLocationAttribute slpAttribute =
                (ServiceLocationAttribute) slpAttributes.nextElement();
            debug("\tAttribute: " + slpAttribute);
        }
    }
}
```

```
        // Create a JMX service URL.
        //
        JMXServiceURL jmxUrl = new JMXServiceURL(surl.toString());

        try
        {
        // Create a JMXConnector using the JMXConnectorFactory.
        //
            JMXConnector client =
                JMXConnectorFactory.newJMXConnector(jmxUrl, null);
            debug("JMX Connector: " + client);

            // Add the connector to the result list.
            //
            if (client != null) list.add(client);
        }
        catch (IOException x)
        {
            System.err.println("Failed to create JMXConnector for " +
                                        jmxUrl);
            System.err.println("Error is: " + x);
            System.err.println("Skipping...");
        }
    }

    return list;
    }
}
```

Using the Jini Network Technology

The Jini Network Technology (Jini) is an open software architecture that enables
developers to create network-centric services that are highly adaptive to change.
Jini offers a standard lookup service. A running Jini Lookup Service can be discovered with a simple API call. A remote service (device, software, application,
etc.) that wants to be registered in Jini provides a serializable Java object. When
looked up by a remote client, a copy of this Java object is returned. Usually, this
object acts as a proxy to the remote service.

In addition, Jini offers various APIs and mechanisms in order to download
code from a remote HTTP server (necessary to get the classes required for
instantiating the proxy objects), and Jini supports security for code download
based on the RMI security manager.

The following steps summarize the procedure defined in the JMX Remote API specification for using the Jini Lookup Service to advertise and find JMX Remote API agents:

1. The agent creates one or more JMX Remote API connector servers.

2. For each connector to expose, the agent registers a JMX Remote API connector stub with the Jini Lookup Service, possibly giving additional attributes that qualify the agent and/or the connector, and can be used as filters.

3. The client queries the Jini Lookup Service, and retrieves one or more connector stubs that match the query.

4. Finally, the client connects directly to the server using the provided connector stub.

The JMX Remoting specification defines bindings with Jini technology–based entries. The specification also defines mandatory and optional entries to specify when registering an agent connector.

JMX Jini Service

Jini is based on service registration. A service is registered through a serializable Java object, which can be a stub, a proxy, or a simple class providing information about the service. Usually, the registered Jini service is a stub that provides a direct link to the underlying service. Thus, although it would be possible to use the JMXServiceURL as the Jini service, the JMX Remoting specification details the use of a JMX connector stub, implementing the JMXConnector interface, as the JMX Jini service. This is consistent with the Jini philosophy, in which objects retrieved from the Jini service are usually proxies implementing the interface of the looked-up service.

The Jini Lookup Service, which is based on RMI, will make use of RMI annotations to automatically download from the server side all the classes needed to deserialize the service object on the client side. This makes it possible for a server to register any private implementation class, and for a client to use that class (through its generic JMXConnector interface) without any presupposed knowledge of the server implementation. However, this requires a certain amount of configuration from the server side. The JMX Remoting specification completely details the JMX connector stubs for the protocols it describes, so that an instance of such a class serialized from the JMX Remote API implementation on the server side can be deserialized in an instance of the same class using the implementation on the client side, without having to download any new classes. Thus, no special configuration is needed on the server side when using standard connectors. Providers and users of nonstandard connectors, however, should perform the required configuration steps if they want to make their nonstandard connectors available to generic JMX clients.

Jini Lookup Attributes

Like SLP, Jini supports the specification of additional lookup attributes, called *entries*. However, the Java class of these attributes must implement the net.jini.core.entry.Entry interface. The JMX Remoting specification does not yet include any JMX-specific entries for Jini lookup—this subject is still under discussion. In particular it is not clear whether those specific entries should be part of the JSR 160 RI or Jini distribution. The Name entry defined by Jini is interpreted as meaning the AgentName, however.

Discovering the Jini Lookup Service

The Jini Lookup Service is represented by the net.jini.core.lookup.ServiceRegistrar class. The following code will get the lookup service using the Jini Lookup Service URL determined by the System property "jini.lookup.url". If no property has been set, the default URL is assumed to be "jini://localhost".

```
import net.jini.core.lookup.ServiceRegistrar;
import net.jini.core.discovery.LookupLocator;
...
    public static ServiceRegistrar getRegistrar()
        throws IOException, ClassNotFoundException, MalformedURLException
    {
        final String jurl =
            System.getProperty("jini.lookup.url", "jini://localhost");
        final LookupLocator lookup = new LookupLocator(jurl);
        final ServiceRegistrar registrar = lookup.getRegistrar();
        return registrar;
    }
```

Registering a JMX Connector with the Jini Lookup Service

A JMXConnector proxy, obtained from JMXConnectorServer.toJMXConnector(Map), is registered with the Jini Lookup Service using an instance of ServiceRegistrar. The following example illustrates this by creating a new ServiceItem instance with the name of the agent and the proxy to be registered. A ServiceRegistration object is returned by the Jini Lookup Service.

```
import net.jini.core.lookup.ServiceRegistration;
import net.jini.core.lookup.ServiceItem;
import net.jini.core.lookup.ServiceRegistrar;
import net.jini.core.entry.Entry;
import javax.management.remote.JMXConnector;

public class ServiceRegistrar
{
    public static ServiceRegistration register(ServiceRegistrar registrar,
                                                JMXConnector proxy,
                                                String name)

        throws IOException
    {
        // Prepare service's attributes entry.
        //
        Entry[] serviceAttrs = new Entry[] {
            new net.jini.lookup.entry.Name(name)
            // Add here the lookup attributes you want to specify.
        };

        System.out.println("Registering proxy:  AgentName=" + name);

        // Create a ServiceItem from the service instance.
        //
        ServiceItem srvcItem = new ServiceItem(null, proxy, serviceAttrs);

        // Register the service with the Lookup Service.
        //
        ServiceRegistration srvcRegistration =
                registrar.register(srvcItem,
                                        Lease.ANY);
        return srvcRegistration;
    }
}
```

Looking Up a JMX Connector from the Jini Lookup Service

JMXConnectors are found by applying a ServiceTemplate to a ServiceRegistrar
lookup. The ServiceTemplate object is composed of the JMXConnector class and the
name by which the JMXConnector should be registered. A ServiceMatches object is
returned as the result. The following code illustrates this process:

```
import net.jini.core.entry.Entry;
import javax.management.remote.JMXConnector;
import net.jini.core.lookup.ServiceMatches;
import net.jini.core.lookup.ServiceTemplate;
...


public class JMXConnectorUtil
{
 public static List lookup(ServiceRegistrar registrar, String name)
     throws IOException
   {
       final ArrayList list = new ArrayList();

       // Returns only JMXConnectors. The filter could be made
       // more strict by supplying e.g. RMIConnector.class
       // (would only return RMIConnectors) or JMXMPConnector.class
       // (would only return JMXMPConnectors) etc.
       //
       final Class[] classes = new Class[]{JMXConnector.class};

       // Will return only those services for which the Name
       // attribute was registered. Since JSR 160 specifies that
       // the Name attribute is mandatory, this makes it possible
       // to filter out all the services that do not conform
       // to the spec.
       // If <name> is null, then all services for which the
       // Name attribute was specified will match, regardless of
       // the value of that attribute. Otherwise, only those services
       // for which Name matches the specified name will be returned.
       //
       final Entry[] serviceAttrs = new Entry[] {
           // Add here the matching attributes.
           new net.jini.lookup.entry.Name(name)
       };

       // Create a ServiceTemplate to do the matching.
       //
       ServiceTemplate template =
           new ServiceTemplate(null, classes, serviceAttrs);

       // Look up all matching services in the Jini Lookup Service.
       //
       ServiceMatches matches =
           registrar.lookup(template, Integer.MAX_VALUE);
```

```
    // Retrieve the matching JMX connectors.
    //
    for (int i = 0; i < matches.totalMatches; i++)
    {
        if (matches.items[i].service != null)
        {
            // Service could be null if it can't be deserialized, because
            // e.g., the class was not found.
            // This will not happen with JSR 160 mandatory connectors
            // however.

            // Get the JMXConnector.
            //
            JMXConnector c = (JMXConnector) (matches.items[i].service);

            // Add the connector to the result list.
            list.add(c);
        }
    }
    return list;
    }
}
```

Using the Java Naming and Directory Interface (LDAP Back End)

The Java Naming and Directory Interface is a standard extension to the Java platform, providing Java technology–enabled applications with a unified interface to multiple naming and directory services in the enterprise. In particular, it provides a means to access X.500 directory services through the LDAP. The JMX Remoting specification defines how an LDAP server can be used to store information about JMX agents, and how JMX clients can look up this information to connect to the JMX agents.

The JMX Remoting specification details how an LDAP server can be used to store and retrieve information about JMX connectors exposed by JMX agents.

The following steps summarize the procedure defined in the JMX Remoting specification for using the JNDI lookup service:

1. The agent creates one or more JMX Remoting connector servers.

2. For each connector to expose, the agent registers the address with the JNDI lookup service, possibly giving additional attributes that qualify the agent and/or the connector, and can be used as filters.

3. The client queries the JNDI lookup service, and retrieves one or more addresses that match the query.

4. Finally, the client obtains a connector that is connected to the server identified by a retrieved address.

The JMX Remoting specification defines an LDAP schema for registering addresses and explains how a client can discover a registered agent. The specification also defines a lease mechanism.

LDAP Schema for Registration of JMX Connectors

Nodes in the LDAP directory tree are typed. A node may have several object classes. JMX connectors should be registered in nodes of class jmxConnector. The jmxConnector class contains two attributes, which are the JMX service URL of the corresponding connector (jmxServiceURL), and the name of the JMX agent exporting this connector (jmxAgentName). The JMX service URL may be absent if the agent is not accepting connections. The jmxConnector class also includes optional attributes, like jmxAgentHost and jmxProtocolType. The JMX agent name makes it possible for a client application to get a connection to a JMX agent it knows by name. Together with jmxAgentHost and jmxProtocolType, it also makes it possible to perform filtered queries, for instance, "Find all the JMXMP connectors of <this> JMX agent," or "Find all connectors of all JMX agents running on <that> node."

The following is the schema definition (as specified in RFC 2252) that should be used to register JMX connectors:

```
-- jmxServiceURL attribute is an IA5 String
( jmxServiceURL-OID NAME 'jmxServiceURL'
          DESC 'String representation of a JMX Service URL'
          SYNTAX 1.3.6.1.4.1.1466.115.121.1.26 SINGLE-VALUE )


-- jmxAgentName attribute is an IA5 String
( jmxAgentName-OID NAME 'jmxAgentName'
          DESC 'Name of the JMX Agent'
          SYNTAX 1.3.6.1.4.1.1466.115.121.1.26 SINGLE-VALUE )


-- jmxProtocolType attribute is an IA5 String
( jmxProtocolType-OID NAME 'jmxProtocolType'
          DESC 'Protocol used by the registered connector'
          SYNTAX 1.3.6.1.4.1.1466.115.121.1.26 SINGLE-VALUE )
```

```
-- jmxAgentHost attribute is an IA5 String
( jmxAgentHost-OID NAME 'jmxAgentHost'
            DESC     'Names or IP Addresses of the host on which the
                             agent is running. When multiple values are
                             given, they should be aliases to the same host.'
            SYNTAX 1.3.6.1.4.1.1466.115.121.1.26 )


-- jmxProperty attribute is an IA5 String
( jmxProperty-OID NAME 'jmxProperty'
            DESC     'Java-like property characterizing the registered object.
                     The form of each value should be: "<property-name>=<value>".
                             For instance: "com.sun.jmx.remote.tcp.timeout=200"'
            SYNTAX 1.3.6.1.4.1.1466.115.121.1.26 )


-- jmxExpirationDate attribute is a Generalized Time
-- see [RFC 2252] - or X.208 for a description of
-- Generalized Time
( jmxExpirationDate-OID NAME 'jmxExpirationDate'
            DESC     'Date at which the JMX Service URL will
                             be considered obsolete and can be removed
                             from the directory tree'
            SYNTAX 1.3.6.1.4.1.1466.115.121.1.24 SINGLE-VALUE )


-- from RFC-2256 --
( 2.5.4.13 NAME 'description'
            EQUALITY caseIgnoreMatch
            SUBSTR caseIgnoreSubstringsMatch
            SYNTAX 1.3.6.1.4.1.1466.115.121.1.15{1024} )
-- jmxConnector class -    represents a JMX Connector.
--                   must contain the JMX Service URL
--                   and the JMX Agent Name

( jmxConnector-OID NAME 'jmxConnector'
            DESC     'A class representing a JMX Connector, and
                             containing a JMX Service URL.
                             The jmxServiceURL is not present if the server
                             is not accepting connections'
            AUXILIARY
            MUST     ( jmxAgentName )
            MAY      ( jmxServiceURL $ jmxAgentHost $ jmxProtocolType $
                         jmxProperty $ jmxExpirationDate $ description ) )
```

The `jmxConnector` class is an AUXILIARY class, which means that its properties can be added to any node in the directory tree—i.e., it does not impose any restriction on the structure of the directory tree.

In order to create a node in the directory tree, you also need a STRUCTURAL class. The JMX Remoting specification does not impose any restriction on the structural classes that may contain JMX connectors.

You may, for instance, reuse the `javaContainer` class from the Java Schema (JNDI—Java Schema) as defined in RFC 2713—i.e., create a node whose object classes would be `javaContainer` (STRUCTURAL) and `jmxConnector` (AUXILIARY). The node containing the `jmxConnector` may also have additional auxiliary classes.

Mapping to Java Objects

The JMX Remoting specification only requires that the JMX service URL is stored in LDAP. JMX agents may additionally store a serialized JMX connector stub—but this is not required by the JMX Remoting specification.

JMX clients should only rely on the JMX service URL. JNDI makes it possible for a client to use `StateFactories` and `ObjectFactories` (JNDI—Java Objects) in order to re-create a `JMXConnector` from the URL when performing a `lookup()`, even if there is no Java object bound to the containing `DirContext`. Alternatively, a client may directly retrieve the `jmxServiceURL` attribute in order to obtain a `JMXConnector` from the `JMXConnectorFactory`. Whether JNDI `lookup()` returns a `JMXConnector` or a `DirContext` depends on the configuration settings on the client side (`InitialContext`), and remains local to that client.

Discovering the LDAP Server

JNDI/LDAP does not provide any standard means for discovering the LDAP server. Assuming the standard port (389) on `localhost` is the entry point is usually not an option, since the LDAP server is usually centralized—i.e., there is not one server per host. JNDI specifies a means to discover the LDAP server(s) through DNS (JNDI—LDAP Servers Discovery), but this is OS dependent, and not always feasible either since the LDAP servers may not always be registered in DNS. The JMX Remoting specification thus does not address the issue of discovering the LDAP server.

Registering a JMXServiceURL with an LDAP Server

The JMX Remoting specification does not impose any structure on the directory tree for registering JMX service URLs. It is assumed that the JMX agent knows where to register its JMX connectors, either from a configuration or from some built-in logic adapted to the environment it is running in. The JMX Remoting specification defines the form of the data that is registered in the directory (the how rather than the where), so that any JMX client can look it up in a generic way.

The following code example registers a JMX connector URL with an LDAP directory. The code expects to find the LDAP DN, with which it will register the JMX connector URL, in the "dn" System property. If that property is not set, then "cn=name" is assumed. If the given DN does not point to an existing node in the directory, then the code will attempt to create it. However, the parent node must already exist in that case. If the DN points to a node that does not have the auxiliary *jmxConnector* object class, then this method will attempt to add this object class to that node.

If the DN points to a node that is already of that class, then the code will simply overwrite its jmxServiceUrl, jmxAgentName, jmxProtocolType, jmxAgentHost, and jmxExpirationDate attributes.

The code assumes a valid DirContext has been located previously.

```
import javax.naming.InitialContext;
import javax.naming.directory.DirContext;
import javax.naming.directory.Attribute;
import javax.naming.directory.BasicAttribute;
import javax.naming.directory.Attributes;
import javax.naming.directory.BasicAttributes;
...


public class LDAPRegistrar
{
    public static void register(DirContext root,
                                            JMXServiceURL jmxUrl,
                                            String name)
        throws NamingException, IOException
    {

        // Get the LDAP DN where to register.
        //
        final String mydn = System.getProperty("dn", "cn=" + name);

        // First check whether <mydn> already exists.
        //
        Object o = null;
        try
        {
            o = root.lookup(mydn);
            // There is already a node at <mydn>.
            //
        }
```

```
catch (NameNotFoundException n)
{
    // <mydn> does not exist! Attempt to create it.
    //

    // Prepare attributes for creating a javaContainer.
    //
    Attributes attrs = new BasicAttributes();

    // Prepare objectClass attribute: you're going to create a
    // javaContainer.
    //
    Attribute objclass = new BasicAttribute("objectClass");
    objclass.add("top");
    objclass.add("javaContainer");
    attrs.put(objclass);
    o = root.createSubcontext(mydn, attrs);
}

// Add the jmxConnector objectClass if needed.
//
final Attributes attrs = root.getAttributes(mydn);
final Attribute oc = attrs.get("objectClass");
if (!oc.contains("jmxConnector"))
{
    // The node does not have the jmxConnector AUXILIARY class.
    // Try to add it.
    //
    final Attributes add = new BasicAttributes();
    add.put("objectClass", "jmxConnector");

    // jmxAgentName is a mandatory attribute for a jmxConnector.
    //
    add.put("jmxAgentName", name);

    // Add the jmxConnector object class and jmxAgentName attribute.
    //
    root.modifyAttributes(mydn, DirContext.ADD_ATTRIBUTE, add);
}

// Now you need to replace jmxConnector attributes.
//
final Attributes newattrs = new BasicAttributes();
newattrs.put("jmxServiceUrl", jmxUrl.toString());
newattrs.put("jmxAgentName", name);
```

```
        newattrs.put("jmxProtocolType", jmxUrl.getProtocol());
        newattrs.put("jmxAgentHost", InetAddress.getLocalHost().getHostName());
        newattrs.put("jmxExpirationDate",
                            getExpirationDate(JMX_DEFAULT_LEASE));
        newattrs.put(new BasicAttribute("jmxProperty"));

        root.modifyAttributes(mydn, DirContext.REPLACE_ATTRIBUTE, newattrs);
    }
}
```

Looking Up a JMX Service URL from the LDAP Server

JMXConnectors are retrieved from an LDAP directory by applying a query string
and search controls to the search method of a DirContext. The following code
example will illustrate this mechanism.

In the code example, the protocol type of the JMXConnectors you want to
retrieve is applied. If the protocol type is null, then the jmxProtocolType attribute
is ignored. Otherwise, only those agents that have registered a matching
jmxProtocolType attribute will be returned.

```
public class JMXConnectorUtil
{
    public static List lookup(DirContext root, String protocolType, String name)
        throws IOException, NamingException
    {
        final ArrayList list = new ArrayList();

        // If protocolType is not null, include it in the filter.
        //
        String queryProtocol =
            (protocolType == null)?"":"(jmxProtocolType=" + protocolType + ")";

        // Set the LDAPv3 query string.
        //
        // Only those nodes that have the jmxConnector object class are
        // of interest, so you specify (objectClass=jmxConnector)
        // in the filter.
        //
        // Specify the jmxAgentName attribute in the filter so that the
        // query will return only those services for which the AgentName
        // attribute was registered. Since JSR 160 specifies that
        // the AgentName attribute is mandatory, this makes it possible
        // to filter out all the services that do not conform
        // to the spec.
```

```
//
// If <name> is null, it is replaced by "*", so that all
// services for which the AgentName attribute was specified match,
// regardless of the value of that attribute.
// Otherwise, only those services for which AgentName matches the
// name or pattern specified by <name> will be returned.
//
// Also specify (jmxServiceURL=*) so that only those nodes
// for which the jmxServiceURL attribute is present will be
// returned. Thus, you filter out all those nodes corresponding
// to agents that are not currently available.
//
String query = "(&" + "(objectClass=jmxConnector) " +
                       "(jmxServiceURL=*) " +
                       queryProtocol +
                       "(jmxAgentName=" + ((name != null)?name:"*") + "))";

System.out.println("Looking up JMX Agents with filter: " + query);

SearchControls ctrls = new SearchControls();

// Want to get all jmxConnector objects, wherever they've been
// registered.
//
ctrls.setSearchScope(SearchControls.SUBTREE_SCOPE);

// Search...
//
final NamingEnumeration results = root.search("", query, ctrls);

for (; results.hasMore();)
{
    // Get result.
    //
    final SearchResult r = (SearchResult) results.nextElement();

    // Get attributes.
    //
    final Attributes attrs = r.getAttributes();

    // Get jmxServiceURL attribute.
    //
    final Attribute attr = attrs.get("jmxServiceURL");
    if (attr == null)
        continue;
```

```
        // Get jmxExpirationDate.
        //
        final Attribute exp = attrs.get("jmxExpirationDate");

        // Check that URL has not expired.
        //
        if ((exp != null) && hasExpired((String) exp.get()))
        {
            continue;
        }

        // Get the URL string.
        //
        final String urlStr = (String) attr.get();
        if (urlStr.length() == 0)
            continue;

        // Create a JMXServiceURL.
        //
        final JMXServiceURL url = new JMXServiceURL(urlStr);

        // Create a JMXConnector.
        //
        final JMXConnector conn =
            JMXConnectorFactory.newJMXConnector(url, null);

        // Add the connector to the result list.
        //
        list.add(conn);
        if (debug) listAttributes(root, r.getName());
    }

    return list;
}
}
```

Summary

The JMX Remoting specification describes how you can advertise and find JMX agents by using existing discovery and lookup infrastructures.

The JMX Remote API specification defines three bindings to lookup services, using existing lookup technologies: SLP Lookup Service, Jini Lookup Service, and JNDI/LDAP Lookup Service. The lookup services allow JMX Remote API clients to find and connect to connector servers that have registered with the lookup services.

To use one of the JMX Remoting lookup services, you implement JMX Remoting agents and JMX Remoting clients. A single JVM can contain many JMX Remoting agents and/or JMX Remoting clients.

A JMX Remoting agent is a logical server application composed of the following features: one MBean server, and one or more JMX Remoting connector servers that allow remote clients to access the MBeans contained in the MBean server.

A JMX Remoting client is a logical client application that opens a client connection with a JMX Remoting agent.

A JMX agent can publish its JMX connector servers with existing lookup and discovery infrastructures, so that a JMX client that does not know about such a server can find it and connect to it.

The JMX Remoting specification specifies JMX connectors that make it possible for a JMX client to access and manage MBeans exposed through a JMX agent (an MBean server) running in a remote JVM. It also defines a JMXServiceURL class, which represents the address of a JMX connector server, and makes it possible for a JMX client to obtain a JMX connector connected to that server. However, the JMX Remoting specification does not provide any specific API that would make it possible for a client to find the address of a connector server attached to a JMX agent it knows about, or to discover which JMX agents are running, or the addresses of the connector servers that make it possible to connect to them. Rather than reinventing the wheel, the JMX Remoting specification instead details how to advertise and find JMX agents using existing discovery and lookup infrastructures.

All three infrastructures considered in the JMX Remoting specification have lookup attributes, which are properties that qualify the registered services. They are passed to the infrastructure when the service is registered, and can be used as filters when performing a lookup.

A client can then query the lookup service in order to find all the connectors registered by a JMX agent that matches one or more attributes. A client that obtains several services as a result of a lookup query can also further inquire about the lookup attributes registered for those services in order to determine which of these returned matching services it wants to use.

In order for a JMX client to be able to format a query to the lookup service independently of the JMX Remote API implementation used on the JMX agent side, and to understand the meaning of the retrieved attributes, the JMX Remoting specification specifies a common set of JMX lookup attributes whose semantics will be known by all JMX agents and JMX clients.

The Service Location Protocol is an IETF standards track protocol (RFC 2608, RFC 2609) that provides a framework to allow networking applications to discover the existence, location, and configuration of networked services in enterprise networks. The SLP white paper provides a brief description of SLP and its positioning with respect to other technologies.

The following steps summarize the procedure defined in the JMX Remoting specification for using the SLP Lookup Service to advertise and find JMX Remoting agents:

1. The agent creates one or more JMX Remoting connector servers.

2. For each connector to expose, the agent registers the address with the SLP Lookup Service, possibly giving additional attributes that qualify the agent and/or the connector, and can be used as filters.

3. The client queries the SLP Lookup Service, and retrieves one or more addresses that match the query.

4. Finally, the client obtains a connector that is connected with the server identified by a retrieved address.

The Jini Network Technology (Jini) is an open software architecture that enables developers to create network-centric services that are highly adaptive to change. Jini offers a standard lookup service. A running Jini Lookup Service can be discovered with a simple API call. A remote service (device, software, application, etc.) that wants to be registered in Jini provides a serializable Java object. When looked up by a remote client, a copy of this Java object is returned. Usually, this object acts as a proxy to the remote service.

In addition, Jini offers various APIs and mechanisms in order to download code from a remote HTTP server (necessary to get the classes required for instantiating the proxy objects), and Jini supports security for code download based on the RMI security manager.

The procedure defined in the JMX Remote API specification for using the Jini Lookup Service to advertise and find JMX Remote API agents is as follows:

1. The agent creates one or more JMX Remote API connector servers.

2. For each connector to expose, the agent registers a JMX Remote API connector stub with the Jini Lookup Service, possibly giving additional attributes that qualify the agent and/or the connector and can be used as filters.

3. The client queries the Jini Lookup Service, and retrieves one or more connector stubs that match the query.

4. Finally, the client connects directly to the server using the provided connector stub.

The JMX Remoting specification defines bindings with Jini technology-based entries. The specification also defines mandatory and optional entries to specify when registering an agent connector.

The Java Naming and Directory Interface is a standard extension to the Java platform, providing Java technology–enabled applications with a unified interface to multiple naming and directory services in the enterprise. In particular, it provides a means to access X.500 directory services through the LDAP. The JMX Remoting specification defines how an LDAP server can be used to store information about JMX agents, and how JMX clients can look up this information to connect to the JMX agents.

The JMX Remoting specification also details how an LDAP server can be used to store and retrieve information about JMX connectors exposed by JMX agents.

The following steps summarize the procedure defined in the JMX Remoting specification for using the JNDI lookup service:

1. One or more JMX Remoting connector servers are created by the agent.

2. The agent registers the address with the JNDI lookup service for each connecter to expose, possibly giving additional attributes that qualify the agent and/or the connector and can be used as filters.

3. The client queries the JNDI lookup service, and retrieves one or more addresses that match the query.

4. Finally, the client obtains a connector connected to the server identified by a retrieved address.

The JMX Remoting specification defines an LDAP schema for registering addresses and explains how a client can discover a registered agent. The specification also defines a lease mechanism.

CHAPTER 9

JMX Clients

THE JMX DISTRIBUTED services level exposes a transparent client/server inter-action. The reason for this transparency is found in the fact that it exposes an API to a remote client that is as close as possible to the API defined by JMX for access to instrumentation within an agent.

Management components cooperate with one another across the network to provide distributed scalable management functions. Customized Java-based management functions can be developed on top of these components in order to deploy a management application.

The combination of the distributed services level with the other agent and instrumentation levels provides a comprehensive architecture for designing and developing complete management solutions. JMX technology brings unique facilities to such solutions: portability, on-demand deployment of management functionality, dynamic and mobility services, and security.

The term *JMX client* (or *client*) is used to identify a logical client application that opens a client connection with a JMX agent. A single JVM can contain many JMX agents and/or JMX clients.

Connector Clients

To recap Chapter 7, the JMX Remoting standard relies on the notion of *connec-tors*. A connector is attached to an MBean server and exposes it to remote Java clients. The client end of a connector is an interface that is virtually the same as the interface exposed by the MBean server. Since connectors have the same interface, no matter the protocol, clients can use the connector most suited to their environment and can even change connectors transparently needed.

A connector consists of a *connector client* and a *connector server*. A connector client is responsible for finding the server and establishing a connection with it.

Even though a client application may contain many connector clients con-nected to different connector servers, a connector client can only be connected to exactly one connector server.

Finding a Connector Server

A JMX agent can register its JMX connector servers with existing lookup and discovery infrastructures, specifically those listed in Chapter 8. This allows a JMX client to create or obtain a `JMXConnector` object and connect to the advertised servers.

Most connector server infrastructures incorporate the notion of lookup attributes or properties that describe the registered services. These attributes can be used as filters when performing a lookup on the server.

A client can pass the desired attributes as part of the lookup service in order to find all the connectors that match one or more of the attributes. A client queries the lookup service, and retrieves one or more `javax.management.remote.JMXServiceURL` addresses (or `javax.management.remote.JMXConnector` stubs) that match the query. Then, it either directly connects to the server using the provided `JMXConnector` stub or it uses `javax.management.remote.JMXConnectorFactory` to obtain a `JMXConnector` connected with the server identified by a retrieved `JMXServiceURL`, as in the following code snippet:

```
int port = 3333;
JMXServiceURL url = new JMXServiceURL("jmxmp", "myserver", port);
JMXConnector jmxc = JMXConnectorFactory.connect(url, null);
mbsc = jmxc.getMBeanServerConnection();
```

Looking Up a JMX Service URL with SLP

SLP is an IETF protocol that provides a framework to allow networking applications to discover the existence, location, and configuration of networked services in enterprise networks.

The following example demonstrates how to use SLP as a lookup service for JMX remote connectors. It shows how to look up a `JMXServiceURL` from the SLP Lookup Service. The `Locator` class is used to perform the SLP lookup.

```
import com.sun.slp.ServiceType;
import com.sun.slp.ServiceLocationEnumeration;
import com.sun.slp.ServiceLocationAttribute;

import javax.management.remote.JMXConnector;
import javax.management.remote.JMXServiceURL;
import javax.management.remote.JMXConnectorFactory;
...
try {
    // Lookup in default SCOPE.
    final Vector scopes = new Vector();
    scopes.add("DEFAULT");
    // Set the LDAPv3 query string.
    // Here you look for a specific agent called "my-jmx-agent",
```

```
    // but you could have asked for any agent by using a wildcard:
    // final String query = "(&(AgentName=*))";
    //
    final String query = "(&(AgentName=my-jmx-agent))";
    // Lookup
    final ServiceLocationEnumeration result =
    slpLocator.findServices(new ServiceType("service:jmx"), scopes, query);
    // Extract the list of returned ServiceURLs.
    while(result.hasMoreElements()) {
        final ServiceURL surl = (ServiceURL) result.next();
        // Get the attributes.
        final ServiceLocationEnumeration slpAttributes =
        slpLocator.findAttributes(surl, scopes, new Vector());
        while(slpAttributes.hasMoreElements()) {
            final ServiceLocationAttribute slpAttribute =
                (ServiceLocationAttribute) slpAttributes.nextElement();
            ...
        }
        // Open a connection.
        final JMXServiceURL jmxUrl = new JMXServiceURL(surl.toString());
        final JMXConnector client = JMXConnectorFactory.connect(jmxUrl);
        ...
    }
}
catch(ServiceLocationException e)
{
}
```

Looking Up a JMX Connector Stub from the Jini Lookup Service

The following example demonstrates how to use Jini (see Chapter 8 for an overview of Jini) as a lookup service for JMX remote connectors. It shows how to look up a JMXConnector from the Jini Lookup Service.

```
import net.jini.core.lookup.ServiceTemplate;
import net.jini.core.lookup.ServiceMatches;
import net.jini.core.lookup.ServiceRegistrar;
import net.jini.core.entry.Entry;

import java.util.*;
import java.rmi.RemoteException;
```

```
import javax.management.MBeanServerConnection;
import javax.management.remote.JMXConnector;
...
// Get the Jini ServiceRegistrar with one of the above methods.
ServiceRegistrar registrar = ...;
// Prepare Service's attributes entry to be matched.
Entry[] serviceAttrs = new Entry[] {
    // Retrieve all services for which a Name entry was registered,
    // whatever the name is (null = wildcard).
    new net.jini.lookup.entry.Name(null)
    // Add here any other matching attribute.
};
// Look for a specific JMXMP Connector (you may also pass
// JMXConnector.class if you wish to get all types of JMXConnector).
//
ServiceTemplate template = new ServiceTemplate(null,
            new Class[] {JMXMPConnector.class}, serviceAttrs);
ServiceMatches matches = null;
try
{
    matches = registrar.lookup(template, Integer.MAX_VALUE);
}
catch (RemoteException e)
{
    e.printStackTrace();
}
// Retrieve the JMX Connector and initiate a connection.
for (int i = 0; i < matches.totalMatches; i++) {
    if(matches.items[i].service != null) {
        // Get the JMXConnector.
        JMXConnector c = (JMXConnector)(matches.items[i].service);
        // Prepare env (security parameters etc...).
        Map env = new HashMap();
        env.put(...);
        // Initiate the connection.
        c.connect(env);
        // Get the remote MBeanServer handle.
        MBeanServerConnection server = c.getMBeanServerConnection();
        ...
    }
}
```

Looking Up a JMX Service URL from an LDAP Server

The following example demonstrates how to use an LDAP directory (see Chapter 8 for an overview of LDAP and JNDI) as a lookup service for JMX Remoting connectors. It shows how to look up a JMXServiceURL from the LDAP directory.

```java
import javax.management.remote.JMXConnectorFactory;
import javax.management.remote.JMXConnector;
import javax.management.remote.JMXServiceURL;
import javax.naming.directory.Attributes;
import javax.naming.directory.Attribute;
import javax.naming.directory.SearchResult;
import javax.naming.directory.SearchControls;
import javax.naming.directory.DirContext;
import javax.naming.directory.InitialDirContext;
import javax.naming.NamingEnumeration;
import javax.naming.InitialContext;
import java.util.Hashtable;

    public connectToLDAP()
    {
        // Create initial context.
        Hashtable env = new Hashtable();
        env.put(InitialContext.PROVIDER_URL, "ldap://ldap.someserver.com");
        env.put(...);
        InitialDirContext root = new InitialDirContext(env);
        // Prepare search filter expression to use for the search.
        // The interpretation of the filter is based on RFC 2254.
        // RFC 2254 defines certain operators for the filter, including substring
        // matches, equality, approximate match, greater than, less than.  These
        // operators are mapped to operators with corresponding semantics in the
        // underlying directory. For example, for the equals operator, suppose
        // the directory has a matching rule defining "equality" of the
        // attributes in the filter. This rule would be used for checking
        // equality of the attributes specified in the filter with the attributes
        // of objects in the directory. Similarly, if the directory has a
        // matching rule for ordering, this rule would be used for
        // making "greater than" and "less than" comparisons.
        String filter = "(&(objectClass=jmxConnector) (jmxServiceURL=*))";
        // Prepare the search controls.
        SearchControls ctrls = new SearchControls();
        // Want to get all jmxConnector objects, wherever they've been
        // registered.
```

```
ctrls.setSearchScope(SearchControls.SUBTREE_SCOPE);
// Want to get only the jmxServiceURL (comment this line and
// all attributes will be returned).
ctrls.setReturningAttributes(new String[]{"jmxServiceURL"});
// Search.
final NamingEnumeration results = root.search("", filter, ctrls);
// Get the URL.
while (results.hasMore())
{
    final SearchResult res = (SearchResult) results.nextElement();
    final Attributes attrs = res.getAttributes();
    final Attribute attr = attrs.get("jmxServiceURL");
    final String urlStr = (String) attr.get();
    // Make a connector.
    final JMXServiceURL url = new JMXServiceURL(urlStr);
    final JMXConnector conn =
        JMXConnectorFactory.newJMXConnector(url, null);
    // Start using the connector.
    conn.connect(null);
}
}
```

Establishing a Connection

A connector client is represented by an object that implements the JMXConnector interface. A connector client may be created in one of two ways. Which way an application uses depends mainly on the infrastructure that is used to find the connector server that the client wants to connect to.

JMXConnectorFactory

If the client knows the address (JMXServiceURL) of the connector server it wants to connect to, it can use the JMXConnectorFactory to make the connection. This is the usual technique when the client has found the server through a text-based discovery or directory service such as SLP.

For example, an application called app1 that includes a JMX MBean server might export that server to remote managers as follows:

1. Create a connector server called cServer.

2. Get cServer's address, addr, either by using the JMXServiceURL that was supplied to its constructor to tell it what address to use, or by calling cServer.getAddress().

3. Put the address where the management applications can find it, for example, in a directory or in an SLP service agent.

A manager can start managing app1 as follows:

1. Retrieve `addr` from where it was stored in step 3.

2. Call `JMXConnectorFactory.connect(addr)`.

Connection Stubs

An alternative way for a client to connect to a server is to obtain a connector stub from somewhere. A connector stub is a `JMXConnector` object generated by a connector server. It is serializable so that it can be transmitted to a remote client. A client that retrieves a connector stub can then call the stub's `connect` method to connect to the connector server that generated it.

For example, an application called app1 that includes a JMX MBean server might export that server to remote managers as follows:

1. Create a connector server `cServer`.

2. Obtain a connector stub, `cStub`, by calling `cServer.getStub()`.

3. Put the stub somewhere the management applications can find it—for example, in a directory, in the Jini Lookup Service, or in an HTTP server.

A manager can start managing app1 as follows:

1. Retrieve `cStub` from where it was stored in step 3.

2. Call `cStub.connect()` to connect to the remote MBean server through `cServer`.

Connecting to an RMI Connector Server

A client can connect to an RMI connector server in one of the following ways:

-   Supply a `JMXServiceURL` to the `JMXConnectorFactory` that specifies the RMI or RMI-IIOP protocol.

-   Obtain a `JMXConnector` stub from an LDAP directory, the Jini Lookup Service, or as the returned value of an RMI method call.

-   Pass an existing `RMIServer` stub as a parameter to the constructor of `RMIConnector`.

Please refer to Chapter 7 for detailed views of the interactions between a connector client and a connector server.

MBean Server Operations Through a Connection

To review the more detailed discussion in Chapter 7, client code can obtain an object that implements the MBeanServerConnection interface. MBeanServerConnection is the parent interface of MBeanServer. MBeanServerConnection contains all of the same methods as MBeanServer except for a small number of methods only appropriate for local access to the MBean server. Because MBeanServer extends MBeanServerConnection, client code can be written that works identically whether it is operating on a local MBean server or on a remote one through a connector.

Distributed Notifications

The JMX specification defines a generic notification model based on the Java event model. Notifications can be emitted by MBean instances, as well as by the MBean server. The JMX Remoting specification describes the notification objects and the broadcaster and listener interfaces that must be implemented by notification senders and receivers.

A JMX Remoting implementation provides services that allow distribution of this notification model, thus allowing a management application to listen to MBean and MBean server events remotely. JMX events transmitted from remote MBeans and remote MBean servers can be very valuable when used with network management monitoring tools and system management monitoring tools.

Adding Remote Listeners

One of the operations in the MBeanServerConnection interface is the addNotificationListener operation. As in the local case, this operation registers a listener for the notifications emitted by a named MBean. A connector will arrange for the notifications to be forwarded from the server end of a connection to the client end, and from there to the listener.

In Figure 9-1, user code calls the addNotificationListener method in the MBeanServerConnection interface, supplying a NotificationListener, L. The client end of the connection notifies the server end of the new listener, and the server reacts by calling addNotificationListener on the MBean server. It supplies the listener proxy L'.addNotificationListener("a:b=c", L).

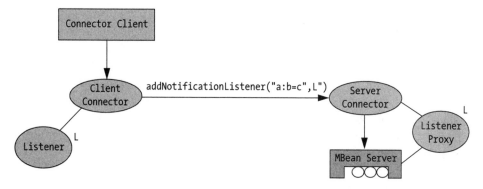

Figure 9-1. The client can add a remote listener using the connection.

Figure 9-2 shows how the remote listener L receives notifications in the same way as a local listener would. When the MBean it is registered with emits the notification N, the listener proxy L' is informed via its handleNotification method. This method causes N to be forwarded through the connection to the client listener L.

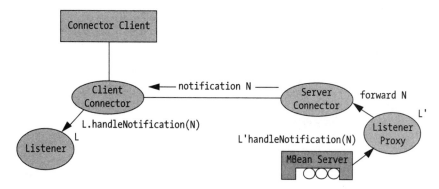

Figure 9-2. The notification N is forwarded through the connection to the remote listener.

Filters and Handbacks

The addNotificationListener method in the MBeanServerConnection interface has four parameters: the object name, the listener, the filter, and the handback. The object name specifies which MBean to add the listener to. The listener is the object whose handleNotification method will be called when a notification is emitted by the MBean. This listener object is local to the client.

The optional filter selects which notifications this listener is interested in. A given connector may execute the filter when the notification arrives at the client, or it may transmit the filter to the server to be executed there. Executing the filter on the server is much more efficient because it avoids sending a notification over the network only to have it discarded on arrival. Filters should be designed so that they work whether they are run on the client or on the server. In particular, a filter should be an instance of a serializable class known to the server. The connectors defined by the JMX Remoting specification execute filters on the server. To force filtering to be done on the client, the filtering logic can be moved to the listener's `handleNotification` method and a null passed in as the filter parameter.

The optional handback parameter to `addNotificationListener` is an arbitrary object that will be given to the listener when the notification arrives. This allows the same listener object to be registered with several MBeans. The handback can be used to determine the appropriate context when a notification arrives. The handback object remains on the client; it is not transmitted to the server and does not have to be serializable.

The `MBeanServerConnection` interface also has an `addNotificationListener` variant that specifies the listener as an `ObjectName`, the name of another MBean that is to receive notifications. With this variant, both the filter and handback are sent to the remote server.

Removing Listeners

In general, a listener that has been added with the following method is uniquely identified by the triple (listener, filter, handback):

```
addNotificationListener(ObjectName name,
                        NotificationListener listener,
                        NotificationFilter filter,
                        Object handback)
```

A listener can subsequently be removed either with the two-parameter `removeNotificationListener`, specifying just the listener, or with the four-parameter `removeNotificationListener` that has the same parameters.

A problem arises with the four-parameter method in the remote case. The filter object that is deserialized in the `removeNotificationListener` method is not in general identical to the filter object that was deserialized for `addNotificationListener`. Since notification broadcaster MBeans usually check for equality in the triple using identity rather than the `equals` method, it would not in general be possible to remove just one triple remotely.

The standard connectors avoid this problem by using listener identifiers. When a connector client adds a triple to an MBean, the connector server returns a unique identifier for that triple on that MBean. When the connector client subsequently wants to remove the triple, it uses the identifier rather than passing the triple itself. To implement the two-parameter `removeNotificationListener` form, the connector client looks up all the triples that had the same listener and sends a `removeNotificationListener` request with the listener identifier of each one.

Every listener identifier corresponds to a different listener proxy in the connector server. If the same listener object is used in several different triples on the client, each one appears as a different listener object on the server.

This technique has the side effect that a remote client can remove a triple even from an MBean that implements `NotificationBroadcaster` but not `NotificationEmitter`. A local client of the MBeanServer interface cannot do this.

Terminating a Connection

As stated in Chapter 7, either end of a connection may terminate a connection at any time. If the client terminates a connection, the server will clean up any state relative to that client, such as listener proxies. If client operations are in progress when the client terminates the connection, then the threads that invoked them will receive an `IOException`.

Typically, a client closes a connection by calling the `close` method on the `JMXConnector` object. If the server terminates a connection, the client will get an `IOException` for any remote operations that were in progress and any remote operations subsequently attempted.

Abnormal Termination

The client end of a session can detect that the server end has terminated abnormally. This might happen, for example, because the JVM software that the server was running in exited, or because the machine it was running on crashed. The connector protocol (or its underlying transport) might also determine that the server is unreachable, because communication to it has not succeeded for a certain period of time. This can happen if there is a physical or configuration problem with the network.

In all of these cases, the client can terminate the session. The behavior seen by code using the client should be the same as if the server had terminated the session normally, except that the details of the exception seen by the client might differ.

Similarly, the server end of a session, or a connection within a session, can detect that the client end has terminated abnormally or become unreachable. It should behave as if the client had terminated the connection normally, except that the notification of connection termination indicates a failure.

Creating a Connector Client

A connector client is represented by an object that implements the JMXConnector interface. As mentioned previously, a connector client may be created in one of two ways, depending on the infrastructure that is used to find the connector server that the client wants to connect to.

Mechanics of the RMI Connector

An RMI connector client that wants to communicate with an RMI connector server obtains a remote stub connected to the server. Any method called on the stub is forwarded to the server. Therefore a client that has a stub for the RMIServer object can call a method on it, and the result will be returned from server's object.

Refer to the figures in Chapter 7 to see the details of two clients that both have stubs for the same server object. The following steps illustrate a typical connection between an RMI server and a remote client:

1. An agent creates an MBean server and an RMI connector server.

2. A remote client creates an RMI connector.

3. Operations are performed on MBeans registered in the MBean server, via the RMI connector.

The Generic Connector Protocol

An optional part of the JMX Remote API is a connector that is based on TCP sockets, known as the *generic connector*. This connector can be configured by adding pluggable modules to define the transport protocol used for requests and notifications, and the object wrapping for objects that are sent from the client to the server. The JMX Messaging Protocol (JMXMP) connector is a configuration of the generic connector using TCP as the transport protocol and Java serialization as the object wrapping.

The following example demonstrates creating and connecting to a connector from a client over JMXMP:

```
import javax.management.remote.JMXServiceURL;
import javax.management.remote.JMXConnector;
import javax.management.remote.JMXConnectorFactory;
import javax.management.MBeanServerConnection;
import java.io.IOException;
```

```
public class JMXMPClient
{
    private MBeanServerConnection mbsc = null;

    public JMXMPClient()
    {
        try
        {
            int port = 3333;
            JMXServiceURL url = new JMXServiceURL("jmxmp", "myserver", port);
            JMXConnector jmxc = JMXConnectorFactory.connect(url, null);
            mbsc = jmxc.getMBeanServerConnection();
        }
        catch (IOException e)
        {
            System.err.println(e);
        }
    }
}
```

SASL, SSL, and TLS

Simple Authentication and Security Layer (SASL) specifies a challenge-response protocol in which data is exchanged between a client and a server for the purposes of authentication and (optional) establishment of a security layer on which to carry on subsequent communications. It is used with connection-based protocols such as LDAPv3 or IMAPv4. SASL is described in RFC 2222.

Secure Sockets Layer (SSL) and Transport Layer Security (TLS) are communication procedures (protocols) to encrypt communication contents. The primary goal of the TLS protocol is to provide privacy and data integrity between two communicating applications. The protocol is composed of two layers: the TLS Record Protocol and the TLS Handshake Protocol.

MBean Server Operation and Connection Message Exchanges

Once the initial handshake phase has been terminated, and all profiles negotiated, the client can retrieve a reference to the remote MBean server by calling the getMBeanServerConnection method on the JMXConnector instance. Through the MBeanServerConnection interface the client can perform operations on the registered MBeans, including registration for receiving notifications. These MBean server operations will be mapped by the protocol to MBeanServerRequestMessage messages. For each such message, the server will receive it, decode it, perform the operation on the MBean server, and return the result of the operation in an MBeanServerResponseMessage message.

If several client threads are performing MBean server operations at the same time, there may be several MBeanServerRequestMessages that have been sent without yet having received the corresponding MBeanServerResponseMessages. There is no requirement that a client receive a response for each request before sending the next request.

Each MBeanServerRequestMessage contains an identifier that the matching MBeanServerResponseMessage must also contain. At any time, the client has a set of identifiers, {id1, id2, ..., idN}, for requests it has sent that have not yet received a response. Each new request must have an identifier that is not in the set, and that is added to the set when the request is sent. Each response must have an identifier that is in the set, and that is removed from the set when the response is received. It is a protocol error for these conditions to be violated. The peer that detects the error must close the connection, optionally after sending a CloseMessage to the other peer.

For notifications emitted by MBeans registered on the MBean server, the server end of the JMX connection will forward them to the client end of the JMX connection encapsulated in a NotificationMessage message.

Figure 9-3 depicts the MBean server operation message exchanges.

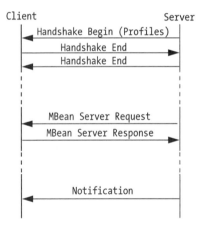

Figure 9-3. MBean server operations message exchanges

At any time after the handshake phase and during the MBean server operation message exchanges, either the client or the server may want to close the connection. On the one hand, the client can achieve that by calling the close method on the JMXConnector instance. On the other hand, the server can achieve that by calling the stop method on the JMXConnectorServer instance. The peer initiating the connection close action will send a message of type CloseMessage in order to inform the other peer that the connection must be closed and necessary cleanup should be carried out.

Summary

The JMX distributed services level exposes a transparent client/server interaction because it exposes an API to the remote client that is as close as possible to the API defined by JMX for access to instrumentation within the agent.

The term JMX client (or client) refers to a logical client application that opens a client connection with a JMX agent. A single JVM can contain many JMX agents and/or JMX clients.

A connector is attached to a JMX MBean server and makes it accessible to remote Java clients. The client end of a connector exports essentially the same interface as the MBean server. Connectors include a remote component that provides end-to-end communications with the agent over a variety of protocols.

A given connector client is connected to exactly one connector server. A client application may contain many connector clients connected to different connector servers. There may be more than one connection between a given client and a given server.

A JMX agent can register its JMX connector servers with existing lookup and discovery infrastructures such as the following, so that a JMX client can create or obtain a JMXConnector object to connect to the advertised servers:

- *Service Location Protocol:* A JMX client can retrieve a JMX Service URL from SLP, and use it to connect to the corresponding server.

- *Jini Network Technology:* A JMX client can retrieve a JMX Connector stub from the Jini Lookup Service (LUS) and connect to the corresponding server.

- *Java Naming and Directory Interface:* A JMX client can retrieve a JMX Service URL from the LDAP directory, and use it to connect to the corresponding server.

A connector client is represented by an object that implements the JMXConnector interface. There are two ways in which a connector client may be created. Which way an application uses depends mainly on the infrastructure that is used to find the connector server to which the client wants to connect.

If the client knows the address (JMXServiceURL) of the connector server it wants to connect to, it can use the JMXConnectorFactory to make the connection. An alternative way for a client to connect to a server is to obtain a connector stub from somewhere. A connector stub is a JMXConnector object generated by a connector server.

From the client end of a connection, user code can obtain an object that implements the MBeanServerConnection interface. This interface is very similar to the MBeanServer interface that user code would use to interact with the MBean server if it were running in the same JVM.

The generic connector protocol defines a set of protocol messages that are exchanged between the client and the server ends of the connection, and the sequence these message exchanges must follow. Implementations of the JMX Remoting specification must exchange these messages in the defined sequence so that they can interoperate with other implementations.

The handshake message exchanges are started by the server end of the connection as soon as the connect method on the JMXConnector class is called by the client and the connection between the client and the server is established.

CHAPTER 10

Security

ONE OF THE PRINCIPAL goals of the distributed services level is security. JMX builds on the Java standards for security including Java Secure Socket Extensions (JSSE), the Simple Authentication and Security Layer (SASL), and the Java Authentication and Authorization Service (JAAS) so that connections between clients and servers can be private and authenticated and so that servers can control what operations different clients can perform.

This chapter discusses the JMX Remote security features, including connector security based on password authentication and file access control, connector security that uses a subject delegation model, and fine-grained connector security.

The simplest type of security is based upon encryption, user name and password authentication, and file access control. A subject-delegation model performs operations on a given authenticated connection on behalf of several different identities. Fine-grained security involves more sophisticated security mechanisms, in which permission to perform individual operations is controlled.

Connector Server Security

Connector servers typically have some way of authenticating remote clients. For the RMI connector, this is done by supplying an object that implements the `javax.management.remote.JMXAuthenticator` interface when the connector server is created. For the JMXMP connector, this is done using SASL.

In both cases, the result of authentication is a JAAS `javax.security.auth.Subject` representing the authenticated identity. Requests received from the client are executed using this identity. With JAAS, you can define what permissions the identity has. In particular, you can control access to MBean server operations using the `javax.management.MBeanPermission` class, provided that a security manager has been set using `System.setSecurityManager(java.lang.SecurityManager)`.

If a connector server does not support authentication or is not set up with authentication, then client requests are executed using the same identity that created the connector server.

As an alternative to JAAS, you can control access to MBean server operations by using a `javax.management.remote.MBeanServerForwarder`. This is an object that implements the `MBeanServer` interface by forwarding its methods to another `MBeanServer` object, possibly performing additional work before or after forwarding. In particular, the object can do arbitrary access checks. You can insert an

MBeanServerForwarder between a connector server and its MBean server using the method setMBeanServerForwarder of the JMXConnectorServer class.

Subject Delegation

Any given connection to a connector server has at most one authenticated Subject. This means that if a client performs operations as or on behalf of several different identities, it must establish a separate connection for each one. However, the two standard connectors also support subject delegation. A single connection is established between client and server using an authenticated identity, as usual. With each request, the client specifies a per-request Subject. The request is executed using this per-request identity, provided that the authenticated per-connection identity has permission to do so. That permission is specified with the permission SubjectDelegationPermission.

For each delegated Subject, the client obtains an MBeanServerConnection from the JMXConnector for the authenticated Subject. Requests using this MBeanServerConnection are sent with the delegated Subject. MBeanServerConnection objects for any number of delegated identities can be obtained from the same JMXConnector and used simultaneously.

Using the JMXAuthenticator Interface

The javax.management.remote.JMXAuthenticator interface defines how remote credentials are converted into a JAAS Subject. This interface is used by the RMIConnectorServer, and can be used by other connector servers.

The user-defined authenticator instance is passed to the connector server in the environment map as the value of the attribute JMXConnectorServer.AUTHENTICATOR. For connector servers that use only this authentication system, if this attribute is not present or its value is null, then no user authentication will be performed and full access to the methods exported by the MBeanServerConnection object will be allowed.

If authentication is successful, then an authenticated Subject filled in with its associated Principals is returned. Authorization checks then will be performed based on the given set of Principals.

The authenticate method of the JMXAuthenticator interface authenticates an MBeanServerConnection client with the given client credentials. The authenticate method takes one parameter, the user-defined credentials Object, to be passed into the server in order to authenticate the user before creating the MBeanServerConnection. The actual type of this parameter, and whether it can be null, depends on the specific connector. The authenticate method returns the authenticated Subject containing its associated principals.

If the server cannot authenticate the user with the provided credentials, the authenticate method throws a SecurityException.

Basic Security with the RMI Connector

The RMI connector provides a simple mechanism for securing and authenticating the connection between a client and a server. This mechanism is not intended to address every possible security configuration, but provides a basic level of security for environments using the RMI connector. More advanced security requirements are better addressed by the JMXMP connector.

To make an RMI connector server secure, the environment supplied at its creation must contain the property jmx.remote.rmi.authenticator, whose associated value is an object that implements the interface RMIAuthenticator. This object is responsible for examining the authentication information supplied by the client and either deriving a JAAS Subject representing the client, or rejecting the connection request with a SecurityException.

A client connecting to a server that has an RMIAuthenticator must supply the authentication information that the RMIAuthenticator will examine. The environment supplied to the connect operation must include the property jmx.remote.rmi.credentials, whose associated value is the authentication information. This object must be serializable.

The JMX Remote specification does not include any predefined authentication system. The simplest example of such a system is a secret string shared between client and server. The client supplies this string as its jmx.remote.rmi.credentials, and the server's RMIAuthenticator checks that it has the right value.

As a slightly more complicated example, the authentication information could be a two-element String array (String[2]) that includes a user name and a password. The RMIAuthenticator verifies these, for example, by consulting a password file or by logging in through some system-dependent mechanism, and if successful derives a Subject based on the given user name.

How Security Affects the RMI Connector Protocol

The authentication information supplied by the client is passed as an argument to the newClient call. The connector server gives it to the RMIAuthenticator. If the RMIAuthenticator throws an exception, that exception is propagated to the client. If the RMIAuthenticator succeeds, it returns a Subject, and that Subject is passed as a parameter to the constructor of the new RMIMBeanServerConnection object. All of the MBean server methods in RMIMBeanServerConnection are executed inside a Subject.doAs operation, so that they have the permissions appropriate to the authenticated client.

Implementing Tighter Security

The solution outlined previously is enough to provide a basic level of security. A number of problems have to be addressed to achieve a real level of security, however

- If the authentication information includes a clear text password, and if the network is not secure, then attackers might be able to see the password sent from client to server.

- Attackers might be able to substitute their own server for the server that the client thinks it is talking to, and retrieve the password that the client sends to authenticate itself.

- Attackers might be able to see the RMI object ID of a legitimately created RMIMBeanServerConnection object as it is accessed remotely. They could then use RMI to call that object, executing MBean server methods using the Subject that was authenticated when the object was created.

- Attackers might be able to guess this RMI object ID, for instance, if object IDs are allocated as consecutive small integers.

The first three problems can be solved by using an RMI socket factory so that the connection between client and server uses SSL.

The fourth problem can be solved by setting the standard RMI system property java.rmi.server.randomIDs to true. This causes the 64-bit object ID of every exported RMI object to be generated using a cryptographically strong random number generator.

Security and the Generic Connector

The JMX Remote API includes a generic connector as an optional part of the API. This connector is designed to be configurable by plugging in modules to define

- The transport protocol used to send requests from the client to the server and to send responses and notifications from the server to the clients

- The object wrapping for objects sent from the client to the server whose class loader may depend on the target MBean.

The JMXMP connector is a configuration of the generic connector in which the transport protocol is based on TCP and the object wrapping is native Java serialization. Security is based on JSSE, JAAS, and SASL.

The generic connector and its JMXMP configuration are optional, which means that an implementation may choose not to include them.

The JMXMP connector provides support for authentication and authorization through the TLS and SASL profiles. The JMX Remote API does not mandate the implementation and support of any specific SASL mechanism. It simply relies on third-party implementations that can be plugged in using the standard SASL interface.

Handshake and Profile Message Exchanges

Handshake-message exchanges are passed between the server end of the connection and the client end of a connection when a connection between the client and the server is established.

The server passes a javax.management.remote.message.HandshakeBeginMessage with the server's supported profiles to an interested client. The client can then exchange profile messages for the desired profiles from the server's supported profiles.

For non-JMXMP profiles, a client must first check that all of its profiles are supported by the server. Then, for each profile asked for in the client's environment map, the client will negotiate that profile. The order in which profiles are negotiated can be very important depending upon the profile. For example, if a client negotiates the SASL/PLAIN profile before the TLS profile, it will send a password in clear text over the connection. If it negotiates TLS first, the connection will become encrypted before the password is sent.

It is recommended that if a server's profiles imply a certain level of security, the server should reject connections from a client whose negotiated profiles do not ensure that level of security. For example, if a server is configured with only the TLS profile, then it should reject connections that do not negotiate TLS. If a server is configured with the TLS profile and with the SASL/DIGEST-MD5 profile specifying the same level of security as regards authentication and encryption, then it should reject connections that do not negotiate either profile.

Figure 10-1 depicts the initial handshake and profile message exchanges.

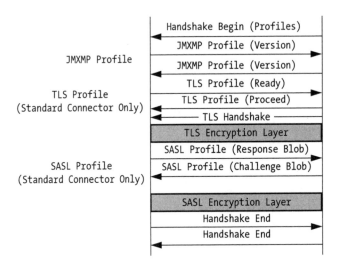

Figure 10-1. Handshake and profile message exchanges

Notice that only the handshake begin and handshake end messages are mandatory. At any time during the handshake phase, if an error is encountered by either peer (client or server), it must send an indication (HandshakeErrorMessage) as to why the operation failed. The peer that encountered the problem will send the error message to the other peer and immediately close the connection. The peer that receives the message on the other end of the connection will also close the connection immediately on reception of a handshake error message. Please refer to Figure 6-6 earlier in this book to see how an error is indicated by either a client or a server to the other peer during the initial handshake message exchanges.

The constructor for the MBeanServerRequestMessage class requires three parameters: an int specifying the method ID, an Object array specifying any parameters to the message, and an instance of Subject specifying the subject on which authorization checks are to be performed. If the Subject parameter is null, the authorization checks are performed on the authentication Subject instead.

TLS Profile

The TLS profile allows the client and server ends of a JMX connection to negotiate a TLS encryption layer. Certificate-based authentication and mutual client/server authentication are optional features configurable through properties in the environment map.

SASL Profile

The SASL profile mechanism uses the JAAS framework to construct a JMXPrincipal based on this authorization identity, and stores this JMXPrincipal in a Subject. Then, when the JMXMPConnectorServer performs any of the subsequent MBean server operations, it must do so using the Subject.doAsPrivileged(subject, action, null) call with the given subject for the required action.

When using a SASL profile, the manner in which authentication is carried out is defined by the selected SASL mechanism and may vary from one mechanism to another. However, at the end of the SASL handshake exchanges, an authorization identity has been negotiated between the SASL client and the SASL server. Thus, the SASL profile has to make this identity available to allow the MBean server and the underlying MBeans to perform access control checks based on this identity.

An MBean interested in retrieving the authorization information can do so (if it has the appropriate permissions) by using the following code snippet:

```
AccessControlContext acc = AccessController.getContext();
Subject subject = Subject.getSubject(acc);
Set principals = subject.getPrincipals();
```

The following example demonstrates how you can create a secured JMXMP connector server that supports the TLS and SASL/PLAIN profiles using the SSLContext class, the SSLSocketFactory class, and the JMXConnectorServerFactory class:

```
import javax.management.remote.JMXConnectorServerFactory;
import javax.management.remote.JMXConnectorServer;
import javax.management.remote.JMXServiceURL;
import javax.management.MBeanServerFactory;
import javax.management.MBeanServer;
import javax.net.ssl.SSLSocketFactory;
import java.io.File;
import java.io.FileInputStream;
import java.security.KeyStore;
import java.security.Security;
import java.security.Provider;
import java.util.HashMap;
import javax.net.ssl.*;
```

```
public class Server
{
    public static void main(String[] args)
    {
        try
        {
            // Create the MBean server.
            //
            MBeanServer mbs = MBeanServerFactory.createMBeanServer();

            HashMap env = new HashMap();

            // Initialize the SSLSocketFactory.
            //
            String keystore = "config" + File.separator + "keystore";
            char keystorepass[] = "password".toCharArray();
            char keypassword[] = "password".toCharArray();
            KeyStore ks = KeyStore.getInstance("JKS");
            ks.load(new FileInputStream(keystore), keystorepass);
            KeyManagerFactory kmf =
                KeyManagerFactory.getInstance("SunX509");
            kmf.init(ks, keypassword);
            SSLContext ctx = SSLContext.getInstance("TLSv1");
            ctx.init(kmf.getKeyManagers(), null, null);
            SSLSocketFactory ssf = ctx.getSocketFactory();

            // Add SASL/PLAIN mechanism server provider.
            //
            Security.addProvider(new ServerProvider());

            // The profiles supported by this server are TLS and SASL/PLAIN.
            //
            env.put("jmx.remote.profiles", "TLS SASL/PLAIN");
```

Once you have initialized the SSL socket factory, you set up your environment to use the TLSv1 protocol and the SSL_RSA_WITH_NULL_MD5 cipher suite.

```
            env.put("jmx.remote.tls.socket.factory", ssf);
            env.put("jmx.remote.tls.enabled.protocols", "TLSv1");
            env.put("jmx.remote.tls.enabled.cipher.suites",
                    "SSL_RSA_WITH_NULL_MD5");
```

```
            // Callback handler used by the PLAIN SASL server mechanism
            // to perform user authentication.
            //
            env.put("jmx.remote.sasl.callback.handler",
                        new PropertiesFileCallbackHandler("config" +
                                                    File.separator +
                                                    "password.properties"));

            // Create a JMXMP connector server.
            //
            JMXServiceURL url = new JMXServiceURL("jmxmp", null, 5555);
            JMXConnectorServer cs =
                JMXConnectorServerFactory.newJMXConnectorServer(url, env, mbs);

            // Start the JMXMP connector server.
            //
            cs.start();
            System.out.println("\nJMXMP connector server successfully started...");
        }
        catch (Exception e)
        {
            e.printStackTrace();
        }
    }
}
```

The following illustrates the ServerProvider class:

```
public final class ServerProvider extends java.security.Provider
{
    public ServerProvider()
    {
        super("SaslServerFactory", 1.0, "SASL PLAIN SERVER MECHANISM");
        put("SaslServerFactory.PLAIN", "ServerFactory");
    }
}
```

And this code illustrates the callback-handler class:

```
import javax.security.auth.callback.*;
import java.util.Properties;
import java.io.FileInputStream;
import java.io.IOException;
```

```
public final class PropertiesFileCallbackHandler
   implements CallbackHandler
{

   private Properties pwDb;
   /**
    * Contents of files are in the Properties file format.
    *
    * @param pwFile name of file containing name/password pairs
    */
   public PropertiesFileCallbackHandler(String pwFile)
      throws IOException
   {
      pwDb = new Properties();
      pwDb.load(new FileInputStream(pwFile));
   }

   public void handle(Callback[] callbacks)
      throws UnsupportedCallbackException
   {
      // Retrieve callbacks.
      //
      NameCallback ncb = null;
      PasswordCallback pcb = null;
      for (int i = 0; i < callbacks.length; i++)
      {
         if (callbacks[i] instanceof NameCallback)
         {
            ncb = (NameCallback) callbacks[i];
         }
         else if (callbacks[i] instanceof PasswordCallback)
         {
            pcb = (PasswordCallback) callbacks[i];
         }
         else
         {
            throw new UnsupportedCallbackException(callbacks[i]);
         }
      }
```

Once you have parsed the callback array, you can check to see if the password for the default user name is available:

```
        if (ncb != null && pcb != null)
        {
            String username = ncb.getDefaultName();
            String pw = pwDb.getProperty(username);
            if (pw != null)
            {
                char[] pwchars = pw.toCharArray();
                pcb.setPassword(pwchars);
                // Clear pw.
                //
                for (int i = 0; i < pwchars.length; i++)
                {
                    pwchars[i] = 0;
                }
            }
        }
    }
}
```

Clients of a secured server can use the SSLContext class, the SSLSocketFactory class, and the JMXConnectorFactory class to assist in connecting securely to a connector server. The following example demonstrates how you can use these to retrieve an MBeanServerConnection securely from a connector server:

```
public void retrieveMBeanServerConn()
{
    try {
        HashMap env = new HashMap();

        // Initialize the SSLSocketFactory.
        String truststore = "config/truststore";
        char truststorepass[] = "trustword".toCharArray();
        KeyStore ks = KeyStore.getInstance("JKS");
        ks.load(new FileInputStream(truststore), truststorepass);
        TrustManagerFactory tmf = TrustManagerFactory.getInstance("SunX509");
        tmf.init(ks);
        SSLContext ctx = SSLContext.getInstance("TLSv1");
        SecureRandom sr = new SecureRandom();
        sr.nextInt();
        ctx.init(null, tmf.getTrustManagers(), sr);
        SSLSocketFactory ssf = ctx.getSocketFactory();
```

```
// Add SASL/PLAIN mechanism client provider.
Security.addProvider(new ClientProvider());

// The profiles required by this client are TLS and SASL/PLAIN.
env.put("jmx.remote.profiles", "TLS SASL/PLAIN");
```

Here you provide the previously initialized SSL socket factory and tell the SSL stack to use the TLSv1 protocol and the SSL_RSA_WITH_NULL_MD5 cipher suite.

```
env.put("jmx.remote.tls.socket.factory", ssf);
env.put("jmx.remote.tls.enabled.protocols", "TLSv1");
env.put("jmx.remote.tls.enabled.cipher.suites",
              "SSL_RSA_WITH_NULL_MD5");
```

You provide a callback handler to be used by the PLAIN SASL client mechanism to retrieve the user credentials required by the server to successfully perform user authentication.

```
env.put("jmx.remote.sasl.callback.handler",
              new UserPasswordCallbackHandler("username", "password"));

// Create a JMXMP connector client and
// connect it to the JMXMP connector server.
JMXServiceURL url = new JMXServiceURL("jmxmp", null, 5555);
JMXConnector jmxc = JMXConnectorFactory.connect(url, env);

// Get the MBeanServerConnection.
MBeanServerConnection mbsc = jmxc.getMBeanServerConnection();
}
catch (Exception e)
{
    e.printStackTrace();
}
}
```

Here you can see the callback-handler class along with the handle method that will used to retrieve a user name and password:

```
import java.io.*;
import javax.security.auth.callback.*;
```

```java
public class UserPasswordCallbackHandler
    implements CallbackHandler
{
    private String user;
    private char[] pwchars;

    public UserPasswordCallbackHandler(String user, String password)
    {
        this.user = user;
        this.pwchars = password.toCharArray();
    }

    public void handle(Callback[] callbacks)
        throws IOException, UnsupportedCallbackException
    {
        for (int i = 0; i < callbacks.length; i++)
        {
            if (callbacks[i] instanceof NameCallback)
            {
                NameCallback ncb = (NameCallback)callbacks[i];
                ncb.setName(user);
            }
            else if (callbacks[i] instanceof PasswordCallback)
            {
                PasswordCallback pcb = (PasswordCallback)callbacks[i];
                pcb.setPassword(pwchars);
            }
            else
            {
                throw new UnsupportedCallbackException(callbacks[i]);
            }
        }
    }

    private void clearPassword()
    {
        if (pwchars != null)
        {
            for (int i = 0 ; i < pwchars.length ; i++)
                pwchars[i] = 0;
            pwchars = null;
        }
    }
```

```
    protected void finalize()
    {
        clearPassword();
    }
}
```

A client and server exchange messages during an SASL authentication challenge. These messages are represented by the javax.management.remote.message.SASLMessage class.

Using the SASL Message Class

The SASLMessage class implements the ProfileMessage interface and represents a challenge or response exchanged between client and server during SASL authentication. This message encapsulates either a challenge or a response generated by the SASL mechanism during the SASL authentication exchanges taking place between the client and the server.

The challenges/responses (blobs) are generated by the SASL mechanism as follows:

- The challenges are generated by the server-side SASL mechanisms.

- The responses are generated by the client-side SASL mechanisms in response to the server challenges.

The status attribute takes one of the two following values:

- CONTINUE: Used by either a client or server to indicate that they require more interaction with the other peer in order to complete the authentication exchange.

- COMPLETE: Used by a server to indicate that the exchange is complete and successful.

At any time during the SASL handshake, if the server encounters a problem, it can notify the client by sending an indication (in the form of a HandshakeErrorMessage) as to why the operation failed.

At any time during the SASL handshake, if the client encounters a problem or wants to abort the authentication exchange, it can notify the server by sending an indication as to why the operation failed or is aborted.

The profile name in this profile message is built by concatenating the prefix "SASL/" with the SASL mechanism name provided by the IANA SASL registry.

The following are some examples of SASL profile names:

- SASL/GSSAPI

- SASL/EXTERNAL

- SASL/CRAM-MD5

- SASL/ANONYMOUS

- SASL/OTP

- SASL/PLAIN

- SASL/DIGEST-MD5

If a peer receives a message from another peer that does not respect the desired protocol version, the recommended behavior is to send a CloseMessage indicating the detected violation and to close the connection immediately afterwards.

Protocol Versioning

The JMX Remote specification identifies version 1.0 of the JMXMP protocol, which is currently the only version. Any given future version of the JMX Remote specification may or may not include an updated version of the protocol. Each protocol version will have a version number that is the same as the version of the JMX Remote specification that first defines it. For example, if version 1.1 of the JMX Remote specification does not change the protocol but version 1.2 does, then the next JMXMP protocol version number will be 1.2.

The first message sent over a newly opened connection is a handshake begin message from the server to the client. This message includes the latest JMXMP version that the server understands. If the client also understands that version, then the subsequent communication will take place using that version. If the client only understands an earlier version, then it will send a JMXMPMessage requesting that the earlier version be used. If the server understands this earlier version, then it will reply with the same JMXMPMessage, and the subsequent communication will take place using that version. Otherwise, the server will send a HandshakeErrorMessage and the communication will be aborted.

In other words, suppose the server version is S and the client version is C. Then the version V to be used for communication is determined as follows:

- Server to client: "Version S."

- If client understands S, V = S.

- Otherwise:

  - Client to server: "Version C."

  - If server understands C:

    - Server to client: "Version C."

    - V = C.

  - If server does not understand C:

    - Server to client: "Handshake error."

  - Connection aborted.

A consequence of this negotiation is that every version of the protocol must understand every other version's HandshakeBeginMessage and JMXMPMessage. This will be true provided that Java serial compatibility is respected.

Properties Controlling Client and Server

When creating a JMXConnector or a JMXConnectorServer, an environment map can be supplied. One of the functions of this environment is to provide configuration parameters for the underlying profiles. The following describes these parameters for the SASL profile:

- jmx.remote.sasl.authorization.id: A string that is the connector client's identity for authorization when it is different from the authentication identity. If this property is unspecified, the provider derives an authorization identity from the authentication identity.

- jmx.remote.sasl.callback.handler: An object of type javax.security.auth.callback.CallbackHandler that is the callback handler to be invoked by the SASL mechanism to retrieve user information. If this property is unspecified, no callback handler will be used.

Using Fine-Grained Security with Connector Servers

A fine-grained level of security can be implemented in your connectors by managing user access through JAAS and Java 2 platform Standard Edition (J2SE) security architecture. JAAS and J2SE security is based on the use of security managers and policy files to allocate different levels of access to different users. Consequently, you can decide more precisely which users are allowed to perform which operations.

The implementation for a fine-grained server is very similar to the server that uses simple security. The only difference is that there is not an access.properties file to map into the environment map. Otherwise, the two servers are identical.

You can use a policy template to create a java.policy file that grants the following permissions:

- All permissions to the server codebase, so that the connector server can create the connectors, and then perform the operations requested by remote user calls

- An MBeanTrustPermission to the MBeans codebase, allowing trusted MBeans to register in the MBean server

- Permission to perform the various MBean and MBean server operations for the user represented by a JMXPrincipal-named user name

The code that follows shows a java.policy.template file that can be used to create a java.policy file for a fine-grained secure RMI connector:

```
grant codeBase
    "file:@JMX_REMOTE_HOME@/lib/jmxremote.jar" {
    permission java.security.AllPermission;
};

grant codeBase "file:@JMX_HOME@/lib/jmxri.jar" {
    permission java.security.AllPermission;
};

grant codeBase "file:server" {
    permission java.security.AllPermission;
};
```

```
grant codeBase "file:mbeans" {
    permission javax.management.MBeanTrustPermission "register";
};

grant principal javax.management.remote.JMXPrincipal "username" {
    permission javax.management.MBeanPermission "*", "getDomains";
    permission javax.management.MBeanPermission "SimpleStandard#-[-]",
        "instantiate";
    permission javax.management.MBeanPermission "SimpleStandard#-
        [MBeans:type=SimpleStandard]", "registerMBean";
    permission javax.management.MBeanPermission
        "SimpleStandard#State[MBeans:type=SimpleStandard]", "getAttribute";
    permission javax.management.MBeanPermission
        "SimpleStandard#State[MBeans:type=SimpleStandard]", "setAttribute";
    permission javax.management.MBeanPermission "SimpleStandard#-
        [MBeans:type=SimpleStandard]", "addNotificationListener";
    permission javax.management.MBeanPermission
        "SimpleStandard#reset[MBeans:type=SimpleStandard]", "invoke";
    permission javax.management.MBeanPermission "SimpleStandard#-
        [MBeans:type=SimpleStandard]", "removeNotificationListener";
    permission javax.management.MBeanPermission
        "SimpleStandard#-[MBeans:type=SimpleStandard]", "unregisterMBean";
    permission javax.management.MBeanPermission
        "javax.management.MBeanServerDelegate#-
        [JMImplementation:type=MBeanServerDelegate]",
        "addNotificationListener";
    permission javax.management.MBeanPermission
        "javax.management.MBeanServerDelegate#-
        [JMImplementation:type=MBeanServerDelegate]",
        "removeNotificationListener";
};
```

The following example demonstrates a secure RMI connector using a security manager and a policy file. This example implements SSL socket factories for encryption; the password authenticator for user authentication; and JAAS and J2SE security, as well as security managers and policy files, for user access-level authorization.

```
import java.io.File;
import java.util.HashMap;
import javax.management.MBeanServer;
import javax.management.MBeanServerFactory;
import javax.management.remote.JMXConnectorServer;
```

```
import javax.management.remote.JMXConnectorServerFactory;
import javax.management.remote.JMXServiceURL;
import javax.management.remote.rmi.RMIConnectorServer;

public class Server
{
    public static void main(String[] args)
    {
        try
        {
            // Instantiate the MBean server.
            //
            MBeanServer mbs = MBeanServerFactory.createMBeanServer();

            HashMap env = new HashMap();

            // Provide SSL-based RMI socket factories.
            //
            RMISSLClientSocketFactory csf = new RMISSLClientSocketFactory();
            RMISSLServerSocketFactory ssf = new RMISSLServerSocketFactory();
            env.put(RMIConnectorServer.RMI_CLIENT_SOCKET_FACTORY_ATTRIBUTE,
                        csf);
            env.put(RMIConnectorServer.RMI_SERVER_SOCKET_FACTORY_ATTRIBUTE,
                        ssf);
```

You must provide a password file to be used by the connector server to perform user authentication. The password file is a property-based text file specifying user name/password pairs.

```
            env.put("jmx.remote.x.password.file",
                        "config" + File.separator + "password.properties");

            // Create an RMI connector server.
            //
            JMXServiceURL url =
                new JMXServiceURL(
                    "service:jmx:rmi:///jndi/rmi://myhost:9999/server");
            JMXConnectorServer cs =
                JMXConnectorServerFactory.newJMXConnectorServer(url, env, mbs);

            // Start the RMI connector server.
            //
```

```
                cs.start();
                System.out.println("\nConnector server successfully started...");
            }
        catch (Exception e)
        {
            e.printStackTrace();
        }
    }
}
```

The following illustrates the RMISSLServerSocketFactory to be used by your connector server:

```java
import java.io.File;
import java.io.FileInputStream;
import java.io.IOException;
import java.net.ServerSocket;
import java.rmi.server.RMIServerSocketFactory;
import java.security.KeyStore;
import javax.net.ssl.KeyManagerFactory;
import javax.net.ssl.SSLContext;
import javax.net.ssl.SSLServerSocket;
import javax.net.ssl.SSLServerSocketFactory;

public class RMISSLServerSocketFactory
    implements RMIServerSocketFactory
{
    private SSLServerSocketFactory ssf = null;

    public ServerSocket createServerSocket(int port)
        throws IOException
    {
        if (ssf == null)
        {
            try
            {
                String keystore =
                    "config" + File.separator + "keystore";
                char keystorepass[] = "password".toCharArray();
                char keypassword[] = "password".toCharArray();
                KeyStore ks = KeyStore.getInstance("JKS");
                ks.load(new FileInputStream(keystore), keystorepass);
                KeyManagerFactory kmf =
                    KeyManagerFactory.getInstance("SunX509");
```

```
            kmf.init(ks, keypassword);
            SSLContext ctx = SSLContext.getInstance("TLSv1");
            ctx.init(kmf.getKeyManagers(), null, null);
            ssf = ctx.getServerSocketFactory();
        }
        catch (IOException e)
        {
            throw e;
        }
        catch (Exception e)
        {
            throw (IOException) new IOException().initCause(e);
        }
    }
    return (SSLServerSocket) ssf.createServerSocket(port);
    }
}
```

Finally, you implement the RMISSLClientSocketFactory to be used by your connector server:

```
import java.io.File;
import java.io.FileInputStream;
import java.io.IOException;
import java.io.Serializable;
import java.net.Socket;
import java.rmi.server.RMIClientSocketFactory;
import java.security.KeyStore;
import javax.net.ssl.SSLContext;
import javax.net.ssl.SSLSocket;
import javax.net.ssl.SSLSocketFactory;
import javax.net.ssl.TrustManagerFactory;

public class RMISSLClientSocketFactory
    implements RMIClientSocketFactory, Serializable
{
    private transient SSLSocketFactory csf = null;

    public Socket createSocket(String host, int port)
        throws IOException
    {
        if (csf == null)
        {
```

```
        try
        {
            String truststore = "config" + File.separator + "truststore";
            char truststorepass[] = "trustword".toCharArray();
            KeyStore ks = KeyStore.getInstance("JKS");
            ks.load(new FileInputStream(truststore), truststorepass);
            TrustManagerFactory tmf =
                TrustManagerFactory.getInstance("SunX509");
            tmf.init(ks);
            SSLContext ctx = SSLContext.getInstance("TLSv1");
            ctx.init(null, tmf.getTrustManagers(), null);
            csf = ctx.getSocketFactory();
        }
        catch (IOException e)
        {
            throw e;
        }
        catch (Exception e)
        {
            throw (IOException) new IOException().initCause(e);
        }
    }
    return (SSLSocket) csf.createSocket(host, port);
    }
}
```

Summary

One of the principal goals of the distributed services level is security. JMX builds on the Java standards for security including JSSE, SASL, and JAAS so that connections between clients and servers can be private and authenticated and so that servers can control what operations different clients can perform.

The JMX Remote security includes connector security based on password authentication and file access control, connector security that uses a subject delegation model, and fine-grained connector security.

The simplest type of security is based upon encryption, user name, and password authentication, and file access control. A subject-delegation model performs operations on a given authenticated connection on behalf of several different identities. Fine-grained security involves more sophisticated security mechanisms, in which permission to perform individual operations is controlled.

Connector servers typically have some way of authenticating remote clients. For the RMI connector, this is done by supplying an object that implements the

JMXAuthenticator interface when the connector server is created. For the JMXMP connector, this is done using SASL.

The JMXAuthenticator interface defines how remote credentials are converted into a JAAS Subject. This interface is used by the RMIConnectorServer, and can be used by other connector servers.

The RMI connector provides a simple mechanism for securing and authenticating the connection between a client and a server that provides a basic level of security for environments using the RMI connector. More advanced security requirements are better addressed by the JMXMP connector.

The JMX Remote API includes a generic connector as an optional part of the API. This connector is designed to be configurable by plugging in modules to define the following: the transport protocol used to send requests from the client to the server and to send responses and notifications from the server to the clients, and the object wrapping for objects sent from the client to the server whose class loader may depend on the target MBean.

Handshake-message exchanges are started by the server end of the connection as soon as the connect method on the JMXConnector class is called by the client and the connection between the client and the server is established.

The server end of the connection sends to the client a HandshakeBeginMessage with the server's supported profiles. These profiles are retrieved from the environment map through the jmx.remote.profiles property. The client then starts the profile message exchanges for the profiles chosen from the server's supported profiles.

The JMXMP profile is used to negotiate the version of JMXMP to use. This profile is always implicitly enabled, but is only negotiated if the client and server differ in their default versions.

The JMXMP connector provides support for authentication and authorization through the TLS and SASL profiles. The JMX Remote API does not mandate the implementation and support of any specific SASL mechanism. It simply relies on third-party implementations that can be plugged in using the standard SASL interface (JSR28).

The TLS profile allows the client and server ends of a JMX connection to negotiate a TLS encryption layer. Certificate-based authentication and mutual client/server authentication are optional features configurable through properties in the environment map.

The SASL profile mechanism uses the JAAS framework to construct a JMXPrincipal based on this authorization identity, and stores this JMXPrincipal in a Subject. Then, when the JMXMPConnectorServer performs any of the subsequent MBean server operations, it must do so using the Subject.doAsPrivileged(subject, action, null) call with the given subject for the required action.

The SASLMessage class implements the ProfileMessage interface and represents a challenge or response exchanged between client and server during SASL authentication. This message encapsulates either a challenge or a response generated by the SASL mechanism during the SASL authentication exchanges taking place between the client and the server.

A fine-grained level of security can be implemented in your connectors by managing user access through JAAS and J2SE Security Architecture. JAAS and J2SE security is based on the use of security managers and policy files to allocate different levels of access to different users. Consequently, you can decide more precisely which users are allowed to perform which operations.

CHAPTER 11

JMX in the Industry

THE JAVA MANAGEMENT EXTENSIONS (JMX) standard is gaining popularity within the Java 2 Enterprise Edition (J2EE) community for the management of applications, application servers, and service-oriented infrastructure software. JMX makes it possible to manage and monitor applications and systems using many of the most popular management systems and consoles.

Many of today's popular J2EE application servers include JMX as integral pieces of their foundational makeup. JMX is being used in application server software to manage configuration information, monitor state changes, organize Web applications and services, and to install individual J2EE services.

This chapter discusses some of the companies that have adopted JMX and some of the products in which JMX is used.

AdventNet

AdventNet has made a major commitment to using JMX throughout their product offerings, with particularly interesting work with subagents and cascading.

Agent Toolkit Java Edition

The AdventNet Agent Toolkit Java Edition (http://www.adventnet.com/products/javaagent/index.html) is a prototyping and development tool used to rapidly build multiprotocol, Java-based agents for SNMP and TL1 agents. The protocols supported include SNMP, RMI, HTTP, CORBA, and TL1.

The multiprotocol agents that are constructed with the AdventNet Agent Toolkit use the AdventNet Multi-Protocol Agent framework to support the standard JMX specification to allow simultaneous management access through multiple protocols.

A high-level view of the AdventNet Multi-Protocol Agent framework is illustrated in Figure 11-1.

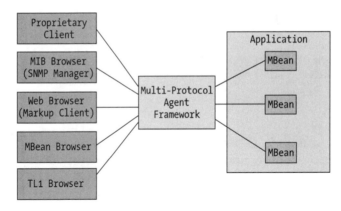

Figure 11-1. AdventNet Multi-Protocol Agent framework

The AdventNet Agent Toolkit provides a technology for constructing agents in a master agent/subagent hierarchy. This technology is called the *Cascader Service*.

Cascader Service

The AdventNet Cascader Service allows you to access the MBeans of a master agent or subagent directly through the MBean server of the master agent. The Cascader Service can use the RMI, CORBA, or HTTP protocols to connect with the master agent or subagent. Figure 11-2 illustrates the relationships involved with the Cascader Service.

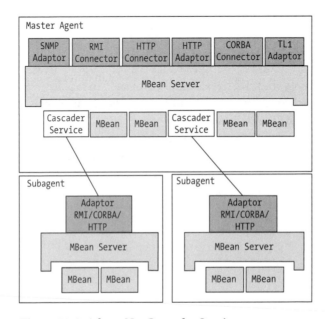

Figure 11-2. AdventNet Cascader Service

ManageEngine JMX Studio

ManageEngine JMX Studio (http://www.adventnet.com/products/manageengine/index.html) from AdventNet is a graphical development environment that facilitates instrumentation of applications without the need to write any code. It generates MBeans for existing applications and provides adaptors that use popular protocols such as SNMP, HTTP, RMI, CORBA, SOAP, and others for existing MBeans built using many varied JMX implementations.

ManageEngine exposes a master agent/subagent architecture and generates MBeans for various Java components and data sources such as plain old Java objects (POJOs), servlets, EJBs, log files, databases, etc.

BEA Systems

From WebLogic Server 6.0 and up, BEA has integrated JMX into the management architecture of its WebLogic server offerings. BEA's support for JMX includes an implementation of the JMX specification as well as using JMX as the foundation for all of BEA's crucial administration and management functionality.

WebLogic Server

BEA has made a very strong statement for JMX by making all WebLogic Server (http://www.bea.com/framework.jsp?CNT=index.htm&FP=/content/products/server) resources manageable through JMX-based services. A WebLogic *administration server* hosts *Configuration MBeans* for all managed resources of all server instances in a particular domain.

Replicas of the Configuration MBeans for each managed server's managed resources are created to enhance performance. WebLogic Server subsystems and applications that interact with MBeans use the replicas on a local server instead of making remote calls to the administration server.

Figure 11-3 illustrates the configuration interactions between an administration server and corresponding managed servers.

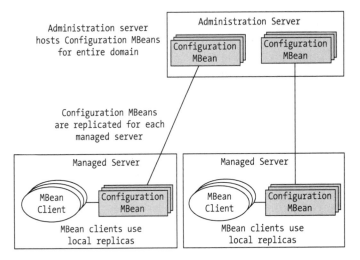

Figure 11-3. WebLogic configuration interactions

WebLogic Server–managed resources provide runtime information and performance metrics through one or more *Runtime MBeans*. Runtime MBeans are not replicated like Configuration MBeans, i.e., they exist only on the same server instance as the managed resources they represent.

Figure 11-4 illustrates the interactions between Runtime MBeans and Configuration MBeans for a given domain.

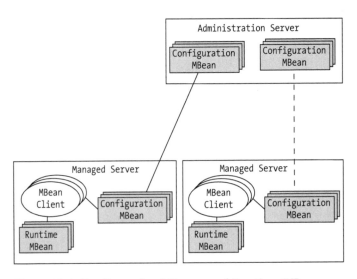

Figure 11-4. Configuration MBeans and Runtime MBeans

All WebLogic Server MBeans implement the `javax.management.NotificationBroadcaster` interface, enabling them to report changes in configuration and runtime information. WebLogic Server also includes Monitor MBeans that can be used to monitor runtime and configuration information.

IBM

IBM has adopted JMX in many of its products, including Tivoli, Web Services Toolkit, WebSphere Application Server, WebSphere Business Components, WebSphere Business Integrator, and WebSphere Voice Server. IBM employees have served as active, contributing members of the JMX expert groups.

WebSphere Application Server

The administration features of Version 5.0 of WebSphere Application Server (http://www.ibm.com/websphere) is based on JMX, including a JMX agent and MBeans representing all of the system components. To support remote access to a server's resources, WebSphere's JMX agent supports connectors for RMI/IIOP and SOAP/HTTP(S). Every process in version 5.0 of WebSphere contains an embedded JMX agent around which additional administrative services are built.

Each managed component of the WebSphere runtime is exposed as a JMX MBean, which is registered with the MBean server and accessed remotely using JMX connectors. Figure 11-5 shows the details of the WebSphere JMX-component interactions.

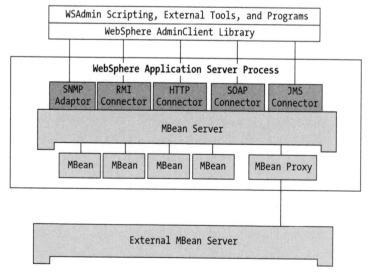

Figure 11-5. WebSphere JMX components

Administrative programs in versions 5.0 and up of WebSphere can register as listeners for distributed event notification from any of the MBeans running in the network. They can also register for operational requests, such as stopping a server, and configuration requests, such as changing an attribute.

Versions 5.0 and up of WebSphere provide a Java/JMX API for developing administrative programs. This API (residing in the `com.ibm.websphere.management` package) is the same API in which all of the administrative tools supplied with the product are written. This API allows you to write your own custom administration client to perform specific administration functions, and it allows you to extend the basic Application Server administration system with your own custom MBeans that expose a management interface meeting your requirements.

Emerging Technologies Toolkit

IBM includes Web services management capabilities in its Emerging Technologies Toolkit (ETTK) (`http://www.alphaworks.ibm.com/tech/ettk`) by providing a JMX-based management interface. An MBean server that tracks Web services statistics—such as the number of times a Web service is invoked, started, stopped, etc.—is embedded globally into the application server's JVM. This allows Web services statistics to be tracked across all installed Web applications.

JMX Bridge

JMX Bridge (`http://dwdemos.dfw.ibm.com/wstk/common/wstkdoc/ettk/wstk/jmxbridge/readme.html`) functions as a bridge between the resources managed by JMX and Web services. JMX Bridge is given information that identifies or describes the MBean instance that represents a specific managed resource. The bridge generates WSDL describing the Web service, a Java class that acts as the Web service implementation, and an Axis deployment descriptor.

The resulting Java class must then be compiled, made available to an application server, and deployed to Axis as a Web service. A client must be written to interact with the Web service. The generated WSDL can be used to make dynamic calls, validate static calls, or generate a client proxy class.

IONA Technologies

IONA sells products that are used to create corporate IT infrastructure for integrating business applications and middleware systems. Many of IONA's products use JMX to provide management functionality.

Orbix E2A Application Server Platform

The Orbix E2A Application Server Platform (http://www.iona.com/products/appserv-enterprise.htm) is a development and deployment environment providing support for enterprise applications using three technologies: CORBA, J2EE, and Web services.

The Management Service of the Orbix E2A Application Server Platform is built on the JMX specification. Using JMX, the Management Service can instrument J2EE components and both Java and C++ CORBA objects.

IONA has instrumented every aspect of their Application Server Platform so that applications built with it and deployed in it can be managed consistently using IONA Administrator.

IONA Administrator

IONA Administrator (http://www.iona.com/support/docs/e2a/asp/5.0/j2ee/DevelopGuide/html/iPA_prog_intro2.html) is a set of tools that enable administrators to configure, monitor, and control distributed applications at runtime. IONA Administrator manages all products in the IONA Suite and any applications developed using those products.

The IONA Administrator management service is the central point of contact for management information in a given domain. A domain is an abstract group of managed server processes in a physical location. The management service can be accessed by both the IONA Administrator Console and by the IONA Administrator Web Console.

Figure 11-6 shows JMX, Orbix E2A, and how they interact to facilitate a comprehensive management system.

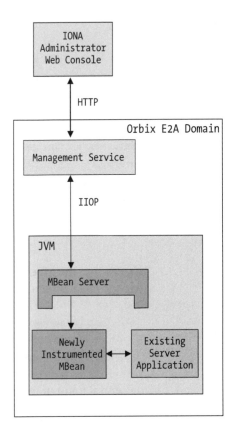

Figure 11-6. Orbix component interactions

XMLBus

XMLBus (http://www.xmlbus.com/) is integrated with all the components of the
Orbix E2A Application Server Platform to provide a platform for Web services
development and deployment. XMLBus includes support for XML, SOAP, WSDL,
UDDI, and HTTP(S). It provides a nonprogrammatic, graphical environment for
defining, assembling, and integrating Web services from existing resources (Java,
J2EE, and CORBA). It includes graphical tools that let you create new Web services, as well as business process models to manage the coordination of Web
services.

The XMLBus Container exposes a JMX-based management service and uses
JMX instrumentation to providing logging facilities and life-cycle management
of a deployed Web service.

JBoss

The JBossMX (http://sourceforge.net/projects/jboss/) project is a very good example of the possibilities of JMX beyond the realm of resource management. JBossMX from JBoss is an incarnation of JMX used to virtually power an application server implementation. JBossMX is called "the core of the JBoss microkernel architecture."

JMX in JBoss is used not only for resource management, but also to provide an unprecedented level of modularity in a distributed application-deployment platform. The JBoss application server sits upon the JMX microkernel, which provides resource management; foundation services such as class-loading, customization, life-cycle management; and service deployment. All JBoss modules are instrumented as MBeans, and therefore can use MBean server as the nucleus for intermodule communication, deployment, etc.

Since JBoss is composed of interrelated modules managed by the MBean server, it enjoys a fine-grained scope of module management, and therefore achieves a high-degree of stability.

The JBoss JMX microkernel allows remote class loading from a central server, making installation and customization of the application server very simple.

JBossMX supports the features of the standard JMX specification, including standard, dynamic, and model MBeans, and all mandatory agent services, including the Timer Service, the MLet Service, etc. In addition to the standard features, JBoss offers extended services such as XML-defined MBeans called *XMBeans,* class loader repositories, interceptor-based invocation, and a pluggable MBean registry.

JBoss allows setting of initial MBean attributes from configuration files, and to make certain that attributes are set and used correctly, JBoss enforces a life-cycle on the MBeans. This life-cycle is shown in Figure 11-7.

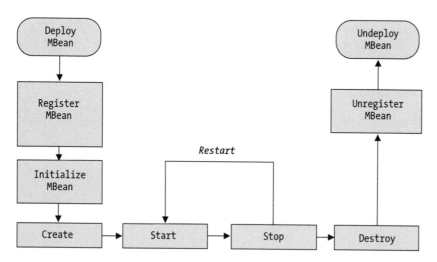

Figure 11-7. The JBoss MBean life-cycle

The life-cycle steps defined in Figure 11-7 are quite self-explanatory, with the exception of the iteration over the start and stop methods. JBoss does not make MBean-attribute changes active until the MBean is restarted. This allows multiple attribute values to be changed and made active at the same time, therefore avoiding any synchronization rules.

JBoss refers to core features such as JNDI, scheduler, mail service, invokers, JBossWeb, JBossMQ, and others, as *services,* and these services are instrumented as MBeans. The deployment of a service MBean in JBoss can be accomplished in one of two ways: by placing a deployment-descriptor file, ending with -service.xml, in the deploy directory or by placing a .sar file containing the deployment-descriptor file in its META-INF directory.

The JBoss service deployment framework allows you to specify dependencies between MBeans, so that actions such as starting an MBean or setting an attribute only occur when a corresponding event takes place on another MBean. An example of this is starting an MBean only when another MBean is started.

JMX4Ant

JMX4Ant (http://jmx4ant.sourceforge.net/) provides build and deploy tasks for J2EE resource creation and management from Ant.

The following JMX-enabled tasks are provided by JMX4Ant:

- configureMBean: Gets or sets attributes on an MBean

- copyMBean: Copies an existing MBean to a new name

- invokeMBean: Makes a method call on an MBean

- removeMBean: Destroys and unregisters an MBean

- showMBean: Writes information about an MBean to a log

- jndiLookup: Performs a JNDI lookup for a specific JNDI object

In addition to the preceding tasks, JMX4Ant provides the following Ant types that allow references to specific MBeans to be reused:

- mbean: Allows references to individual MBeans to be reused across JMX4Ant tasks

- context: Allows references to a JNDI server to be reused

JMX4Ant provides support for many Java types that are used in MBean methods and properties for WebLogic and JBoss. These types are as follows:

- Java primitives `boolean`, `byte`, `char`, `double`, `float`, `int`, `long`, and `short`

- `java.lang.String`, `java.util.Properties` and `java.util.Set`

- Any class with a static `valueOf()` method

- Any class exposing a constructor with a single argument of type `java.lang.String`

- Any descendents of `weblogic.management.WebLogicMBean`

- Arrays of any of the preceding types

JMX4Ant allows additional types to be added by providing an implementation of the `ValueConverter` interface and registering the implementation by calling the `registerValueConverter` method of `ValueFactory`.

Tomcat

Tomcat (`http://jakarta.apache.org/tomcat/index.html`) uses MBeans as the technology for implementing manageability. JMX-based administration features were added as of version 4.1.x of Tomcat, and version 5.0.x added complete server monitoring using JMX, embedding of Tomcat using JMX, and a JMX-enabled, Web-based manager application. MBean support in Tomcat is enabled by default in Tomcat's server.xml configuration file.

MBeans registered in Tomcat are categorized by *group name* and *MBean name*. MBean names are defined in a resource file named mbeans-descriptors.xml and are used within the Tomcat manager web application.

The JMX Proxy Servlet

Tomcat provides a lightweight proxy servlet, known as the *JMX Proxy Servlet*, to get and set the Tomcat internals and any class that has been exposed via an MBean. The JMX Proxy Servlet is used to get information and set information through the `Query` command and the `Set` command.

The Query Command

The `Query` command enables a URL query string with JMX query capabilities using the following syntax:

```
http://mytomcatserver/manager/jmxproxy/?qry=<QUERY>
```

where <QUERY> is the JMX query you wish to perform.

The Set Command

The Set command allows you to modify Tomcat's internals. The general form of the Set command is

```
http://mytomcatserver/manager/jmxproxy/?set=<BEANNAME>&att=<ATTRIBUTENAME>&
val=<NEWVALUE>
```

To use the Set command, simply replace <BEANNAME>, <ATTRIBUTENAME>, and <NEWVALUE> with your desired values. Remember to encode any reserved characters that may exist in values passed to the Query or Set command. A detailed explanation of URL encoding can be found at http://www.cis.ohio-state.edu/cgi-bin/rfc/rfc2396.html.

XMOJO

The XMOJO project is a free open source implementation of the JMX specification that is spawned from AdventNet's JMX implementation. XMOJO provides a complete implementation of the standard JMX specification, as well as an MBean browser and adaptors for HTML and RMI.

XMOJO works with many different application and integration platforms, including WebLogic, WebSphere, JBoss, and Oracle9iAS. XMOJO works with enterprise management systems such as CA, Tivoli, BMC, HP, etc.

MX4J

MX4J is an open source implementation of the JMX TM technology. MX4J implements both the standard JMX specification and the JMX Remoting specification. MX4J's implementation of the JMX specification runs in J2SE version 1.3 or higher and provides some nonstandard extensions.

The MX4J implementation also provides some useful services and tools, and several examples demonstrating the use of JMX in applications. Some of the tools, extensions, and utilities are

- An HTTP adaptor

- A ConfigurationLoader to read MBean configuration from XML

- An AbstractDynamicMBean to ease DynamicMBean development

- Utility MBeans for

  - RMIRegistry

  - TNameServ

  - Statistics

  - E-mail

  - Remote MBean proxying

- Automatic generation of management interfaces for standard MBeans via XDoclet (http://xdoclet.sourceforge.net/)

MX4J provides an MBean that acts as a remote proxy, through which you can register with a local MBean server to act as a proxy for a remote MBean hosted in a remote MBean server.

The mx4j.remote.RemoteMBeanProxy MBean is a transparent proxy for a remote MBean. Invoking a method on the proxy MBean results in the method being invoked on the remote MBean. Also, registering a local NotificationListener on the MBean proxy results in registration on the remote MBean, and therefore the local listener will receive notifications emitted by the remote MBean.

MC4J Management Console

The MC4J project (http://mc4j.sourceforge.net/) is a Swing/OpenIDE application facilitating remote administration of JMX-enabled servers and applications using JMX. MC4J supports most major application servers and platforms. MC4J provides advanced features such as live attribute graphing and remote connections to JMX servers.

The primary features of MC4J are

- A Tree view of MBeans and their attributes, operations, and notifications

- The ability to connect to multiple servers

- Descriptor information for MBeans, attributes, and operations

- Live graphs of numeric MBean attributes

- The ability to execute operations on MBeans

- The ability to set attribute values of many common types

- The ability to listen to MBean notifications

- Definitions of a layout and interface, for specific use cases within a JMX-enabled server, using Dashboards

- The ability to search and filter MBeans for a JMX-enabled server using queries

MC4J Layout

The default layout for MC4J exposes a four-section window that provides standard locations for information and functionality. Most of these panels can be rearranged to suit a desired style. Figure 11-8 illustrates the default sections for MC4J.

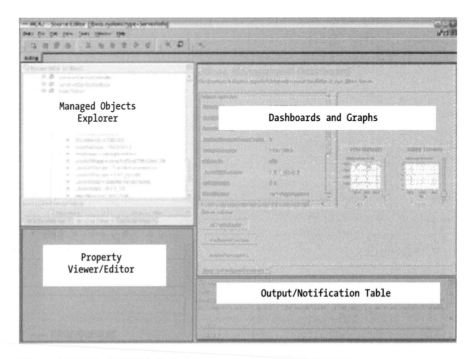

Figure 11-8. The MC4J default layout

The top-left section is the Explorer section and it provides the primary interface for the information and servers that MC4J exposes. This area includes one tab for each of the supported server types. Each tab holds a tree structure of the servers that are configured for that type. This section is where new connections to servers are configured and where those connections are managed.

The lower-left panel is the property display section. This section contains a list of properties for a selected node within the Explorer section. Supported attribute types can be directly edited when their managed objects are selected.

The top-right section can contain richer interfaces, called *Dashboards*, for selected managed objects. Dashboards are custom interfaces for specific functionality, defined in XML.

The lower-right section is a set of tabs for informational display. The tabs contain an output window with messages about the operation of MC4J, and a table of notification information from JMX notifications.

MC4J and JBoss

MC4J uses RMI to connect to JBoss Application Servers and provide access to JMX MBeans running within a JBoss server.

MC4J and WebLogic

MC4J uses RMI and the T3 protocol to connect to WebLogic Application Servers and to provide access to JMX MBeans running within that server.

MC4J and Tomcat

MC4J also supports connections to Tomcat 4.1 servers.

Summary

The JMX standard is gaining popularity within the J2EE community for the management of applications, application servers, and service-oriented infrastructure software. JMX is being used as the foundation service to manage and monitor applications and systems employing many of the most popular management systems and consoles.

Many of today's popular J2EE application servers include JMX as integral pieces of their core services. JMX is being used in application server software to manage configuration information, monitor state changes, organize Web applications and services, and install individual J2EE services.

Companies like AdventNet, BEA Systems, IONA, and JBoss have incorporated JMX into their products as critical components to their core services. These companies have implemented entire toolkits, platforms, and product offerings around the capabilities that JMX offers.

Open source technologies such as JMX4Ant, Tomcat, XMOJO, and MC4J have realized the power and flexibility that JMX offers, and therefore have built their offerings around the JMX standard.

CHAPTER 12

A Summary of JMX

THE ENTERPRISE SYSTEMS and applications of today exist in environments composed of an ever-changing list of resources such as applications, devices, services, and processing power. These dynamic resources can appear, change, and disappear arbitrarily at runtime, making static management technologies powerless in their attempts to maintain administrative control.

JMX (http://java.sun.com/jmx) solves dynamic system challenges for systems of all sizes by presenting a standardized and modular management framework and programming interface that can be used to instrument resources and build dynamic management tools through the Java programming language.

Instrumentation, Agents, and Distributed Services

JMX defines a three-level technological model targeting different levels of developer communities. This allows teams of developers to target the area of management that best suits their experience level and business needs.

The JMX *instrumentation* level allows developers to augment Java resources with management semantics from any level of the development cycle. Once instrumented, these resources are referred to as MBeans. MBeans provide the foundation for a comprehensive and powerful management platform. This design, along with the component-oriented nature of JMX, ensures that system and application services are not only manageable, but also very modular in nature.

The JMX specification defines the *agent* level, which targets the management solutions development community by providing a comprehensive and flexible framework for building management agents.

Agents expose instrumented resources in a manner that allows management applications to discover them and invoke operations on them in a standard fashion. An agent can reside in a local JVM or in a remote JVM. This makes it possible to build management applications that interact with agents and resources in a generic way, thus allowing management applications the ability to administrate any system that adheres to this framework. JMX clients and managers interact with JMX agents. A single JVM can contain many JMX agents and/or JMX clients.

In addition to facilitating access to instrumented resources, an agent broadcasts notifications to interested notification receivers that have previously registered with it. An agent exposes an *MBean server,* at least one protocol *adaptor* or *connector,* and several mandatory services, known as *agent services.* The mandatory agent services are registered as MBeans and include a monitoring service, a timer service, a relationship service, and a dynamic class-loading service.

The JMX *distributed services* level facilitates management solutions that are interoperable, flexible, secure, and portable. Management solutions constructed within the technological sphere of the JMX distributed services level can benefit from its communication standards, protocol flexibility and transparency, location transparency, and standard security mechanisms.

Figure 12-1 illustrates the three-level model of JMX.

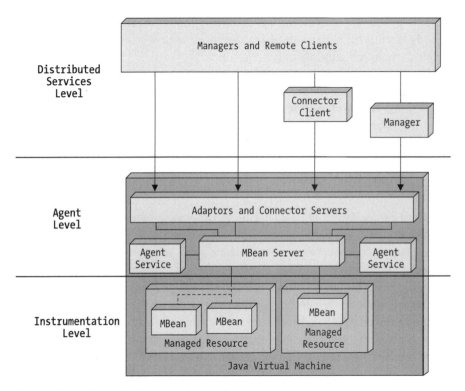

Figure 12-1. The JMX three-level model

All levels of JMX are inherently interested in managed resources, which are represented as MBeans. MBeans are registered and maintained by MBean servers.

MBean Servers

The MBean server is the principal component of the JMX agent layer and acts as a registry and repository for all of an agent's MBeans. An MBean server provides an abstraction layer between managed resources and management applications, and acts as a proxy object between MBeans and the external environment. Within the MBean server environment, events/notifications are passed to interested listeners by the MBean server.

An MBean server is created by invoking one of the static `createMBeanServer` methods or `newMBeanServer` methods on the `javax.management.MBeanServerFactory` class.

An MBean server's management interface is described and presented by an object known as an `MBeanServerDelegate`. Each MBean server must define and reserve a domain called `JMImplementation` in which to register one MBean of type `javax.management.MBeanServerDelegate`. The `MBeanServerDelegate` MBean is automatically created and registered with an MBean server when the MBean server is started.

The `javax.management.MBeanServer` interface specifies methods for creating and registering new MBeans and a method for registering and unregistering existing MBeans. When an object is registered as an MBean with an MBean server, all JMX requests to the MBean must go through the MBean server. Likewise, all operations that retrieve a reference to an MBean return only a proxy object or name representing the MBean. This ensures that a loose coupling exists between any application or service and the MBeans. This loose coupling allows modifications to be made on the resources that MBeans represent without altering the components and applications that access them.

Figure 12-2 illustrates the request/response interactions between an MBean server, MBeans, and interested clients.

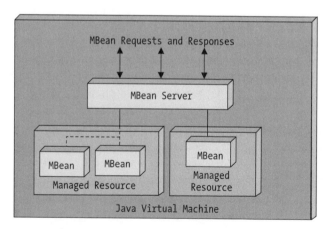

Figure 12-2. The MBean server interaction mechanism

An MBean server uses callback methods, defined in the `MBeanRegistration` interface, to allow an MBean a certain amount of control when it is registered or deregistered with the MBean server.

Interested components can register as a NotificationListener object with an MBean server in order to be notified when any MBean is registered or deregistered. All components registered as listeners will receive a notification event from the MBean server whenever an MBean is registered and an unregistration event when an MBean is deregistered.

MBean servers can be queried for the presence of one or more registered MBeans using the queryMBeans method or the queryNames method. MBeans can be searched for by object name, attribute values, or both.

Query methods provided by an MBean server take query expression objects as parameters. Query expression objects are used to construct query expressions. The query expression objects are then passed as parameters to the MBean server's query methods. The queryMBeans method retrieves a Set of ObjectInstance objects and the queryNames method retrieves a Set of ObjectName objects.

Designs of Distribution

A management system serves many purposes. These include discovering and disseminating information about specific resources, modifying information about specific resources, and returning the results of modifications to users and devices. Modifications to information can take the form of computations on data, data mediation, or conversion of data from one format to another.

A management system must also meet a number of different challenges such as controlling, monitoring, updating, and reporting the state of devices, applications, and services.

The evolution of large, complex software systems has presented systems managers with a high risk of errors and system failure. Also, the demand for new management system services and features has increased over the years almost in parallel with the increase in management system complexity. Increased bandwidth, transmission quality, and more sophisticated equipment have all helped to fuel this demand.

Management system providers have scrambled to retrofit and redesign their products with increased complexity to meet these demands. Also, many equipment manufacturers are installing their own management tools into their hardware to manage hardware configurations and faults. These sophisticated machines are being integrated with advanced software systems in order to provide a centralized and integrated solution for handling management needs.

The increased complexity of management systems, the increased risks of errors and failures, and the diversity of hardware and software solutions has led to the following approximate history of standards and initiatives.

System management standards and initiatives have evolved from modest beginnings into complex and advanced distributed management systems. This evolution of management standards and initiatives has included the OSI Management Framework, CMIS/CMIP, the Guidelines for Definition of Managed Objects, and others.

System management designs have evolved along with the changes in standards from simple hardware configurations into decentralized distributed system configurations. This evolution has included many different configuration designs such as terminal-configurable devices, in-band and out-of-band network management, and policy-based network management, to name a few.

System management frameworks tend to follow four different architectural patterns as follows:

- Specialized/Detached

- Centralized

- Hierarchical

- Distributed/Cooperative

Management design has brought about a management framework that defines a manager/agent concept. Managers and agents share status and control information about resources in order to build a unified management view of a network.

Within a manager/agent framework, managed resources are controlled and manipulated in order to maintain and modify management structure. The interaction between a manager and an agent usually involves the manager directing the agent to manipulate its managed resources using operations on attributes of the managed resource. An agent responds to a manager with managed resource attribute values and transmits notifications pertaining to events that affect managed resource attribute values.

A manager is an application or service that acts on behalf of a client in order to connect with and use an agent to perform operations on managed resources. A manager invokes operations on an agent with the aim of gathering information about the agent's managed resources or manipulating the resources. A manager receives information from an agent in response to operation invocations and as event notifications from an agent.

Figure 12-3 shows a typical manager/agent environment.

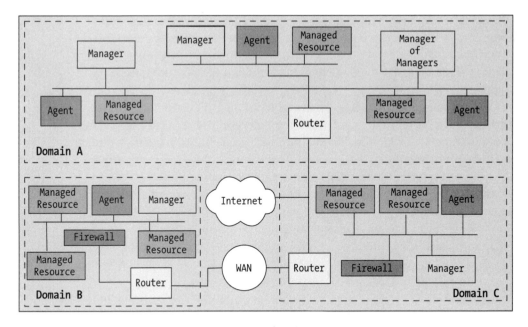

Figure 12-3. The MBean server interaction mechanism

A management agent is a software entity that accepts management requests from managers or management clients, services the requests, and then waits for the next request. Management agents are responsible for exposing to managers or management clients information associated with a managed resource exposed as attributes of the resource. An agent invokes operations that are received from a manager and returns responses to the manager. An agent can also notify a manager in the event that attributes of a managed resource change or an error or exception has occurred. An agent can service requests from multiple managers.

Applications or services that expose management interfaces are typically thought of as operating in an agent role, and applications or services that employ those interfaces are typically thought of as operating in a manager role.

Managers and agents can take on similar roles, depending on the circumstances. For example, agents and managers can interact in a peer-to-peer model; agents may operate in a hierarchical model; managers may interact with each other on a peer-to-peer basis. Even though many different types of manager-agent models are possible, the following four typically occur:

- Horizontal

- Centralized

- Hierarchical

- Distributed

Management systems maintaining a large network of agents can be optimized using a hierarchy of agents and subagents that are controlled by a master agent. Within this structure, the master agents act as liaisons between managers and subagents. Managers are shielded from the details of the agent hierarchy by the master agents. Managers connect and communicate only with the master agents.

For efficient administration of large distributed systems, such systems often need to be partitioned into multiple logical segments that are controlled by individual managers. These segments are often referred to as *manager domains*.

When a system becomes too complex, it is often necessary to introduce a manager that is responsible for coordinating and administrating the managers of each domain. This manager is referred to as *manager of managers,* or *MoM.* In a MoM-administered environment, domain managers rely on the MoM to communicate with other managers.

Managers that are developed using JMX and the Java programming language request information from other managers and agents. Agents in turn retrieve the information from MBeans.

In a distributed system, remote communication processes can be complex and fraught with fragile interactions. The remote access framework of the JMX distributed services level is designed to alleviate these challenges.

Distributed Services and Remote Access

Using the distributed services level of JMX allows client and server components to easily connect with each other to conduct management sessions and to promote distributed service use with existing or proprietary lookup services.

The distributed services level is embodied in the JMX Remoting specification and defines *Remoting agents* and *Remoting clients.*

A JMX Remoting agent is a logical server application composed of the following features:

- One MBean server

- One or more JMX Remoting connector servers that allow remote clients to access the MBeans contained in the MBean server

A JMX Remoting client is a logical client application that opens a client connection with a JMX Remoting agent. Remoting agents and Remoting clients interact with each other through the use of *connector servers* and *connector clients.*

Connectors

The JMX-Remoting specification defines a remote communication entity known as a *connector.* A connector is used by an agent to publicize its MBean server to remote managers and management clients, and it consists of a connector client and a connector server. Connectors make it possible for a JMX client to access and manage MBeans exposed through an MBean server running in a remote JVM.

A connector client is embodied in a `javax.management.remote.JMXConnector` and is essentially the remote publication of an agent's management interface. Since all connectors have the same Java technology–based interface, management applications use the connector most suited to their networking environment and even change connectors transparently as needs evolve.

A connector server is represented by an object of a subclass of `javax.management.remote.JMXConnectorServer`. To create a connector server, you must instantiate such a subclass. The connector server for the JMXMP connector is represented by the `JMXMPConnectorServer` class. The `javax.management.remote.generic.GenericConnectorServer` class can be used to create nonstandard connectors. To be useful, a connector server must be attached to an MBean server, and it must be active.

A connector client is responsible for finding a connector server and establishing a connection with it. A connector client and a connector server have a one-to-one physical relationship; however, more than one logical connection may exist between a connector client and a connector server. A client application or manager also may contain many connector clients connected to different connector servers.

A connector server or a connector client may terminate a connection at any time. If the client terminates the connection, the server will clean up any state relative to that client, such as listener proxies. If client operations are in progress when the client terminates the connection, then the threads that invoked them will receive a `java.io.IOException`.

The RMI connector is the only connector that must be present in all implementations of the JMX Remoting specification. It uses the RMI infrastructure to communicate between client and server.

The JMX Remoting API includes a generic connector as an optional part of the API. This connector is designed to be configurable by plugging in modules to define the transport protocol used to send requests from the client to the server and to send responses and notifications from the server to the clients. It is also designed to allow modules to be plugged in to define the object wrapping for objects sent from the client to the server whose class loader may depend on the target MBean.

Connector servers are exposed to clients through connector server addresses.

Connector Server Addresses

Most connector servers expose an address that clients can use to establish connections to it. Some connectors may provide alternative ways to establish connections, such as through connection stubs.

The JMX Remoting specification defines a `javax.management.remote.JMXServiceURL` class that represents the address of a JMX connector server and makes it possible for a JMX client to obtain a JMX connector connected to that server.

If a connector server has an address, this address is typically described by the `JMXServiceURL` class. A user-defined connector may choose to use another address format, but it is recommended to use `JMXServiceURL` where possible.

The JMX Remoting specification does not provide any specific API that would make it possible for a client to find the address of a connector server attached to a JMX agent it knows about, or to discover which JMX agents are running, or the addresses of the connector servers that make it possible to connect to them. Rather, the distributed JMX specification details how to advertise and find JMX agents using existing discovery and lookup infrastructures.

This specification discusses three such infrastructures as follows:

- The Service Location Protocol

- The Jini Network Technology

- The Java Naming and Directory Interface with an LDAP back end

The standard protocols defined by the JMX Remoting specification may not correspond to all possible environments. There are two ways to implement a user-defined protocol. One is to define a transport for the generic connector using the `javax.management.remote.generic.MessageConnection` and `javax.management.remote.generic.MessageConnectionServer` classes. The other is to define a new provider for the `javax.management.remote.JMXConnectorFactory`. User-defined protocols must implement a protocol-message exchange sequence defined by the JMX Remoting specification.

Protocol Message Exchanges

The generic connector protocol defines a set of protocol messages that are exchanged between the client connector and the server connector, and the sequence these message exchanges must follow. Implementations of the distributed JMX specification must exchange these messages in the defined sequence so that they can interoperate with other implementations.

Each configuration of the generic connector includes a transport protocol, which is an implementation of the interface `MessageConnection`. Each end of a connection has an instance of this interface.

The handshake message exchanges are started by the server end of the connection as soon as the connect method on the `JMXConnector` class is called by the client and the connection between the client and the server is established.

The server end of the connection sends to the client a `HandshakeBeginMessage` with the server's supported profiles. These profiles are retrieved from the environment map through the `jmx.remote.profiles` property. The client then starts the profile message exchanges for the profiles chosen from the server's supported profiles.

The JMXMP profile is used to negotiate the version of JMXMP to use. This profile is always implicitly enabled, but is only negotiated if the client and server differ in their default versions.

Remote Notification Events

The distributed JMX specification defines a model for transmitting notification events remotely. This model is based on the standard Java event model. As with the local notification event model, remote notification events can be transmitted by MBean instances and by an MBean server.

A JMX implementation may provide services that allow distribution of this notification event model, thus allowing a management application to listen to MBean events and MBean server events remotely.

When a user of the `JMXConnector` interface for an RMI connector client adds a listener, the listener proxy queues notifications at the server end of the connection. When the client calls the remote `fetchNotifications` method, any queued up notifications are returned to it. If there are no queued notifications when `fetchNotifications` is called, it blocks until at least one arrives.

Remote Agent and Server Lookup

The JMX Remoting specification defines a lookup service API and also describes how you can advertise and find JMX agents by using existing discovery and lookup infrastructures.

The lookup service API allows JMX Remoting clients to find and connect to connector servers that have registered with the lookup services.

To use one of the JMX Remoting lookup services, you must implement JMX Remoting agents and JMX Remoting clients. A single JVM can contain many JMX Remoting agents and/or JMX Remoting clients.

A JMX agent can register its JMX connector servers with existing lookup and discovery infrastructures, so that a JMX client can create or obtain a `JMXConnector` object to connect to the advertised servers. In particular, the JMX Remoting specification defines the following three lookup service bindings:

- *Service Location Protocol:* A JMX client can retrieve a JMX service URL from SLP and use it to connect to the corresponding server.

- *Jini Network Technology:* A JMX client can retrieve a JMX connector stub from the Jini Lookup Service and connect to the corresponding server.

- *Java Naming and Directory Interface:* A JMX client can retrieve a JMX service URL from the LDAP directory and use it to connect to the corresponding server.

All three infrastructures incorporate lookup attributes. These attributes are properties that qualify the registered services. They are passed to the infrastructure when the service is registered, and can be used as filters when performing a lookup. A client can then query the lookup service in order to find all the connectors registered by a JMX agent that matches one or more attributes. A client that obtains several services as a result of a lookup query can also further inquire about the lookup attributes registered for those services in order to determine which of these returned matching services it wants to use.

Remote Clients

The JMX distributed services level exposes a transparent client/server interaction because it exposes an API to the remote client that is as close as possible to the API defined by JMX for access to instrumentation within an agent.

A given connector client is connected to exactly one connector server. A client application may contain many connector clients connected to different connector servers. There may be more than one connection between a given client and a given server.

From the client end of a connection, user code can obtain an object that implements the MBeanServerConnection interface. This interface is very similar to the MBeanServer interface that user code would use to interact with the MBean server if it were running in the same JVM.

A connector client is represented by an object that implements the JMXConnector interface. There are two ways in which a connector client may be created. Which way an application uses depends mainly on the infrastructure that is used to find the connector server that the client wants to connect to.

If the client knows the address (JMXServiceURL) of the connector server it wants to connect to, it can use the JMXConnectorFactory to make the connection. An alternative way for a client to connect to a server is to obtain a connector stub, which is a JMXConnector object generated by a connector server.

From the client end of a connection, user code can obtain an object that implements the MBeanServerConnection interface. This interface is very similar to the MBeanServer interface that user code would use to interact with the MBean server if it were running in the same JVM.

Security

One of the principal goals of the distributed services level in JMX is security. JMX builds on the Java standards for security, including Java Secure Socket Extension (JSSE), the Simple Authentication and Security Layer (SASL), and the Java Authentication and Authorization Service (JAAS) so that connections between clients and servers can be private and authenticated and so that servers can control what operations different clients can perform.

The JMX Remoting security includes connector security based on password authentication and file access control, connector security using a subject delegation model, and fine-grained connector security.

The simplest type of security is based upon encryption, user name and password authentication, and file access control. A subject-delegation model performs operations on a given authenticated connection on behalf of several different identities. Fine-grained security involves more sophisticated security mechanisms, in which permission to perform individual operations is controlled.

Connector servers typically have some way of authenticating remote clients. For the RMI connector, this is done by supplying an object that implements the `javax.management.remote.JMXAuthenticator` interface when the connector server is created. For the JMXMP connector, this is done using SASL.

In both cases, the result of authentication is a JAAS `javax.security.auth.Subject` representing the authenticated identity. Requests received from the client are executed using this identity. With JAAS, you can define what permissions the identity has. In particular, you can control access to MBean server operations using the `javax.management.MBeanPermission` class. For this to work, though, you must have a `SecurityManager`.

The `javax.management.remote.JMXAuthenticator` interface defines how remote credentials are converted into a JAAS `javax.security.auth.Subject`. This interface is used by the `javax.management.remote.rmi.RMIConnectorServer`, and can be used by other connector servers.

The RMI connector provides a simple mechanism for securing and authenticating the connection between a client and a server. This mechanism is not intended to address every possible security configuration, but provides a basic level of security for environments using the RMI connector. More advanced security requirements are better addressed by the JMXMP connector.

The JMXMP connector provides support for authentication and authorization through the `TLS` and `SASL` profiles. The JMX Remoting API does not mandate the implementation and support of any specific SASL mechanism. It simply relies on third-party implementations that can be plugged in using the standard SASL interface.

The TLS profile allows the client and server ends of a JMX connection to negotiate a TLS encryption layer. Certificate-based authentication and mutual client/server authentication are optional features configurable through properties in the environment map.

The SASL profile mechanism uses the JAAS framework to construct a javax.management.remote.JMXPrincipal based on this authorization identity, and stores this javax.management.remote.JMXPrincipal in a Subject. Then, when the javax.management.remote.jmxmp.JMXMPConnectorServer performs any of the subsequent MBean server operations, it must do so using the javax.security.auth.Subject.doAsPrivileged(subject, action, null) call with the given subject for the required action.

The javax.management.remote.message.SASLMessage class implements the javax.management.remote.message.ProfileMessage interface and represents a challenge or response exchanged between client and server during SASL authentication. This message encapsulates either a challenge or a response generated by the SASL mechanism during the SASL authentication exchanges taking place between the client and the server.

A fine-grained level of security can be implemented in connectors by managing user access through JAAS and Java 2 platform Standard Edition (J2SE) Security Architecture. JAAS and J2SE security is based on the use of security managers and policy files to allocate different levels of access to different users.

Industry Appeal

The JMX standard is gaining popularity within the J2EE community for the management of applications, application servers, and service-oriented infrastructure software. JMX is being used as the foundation service to manage and monitor applications and systems using many of the most popular management systems and consoles.

Many of today's popular J2EE application servers include JMX as integral pieces of their core services. JMX is being used in application server software to manage configuration information, monitor state changes, organize Web applications and services, and install individual J2EE services.

Companies like AdventNet, BEA Systems, IONA, and JBoss have incorporated JMX into their products as critical components to their core services. These companies have implemented entire toolkits, platforms, and product offerings around the capabilities that JMX offers.

Open source technologies such as JMX4Ant, Tomcat, XMOJO, and MC4J have realized the power and flexibility that JMX offers, and therefore have built their offerings around the JMX standard.

Conclusion

The dynamic nature of today's enterprise systems presents significant challenges to management systems and application frameworks. It has become imperative for systems to be able to adapt to changes with little or no impact on the run-time environment.

The three-level JMX model provides the necessary abstractions and technologies to enterprise developers through which robust, fault-tolerant, and distributed solutions can be produced to meet these challenges.

Index